HER
UNSEEN BATTLE

Stories of Conquering Personal Battles, Accompanied by
Practical Tips, Empowering Affirmations, and Actionable Steps

HANNA OLIVAS & ADRIANA LUNA CARLOS
along with 24 inspiring authors

ISBN: 978-1-964619-74-3

Table of Contents

INTRODUCTION

Welcome to *Her Unseen Battle: Stories of Conquering Personal Battles, Accompanied by Practical Tips, Empowering Affirmations, and Actionable Steps*. This book is not just a collection of powerful stories; it is a celebration of the strength, resilience, and courage that resides within every woman.

In a world that often overlooks the struggles that go unseen, this book brings those quiet battles into the light. Here, women from all walks of life—different backgrounds, experiences, and journeys—share their raw, unfiltered stories of overcoming personal hardships. From navigating the heartache of loss to breaking free from self-doubt, battling societal expectations, or confronting invisible struggles with mental health, these stories offer a window into the real, unspoken challenges that shape who we are.

As you read through these intimate narratives, you will witness the strength of the human spirit in its most vulnerable and triumphant forms. The women in this book speak from a place of honesty, sharing not only the darkness they've endured but the lessons they've learned, the victories they've won, and the wisdom they've gained along the way. Their stories are a testament to the power of resilience and the capacity we all have to rise—even when we feel defeated, lost, or invisible.

But *Her Unseen Battle* is more than just a book of stories—it's a guide to help you navigate your own struggles. Interwoven throughout these pages are practical tips, empowering affirmations, and actionable steps that provide tools for building resilience, healing, and self-empowerment. These insights are designed to support you in your own journey—whether you're coping with grief, facing a major life transition, battling inner fears, or simply seeking to find more strength in your day-to-day life.

Each chapter offers something tangible to help you move forward. From mindfulness exercises and self-care strategies to affirmations that encourage self-love and empowerment, you'll find guidance that can be immediately applied to your own battles. These steps are designed to help you reclaim your power, embrace your vulnerabilities, and step into your true strength.

While the women in these stories may come from different walks of life, their experiences are universal. *Her Unseen Battle* reminds us all that every struggle, no matter how private or silent, is part of the larger human experience. It speaks to the strength of the female spirit, showing that, while we may face our battles in solitude, we are never truly alone.

As you turn the pages of this book, remember: your battle is seen. Your pain is valid. And within you lies a warrior who is capable of more than you may ever realize. May these stories inspire, comfort, and guide you on your own path toward healing, empowerment, and self-discovery.

Welcome to **Her Unseen Battle.** May this be the first step toward your own personal transformation.

SHE RISES STUDIOS
Hanna Olivas
Founder & CEO

Author, Speaker, and Founder. Hanna was born and raised in Las Vegas, Nevada, and has paved her way to becoming one of the most influential women of 2022. Hanna is the co-founder of She Rises Studios and the founder of the Brave & Beautiful Blood Cancer Foundation. Her journey started in 2017 when she was first diagnosed with Multiple Myeloma, an incurable blood cancer. Now more than ever, her focus is to empower other women to become leaders because The Future is Female. She is currently traveling and speaking publicly to women to educate them on entrepreneurship, leadership, and owning the female power within.

https://www.linkedin.com/company/she-rises-studios/
https://www.facebook.com/sherisesstudios
https://www.instagram.com/sherisesstudios_llc/
http://www.sherisesstudios.com

THE WARRIOR WITHIN

By Hanna Olivas

There are moments in life that can change the very fabric of who we are, moments that carve deep scars in our souls and test every ounce of our strength. For me, those moments began long before I had the words to fully describe them. My life has been a journey through fire, a journey that has left me raw and vulnerable, but also fiercely determined to survive, thrive, and rise above the darkness.

Growing up, I didn't understand why the world could be so cruel. I was just a little girl when I first learned what it meant to feel small, insignificant, and powerless. Sexual abuse is not something anyone should ever have to endure, especially a child. But there I was, faced with a reality no one had prepared me for. The innocence of childhood was shattered in an instant, replaced by confusion, fear, and shame.

I was just a child, and yet, I felt as though a weight had been placed on my shoulders that I would carry for the rest of my life. The abuse left scars that no one could see, but that I felt every day. It was a wound that ran deep, cutting into the core of my being and leaving me with a sense of worthlessness that lingered for years.

"I learned early on that pain can silence you, but only if you let it. I made a vow to myself that I would not be defined by the darkness that had been forced upon me."

As the years went on, the world continued to test me in ways I never could have imagined. I fell in love for the first time, thinking that maybe, just maybe, I could find safety in someone else's arms. But love, at least the kind I had found, wasn't the healing balm I had hoped for. Domestic violence crept into my life like a thief in the night. It started small, subtle—a raised voice, a door slammed too hard, a bruise hidden beneath the fabric of my clothes.

At first, I made excuses. I told myself that it wasn't that bad, that maybe I had done something to deserve it. But deep down, I knew that no one deserved to be treated like that. I knew that love isn't supposed to hurt, that love isn't supposed to leave you broken and bleeding, both inside and out.

Leaving wasn't easy. It never is. Domestic violence has a way of trapping you, making you feel like you have no options, no way out. But I had already survived so much by that point. I knew I had more fight in me. So, I left. I walked away from the man who claimed to love me, knowing that I deserved better.

"Walking away from the ones who hurt us is not a sign of weakness. It's the ultimate act of strength, of self-love, of choosing yourself over the pain they cause."

Life didn't give me much time to catch my breath. Shortly after leaving that toxic relationship, I experienced one of the greatest losses of my life—a miscarriage. The pain of losing a child, even one you've never held, is something that stays with you forever. I remember the hope I had felt when I found out I was pregnant, the dreams I had for the future, the plans I had started to make.

And then, in an instant, it was gone. There was nothing I could do to bring that little life back, nothing I could do to fix what had been taken from me. The grief was overwhelming, suffocating. I didn't know how to move forward, how to make sense of a world where such loss could exist.

But even in my darkest moments, I found a glimmer of hope. I found strength in the knowledge that I had survived before, and that I could survive again. I had to believe that there was a reason for the pain, that there was a purpose for my life that I had yet to uncover.

"Grief can break you if you let it, but it can also make you. It can forge a fire in your soul that refuses to be extinguished."

As if life hadn't tested me enough, financial disruption soon followed. The stability I had worked so hard to build was crumbling beneath my feet. Bills piled up, and the weight of the financial burden felt crushing. There were days when I didn't know how I was going to make it through, or how I was going to provide for myself or my family. But I had learned by then that no matter how heavy the load, I was strong enough to carry it.

And yet, amidst all the chaos, one of the hardest moments of my life was when my father walked out. He wasn't there when I needed him most, not there to help pick up the pieces of my shattered world. The abandonment stung in ways that words can never fully capture. I had looked up to him and believed in him, and when he left, it felt like a part of me had left too.

But I kept going. I kept pushing forward because that's what warriors do. They keep fighting, even when the world tries to tear them down. And then came the diagnosis.

Cancer.

The word itself is enough to send chills down your spine. When I heard the doctor say it, I felt as though the ground had been ripped out from beneath me. Cancer was something that happened to other people, not to me. Not to someone who had already endured so much.

But there it was, staring me in the face, forcing me to confront my own mortality in a way I never had before. Multiple myeloma. A cancer that would challenge me in ways I had never imagined. The treatments were grueling, and the uncertainty was terrifying, but through it all, I refused to give up. I refused to let cancer define me or take away the strength I had fought so hard to build.

"Cancer may have been a part of my story, but it was never the end of it. I am more than my diagnosis. I am a warrior, and I will not be defeated."

Through it all, I learned that life is not about avoiding pain. It's about finding the courage to face it head-on, to rise from the ashes, and to become stronger for having lived through it. Each battle I faced, each wound I carried, was a testament to my resilience, tenacity, and perseverance.

I also learned that self-love is not a luxury—it is a necessity. It is the foundation upon which all other forms of strength are built. Without self-love, we cannot heal, we cannot grow, we cannot move forward.

Self-love is about more than just treating yourself with kindness. It's about recognizing your worth, even when the world tries to tell you otherwise. It's about choosing yourself, over and over again, no matter how many times life tries to knock you down.

"In the end, the most important relationship you will ever have is the one you have with yourself. Love yourself fiercely, unapologetically, because you are worth every ounce of that love."

I found solace in laughter, in moments of joy that seemed to come out of nowhere, reminding me that even in the darkest of times, there is still light to be found. I found healing in self-care, in taking the time to nourish my mind, body, and soul. I found strength in the women who walked this journey with me, women who had also faced their own battles and come out stronger on the other side.

And most of all, I found hope—hope that the pain I had endured was not in vain, hope that my story could inspire others to keep going, to keep fighting, to keep believing in the possibility of a better tomorrow.

"Hope is the thread that connects us to the future, the light that guides us through the darkest of nights. Hold onto it, even when it feels like all is lost."

As I look back on my journey, I see a woman who has faced unimaginable challenges and emerged victorious. I see a woman who has learned to love herself, to care for herself, and to believe in her own strength. I see a warrior who refuses to be defeated, no matter what life throws her way.

"Becoming a warrior is not about never falling. It's about rising, again and again, no matter how many times you are knocked down."

In my quest for healing, I discovered the importance of community. Surrounding myself with like-minded women who understood my struggles brought me a sense of belonging and strength that I desperately needed. We laughed together, cried together, and supported one another through our darkest hours. There is power in shared experiences, in knowing that we are not alone in our battles.

In these connections, I found the courage to speak out about my own experiences and share my story in hopes of reaching others who might be fighting their own unseen battles. Each time I opened my heart to someone new, I felt a weight lifting off my shoulders, and I realized the power of vulnerability. By sharing my truth, I could help others feel less isolated in their struggles.

"Vulnerability is not weakness; it is the strength to show your true self to the world, to let others in, and to find solace in shared experiences."

As I navigated through the complexities of life, I also began to understand the importance of embracing joy amidst the chaos. I sought out moments of happiness, however small, and learned to celebrate them fiercely. A sunny day, a kind word from a friend, the laughter of children— each moment became a treasure that filled my heart with gratitude.

"Joy is not the absence of pain; it is the presence of hope. Seek it out in the little things, for they hold the power to illuminate even the darkest days."

In moments of despair, when the weight of the world felt unbearable, I learned to lean into my passions. Writing became my sanctuary, a space where I could pour out my heart and find clarity amidst the chaos. With each word, I felt a piece of my spirit reclaiming its power. I wrote about my journey through trauma, healing, and ultimately, empowerment. I wrote for myself, and I wrote for others who might find solace in my words.

Through writing, I discovered my voice. I learned that my story was not just a narrative of pain but also one of resilience and strength. I began to share my experiences openly, speaking to groups of women about the battles I had faced. I saw their eyes light up with understanding as I articulated feelings they had long kept hidden. In those moments, I felt a connection that transcended words, a bond forged through shared experiences and mutual healing.

"Your voice is a powerful tool; use it to tell your story. You never know who needs to hear it."

As I moved through the healing process, I realized that becoming an unstoppable woman required more than just overcoming the challenges life threw my way. It was about embracing every facet of who I am—the good, the bad, and everything in between. It was about understanding that while my past shaped me, it did not define me. I was not a victim; I was a survivor, a thriver, a warrior.

With each day, I focused on cultivating my well-being—mind, body, and spirit. I embraced mindfulness practices that allowed me to stay present, grounding me in the reality of each moment. Meditation and yoga became integral parts of my life, helping me connect with my inner self and fostering a sense of peace that had eluded me for so long.

"In the stillness, I found my strength. In the quiet moments, I learned to listen to my heart."

Nutrition also became a vital aspect of my journey. I discovered the power of nourishing my body with wholesome foods that fueled my spirit. I learned that what I put into my body could significantly impact my emotional and physical well-being. Cooking became a joyful ritual, a way to celebrate my body and honor the warrior within. I experimented with flavors, colors, and textures, creating meals that were not only nourishing but also vibrant and alive.

Fitness took on a new meaning as well. I began to exercise not just as a means to an end but as a celebration of what my body could do. Each workout was a reminder of my strength, my resilience, and my unwavering determination. I pushed my limits, ran farther, lifted heavier, and danced freely, all while embracing the joy of movement.

"When you move your body, you honor your spirit. Dance, run, lift— do what makes your heart sing."

I also prioritized self-care in ways I had never done before. I learned to set boundaries, to say no when I needed to, and to carve out time for myself without guilt. I indulged in bubble baths, long walks in nature, and quiet evenings with a good book. I surrounded myself with uplifting energy, choosing to be around those who inspired me to grow and evolve. In doing so, I created a sanctuary where I could recharge and reconnect with my true self.

"Self-care is not selfish; it is essential. You cannot pour from an empty cup. Fill yours first."

Throughout my journey, I often reflected on the concept of resilience. I realized that resilience is not just about bouncing back; it's about evolving. It's about embracing the lessons learned through pain and using them to forge a stronger, wiser self. Every scar tells a story, and each story holds the potential for healing—not only for ourselves but for others as well.

"We are not defined by our scars; we are defined by how we rise from our struggles."

As I continued to share my story and my journey, I found myself surrounded by a community of incredible women who were also on their paths to healing. Together, we created a safe space where we could be vulnerable, and share our truths without fear of judgment. We lifted each other up, celebrated each other's victories, and provided solace in moments of pain.

In this community, I learned that healing is not a solitary journey; it's a collective one. We are stronger together, and our shared experiences create a tapestry of resilience that weaves us together in profound ways. Each woman brought her own unique story, and in our sharing, we found strength, understanding, and hope.

"There is power in community. Together, we can create a ripple effect of healing and empowerment."

As I moved forward, I became more intentional about living my life with purpose. I recognized that I had a voice, a platform, and a responsibility to use them to uplift others. I started speaking at events, sharing my story and the lessons I had learned along the way. My mission became clear: to inspire other women to reclaim their power, to heal from their past, and to embrace their true selves.

"Your story is your power. Share it boldly, for it has the potential to ignite the fire in someone else's soul."

I also began to explore ways to give back. I volunteered with organizations that supported women in crisis, those who had experienced domestic violence, sexual abuse, and other forms of trauma. I wanted to be a beacon of hope for those still trapped in their battles, to show them that healing is possible and that they are not alone.

In doing this work, I encountered countless women who, like me, had faced unimaginable challenges. Their stories touched my heart and fueled my passion for advocacy. I learned that every woman has a warrior within her, waiting to be awakened. And I made it my mission to help others discover that strength.

"We are not just survivors; we are thrivers. We have the power to change our narratives and inspire others to do the same."

As I embraced my own journey of self-discovery, I also became more attuned to the importance of mental health. I recognized that healing is not just physical; it encompasses our emotional and psychological well-being. I sought therapy and counseling to process my trauma, to unpack the pain I had carried for so long. It was a brave step, one that required vulnerability, but it ultimately became a source of empowerment.

"Seeking help is not a sign of weakness; it is an act of courage. It takes strength to confront our demons and work toward healing."

Through therapy, I learned to rewrite my story, to reclaim the narrative that had once felt so heavy. I transformed my pain into power, using my experiences to fuel my passion for advocacy. I began to see my struggles as stepping stones rather than stumbling blocks. Each challenge became a lesson, each tear a testament to my resilience.

Now, as I reflect on my journey, I stand tall as an unstoppable woman—a woman who has faced the unseen battles of sexual abuse, domestic violence, miscarriage, financial disruption, and cancer. I embrace my past, not as a source of shame, but as a powerful testament to my strength.

"I am not just a survivor; I am a warrior. I am proof that healing is possible, that hope exists even in the darkest of times."

In every woman's journey lies the potential for transformation. We are capable of incredible strength, and our stories can inspire others to rise up and claim their power. Embracing our journeys, sharing our truths, and supporting one another creates a ripple effect that can change lives.

"Together, we can create a world where every woman knows her worth, recognizes her power, and embraces the warrior within."

As I move forward, I carry with me the lessons learned through every battle, every tear, and every moment of joy. I am committed to nurturing my well-being—mind, body, and spirit. I will continue to advocate for those who feel voiceless, to shine a light on the unseen battles that so many face, and to celebrate the strength that exists within each of us.

I am an unstoppable woman, and I will continue to rise, to inspire, and to empower others to do the same. Together, we can change the narrative, heal our wounds, and create a brighter, more hopeful future for all women.

"Our stories are powerful, and our voices deserve to be heard. Let us rise together, unstoppable and unbreakable."

SHE RISES STUDIOS & FENIX TV
Adriana Luna Carlos
Founder & CEO

Adriana Luna Carlos is an accomplished web and graphic designer, author, and mentor with a passion for helping women succeed in life and business. With over 10 years of experience in graphic and web arts, Adriana has built a reputation as an innovative leader and entrepreneur. In 2020, she co-founded She Rises Studios, a multi-digital media company and publishing house that has helped countless clients achieve their branding and marketing goals. In 2023, she co-created FENIX TV, an online streaming platform that showcases stories of people breaking barriers, shattering stereotypes, and triumphing against the odds.

As an advocate for women's success, Adriana challenges her clients and mentees to strive for nothing less than excellence. She has a deep understanding of the insecurities and challenges that women often face in the business world and provides the guidance and resources needed to overcome them. Her success as a business leader and entrepreneur has made her a sought-after mentor and speaker at events around the world.

Through her work, Adriana has demonstrated a commitment to

creating opportunities for women to succeed in business and life. Her passion for innovation, leadership, and women's empowerment has made her a respected figure in the business community, and her impact will undoubtedly continue to inspire and empower women for years to come.

https://www.linkedin.com/in/adriana-luna-carlos/
https://www.facebook.com/adrianalunacarlos
https://www.instagram.com/sherisesstudios_llc/
https://www.sherisesstudios.com/
https://fenixtv.app/

RISING THROUGH THE SHADOWS

By Adriana Luna Carlos

Life's battles aren't always visible, yet they shape us in ways that are both profound and deeply personal. I'm sharing my story because I know the power of connection and understanding. If you're fighting a battle that no one else sees, I want you to know you're not alone. There is strength, even in the struggle, and every challenge holds a pathway to resilience.

The Unseen Struggles

For years, I dealt with health issues that made every day feel like a mountain to climb. My most personal battle was the struggle with heavy, prolonged periods that at one point lasted an entire year without a break. It's something I've never shared publicly before, and the toll it took on my life was both physical and emotional. The constant fatigue, the pain, and the discomfort became daily hurdles, making even the smallest tasks feel overwhelming. My energy would drain, and I felt a weight settle on me that I could never quite shake.

Over time, dealing with these health issues started to affect my fertility, which has been incredibly painful for me. Having children has always been something I envisioned for myself, and it's tough to accept that this dream might not happen. Every time I think about a future without my own kids, I feel a deep sadness and disappointment.

It's not about feeling inadequate; it's simply the reality of losing something I've always pictured in my life. Not knowing what my future looks like without this dream is hard to come to terms with, and it's something that sits heavily with me every day.

Facing these health issues has also led me to confront difficult questions about my identity and purpose. When life throws curveballs that alter the path you thought you'd take, it can leave you questioning everything. For a long time, I felt adrift, wondering if the life I'd imagined was ever truly within reach. But through this process, I've come to realize that while I may not have control over certain aspects of my future, I do have control over how I respond to them. I can choose to find strength, to create new dreams, and to focus on what I can control.

Embracing the Power of Resilience

This journey taught me that resilience isn't about pretending to be okay. It's about acknowledging where you are, accepting the pain, and taking one step at a time toward healing. I had to let go of the idea that I needed to "fix" everything and instead focus on simply being present with myself, imperfections and all. I've come to understand that resilience is built not in moments of victory but in the quiet persistence of facing each day, even the hardest ones, with a sense of purpose.

Living with these health challenges has shown me that strength doesn't always come from overcoming the pain. Sometimes, it comes from simply enduring, from choosing to live fully despite the weight of what you carry. Every setback, every moment of uncertainty, has reinforced my belief in my own capacity to keep going. This journey has become a testament to my inner strength, a reminder that I can continue to rise no matter how many times life tries to pull me down.

When I look at my journey, I see more than just struggle; I see growth, self-compassion, and resilience. I'm not defined by my health challenges, nor am I limited by them. Instead, they have become part of the fabric of who I am—a woman capable of facing difficult truths, of creating new dreams, and of finding beauty in a life that might look different than I once imagined.

Practical Tips for Navigating Unseen Battles

Living with ongoing health challenges can feel isolating. Over time, I've developed a few practices that help me navigate these unseen struggles, and I hope they can help you too.

1. **Track Your Health Patterns**: Keeping a journal of your symptoms and how you feel each day can give you insights into what triggers your challenges. Knowing your patterns also helps you communicate better with your healthcare providers, ensuring you get the support you need.
2. **Create a Self-Care Toolkit**: Find simple activities that bring you comfort and relief. For me, this includes listening to music, watching a favorite movie, or spending time outdoors. Having a go-to list of activities for difficult days reminds you that there are moments of light, even in the darkest days.
3. **Prioritize Gentle Movement**: Moving your body, even in gentle ways, can make a significant difference in managing chronic conditions and uplifting your mood. Try simple stretches, a short walk, or deep breathing exercises to help reduce tension.
4. **Celebrate Small Wins**: It's easy to focus on the things we can't do, but celebrating small wins each day can shift your perspective. On a tough day, making it through work or even preparing a meal might be a win, and that's worth recognizing.
5. **Seek Support**: You don't have to go through this alone. Whether it's through online communities, local support

groups, or trusted friends, surround yourself with people who understand and respect your journey.

Empowering Affirmations

Affirmations have become a vital part of my journey. They serve as reminders of the strength within me, even when I feel at my lowest. Here are some affirmations I return to often, and I encourage you to say them out loud or write them down as part of your own journey:

- "I am resilient. My challenges are an opportunity for growth."
- "My worth is not defined by my struggles. I am enough just as I am."
- "Every step, no matter how small, is progress on my journey."
- "I am deserving of compassion, especially from myself."
- "My body is doing the best it can, and I honor its journey."

Actionable Steps for a Stronger You

If there's one thing I've learned, it's that resilience isn't built in a single moment. It's the sum of small actions, repeated over time, that creates a solid foundation of strength and self-belief. Here are a few actions that have helped me, and I hope they can guide you as well:

1. **Establish a Routine of Self-Care**: Whether it's a morning ritual, a midday break, or an evening routine, create a small moment each day that's just for you. Use this time to check in with yourself and recharge. Small rituals, like making tea or journaling, can provide a sense of control and peace.
2. **Set Realistic Goals**: Rather than overwhelming yourself with big tasks, break your goals into small, achievable steps. This approach helps you maintain a steady pace and keeps your motivation high, even on difficult days.
3. **Learn to Say "No" When Needed**: One of the hardest lessons I had to learn was saying "no" without feeling guilty.

Respecting your boundaries, especially when managing health issues, is essential. Give yourself permission to prioritize your well-being without feeling like you're letting anyone down.

4. **Celebrate Your Progress**: Take time to acknowledge how far you've come, even if the journey still feels long. Recognize that resilience isn't about being perfect; it's about showing up for yourself day after day, despite the setbacks.

5. **Give Yourself Grace**: Healing, both physically and mentally, is not a linear path. There will be good days and challenging ones. Allow yourself to rest when you need it and know that asking for help or taking a break does not diminish your strength.

Your journey may be uniquely your own, but in this shared human experience, know that there are others who walk a similar path. Remember that strength isn't always loud or visible. Sometimes, it's quiet and unseen, found in the gentle acts of self-care and the courage to keep going.

As you navigate your own battles, take comfort in knowing that resilience is within you, waiting to be discovered and nurtured. Let go of any expectations about what healing "should" look like and trust that you are exactly where you need to be in this moment. The road may be long, but with each step, you are building a foundation of strength and courage that will serve you in ways you can't yet imagine.

To all who read this, may your journey of resilience inspire others, and may you find peace in the knowledge that you are never truly alone in your unseen battles. Stand tall, keep moving forward, and believe in your own ability to rise. Your story is still unfolding, and it holds the power to inspire countless others.

THE FULFILLMENT COACH
Tomia Minnis
Founder

Hello Lovely! My name is Tomia Minnis! Professional transformation & performance coach, author, speaker, and course creator on a mission of helping women just like her! Tenacious women who have experienced feeling incapable as a result of their self-defeating behaviors. Women who have struggled with mental health and self-perception and have difficulties getting out of their own way in life.

What inspires me to be on this journey the most, is that I too am someone who knows all too well what it is like to experience pain in the deepest forms. Pain that cannot be seen by the naked eye and truly shakes you to your core.

I am also a firm believer that we are not given the privilege of making it through our darkest valleys and deepest despair's without a moral obligation of lending a hand to others who need guidance on how to do the same.

https://www.facebook.com/TheFulfillmentCoach/
https://linktr.ee/TheFulfillmentCoach

NOTE TO SELF

By Tomia Minnis

DEDICATION

To my mom in heaven,
Your life was not in vain.
I vow that for as long as I live, you will never be forgotten.
For everyone will hear my story and how amazing you were and
what a blessing it is to be my mother's daughter.

"There are wounds that never show on the body that are deeper and more hurtful than anything that bleeds."—Laurell K. Hamilton

"Your mother is going to die."

These are the words my 12-year-old self could have never imagined, fathomed, or prepared to have to ever hear. Especially directly by someone on the hospital staff.

When I heard those words and was essentially told to prepare for her passing, I was in denial. What do you mean my mother is going to die? MY mother? No, you must be mistaken. I know she has cancer, and I know this may look bad, but she can bounce back from this, right?

In hindsight, I could have NEVER prepared my adolescent brain enough to understand the weight of what was spoken or what my life would look like without my best friend, my #1 supporter, my ride or die, my incredibly faithful and believing mother, and still to this day, my hero.

Watching my single mother have the ability to not only take care of herself and me, but also carry the weight of the world on her shoulders like it was a feather, transition into skin and bones, and be put into a medically induced coma in less than a year truly is one of the hardest battles I have ever experienced in my entire life.

There is something that is so wicked and indescribable about the capability cancer has to completely destroy someone's body and suffocate the life out of them. My mother looked nearly unrecognizable before she passed, and to watch as cancer was taking her from me and not be able to do anything about it was heartbreaking. A feeling of powerlessness I hope to never have to experience again.

Now that I am 25, my mother has not been earth side for more than half of my life. This is something that sometimes is still hard to swallow, and now that I am at a point in my life where I am: Striving to heal from past hurts, make my dreams of being a business owner, a wife, and hopefully, half as amazing as a mother she was, the reality is that the hurt seems to bubble to the surface more often.

The pain that is felt within your heart and in the back of your throat when you just want to call them, to hear their voice, their laugh, to tell them you love them and be able to hear it back is some of the deepest pain I have ever encountered, and I would not wish that on my worst enemy.

I truly wish that my mother no longer being by my side in the physical sense was the only detrimental hardship I have faced. However, it is not. Nothing will ever compare to losing her, but in hindsight, the years that followed and the weight of some deep traumas that occurred afterward come to a close second.

I experienced some things that I am and continue to work on healing from in trauma-informed therapy. My mental health issues that started to show their face to me while my mother battled cancer became ones that are familiar and recognizable. And all too often come to visit, especially at the most unexpected times.

Without the guidance and love of my mother, my rock, my backbone, and so much more, I lost my way in life.

I lost my faith in God for years. I grew up in the church and learned to love God and the love he has shown me and all of us. However, after this tragedy, I found myself questioning him and placing blame where it should not have been but, at the time, felt right. Without guidance and connection with Jesus, I gave my love out to people who hurt me deeply, I trusted people I sometimes wish I never did, and I developed a version of myself that didn't wish to fight to see another sunrise.

The number of occurrences and long nights where I basically begged and pleaded that this life journey of mine come to an end so that I no longer had to feel pain is innumerable.

After my mom passed, I developed a hard shell that I have been working diligently to be able to penetrate and decipher. A hard shell that presents itself in a friendly, extroverted, laughter kind of way. But also a quiet, irritable, standoffish way at times, too.

I lost touch with my emotions and who I was in the mix of all the BS my mental health and traumas, unfortunately, fed me for more years than they have not.

For as long as I can remember, especially being the youngest, and while my mother battled cancer, I always felt I needed to be strong and did not want others to worry about me. So much so that I couldn't bring myself to cry at my mother's funeral. I hid and became out of touch with my true emotions, so much so that I returned back to school two days later, and I just kept pushing. Something I now know was not the best option for me, but hindsight is always 20/20.

You see, I have suffered from some level of mental health issue since I was roughly 11 years old. And as many of you unfortunately can relate to, this journey is quite literally not for the faint of heart.

It feels as if I have cried more tears than the deepest of seas and, that I have carried more weight than any world-class bodybuilder could even begin to fathom. I have run more mental marathons than the greats.

"The path out of hell is through misery. By refusing to accept the misery that is part of climbing out of hell, you fall back into hell."— Marsha Linehan

People like you and me have been through the unimaginable and continue to fight toward a life worth living. However, because of our thoughts, negative self-talk, self-perception, emotions, and so much more that cannot be seen by the naked eye, it is often written off as minuscule.

We are pelted with unsolicited advice that we never requested (and shitty advice at that) from people who cannot fathom what it is like to walk in our shoes, or how much of a war is going on inside our heads.

People like you and I have seen the light at the end of the tunnel slowly fade away and not even return or flicker for months on end, and yet, because a mass majority of society has this "see it to believe it" mentality, mental health and other conditions get written off like they are nothing. When in reality, I have felt the deepest levels of pain inside my body than I ever have externally.

Life can seem unfair. The "normies" are privileged enough to go through life without a voice in their heads telling them that they aren't capable or that they are worthless, what sometimes seems like every second of the day.

I've pondered, questioned, and wondered why is it some of us have cards dealt to us that appear to be such shit hands, and I am thankful to the one above that I found a philosophy that sincerely comforts my soul.

We fight through and experience hardships so that we can be molded into who we need to become. What is gained in the valley will and never can be experienced on the highest of the mountain tops. That there truly is a purpose in our pain and that the mess can become our greatest message and lesson. What we learn and unlearn from our hardest points of just trying to survive in this world should be our badges of honor and not our reasoning for hanging our heads low in guilt and shame.

One of my all-time most adored Bible verses sums this up pretty perfectly:

"Consider it pure joy, my brothers and sisters, whenever you face trials of many kinds, because you know that the testing of your faith produces perseverance. Let perseverance finish its work so that you may be mature and complete, not lacking anything."—James 1:2-4

I find comfort in understanding that you and I were not meant to always have peaches and rainbows experiences. That realization of life has kept me pushing forward and given me hope in some of my darkest moments in my life's journey.

Also, I don't know about you, but I personally have found myself mentally suffering. I mean, going through the thickest parts of the woods in my mind because I believed some false societal expectation that I should not have hard times or that the grass should always be green, and my sky should always be blue with sun rays as far as the eye can see.

The reality that continues to free my soul each and every day is that this life is not and was not meant to always be that way.

It's so easy to get wrapped up in people's "highlight reels" on social media and let comparison creep in. Comparisons that guide us into thinking we don't have a life worth living because we, too, aren't sipping "Margs" at an all-inclusive resort in the Bahamas every weekend.

But the thing is, maybe we aren't. Maybe that isn't in the cards we have available to us right now. And that is OKAY!

Someone wise once told me something that has stuck with me ever since. "Do not compare your inside with someone else's outside."

Meaning, what in the world does what someone else has going on in their life have anything to do with you, your worth, your character, your ability, your personality, your love, your anything.

And I know it is easier said than done to stop comparing ourselves to others so negatively. In fact, comparison can be a good coping strategy if used effectively.

What I am saying is (and what is beautiful about this life) that we have our own mission, purpose, and passion to fulfill. As much as we may desire to do so, we cannot live our life through someone else's. And I know sometimes that feels like some bad juju, but it can also be so freeing to know that you do not need to be on anyone else's timeline but your own and the one God set out for you.

Regardless of what society says or what incredibly high and unrealistic expectations you have set out for yourself. You can, and you will make it in this world. No matter what the wicked ways of this world throw your way, you will make it! And I know that can seem like a load of crap some days, but if you start to believe it, you will see it, too.

And trust me when I say this: We all have our moments. We all have days when things get hard, days when even taking care of foundational things seems like they are impossible tasks. Days when said tasks are done with what appears to be minimal effort, and days when said things aren't done at all. And guess what? That is okay, too!

As a society, we need to stand up for ourselves and flip the script on measuring our self-worth in productivity, and things checked off of to-do lists. (Don't get me wrong, I love me a good to-do list!) We need to focus on what is most important. Your needs, your physical and mental health, creating core memories that last, and not just going through the motions of life on autopilot trying to keep up with obligations and tasks that are never 100% complete.

Trust me, I know that it can be difficult to get out of the rat race and I promise I won't talk your ear off about how much society plays a pivotal role in why that race even exists to begin with. But for the love of all things holy, please stop running in circles on the hamster wheel!

I know all of this is easier said than done, and trust me, Rome was not built in a day. But it's worth considering so that you can be free from despair.

Here are some things that have helped me immensely to work towards striving to thrive in my day to day regardless of what invisible battles I may be facing!

1. Journaling! Now, this is not always everyone's cup of tea, and there are probably a million different ways to journal nowadays. What might work for you may not work for everyone, so I suggest doing some research on the different types and ways to journal as well.

I personally enjoy starting out my writing with prompts about how my day or week has gone, what went well, and what maybe went not as hot. Gratitude is a BIG ONE. Regardless of where we are in life, there is always something to be grateful for! I also like to do a personal check-in on how I am really doing lately.

2. Prayer and worship! This somewhat piggybacks on the last one. If you are like me and when you try to pray, your mind wanders into other things, I have a specific journal for my prayers written in letter format. I always try to include what I am thankful for, what I am worried about, and my prayer request.

3. Affirmations! I personally find them via Pinterest, but any resource will be sufficient. You can search for affirmations regarding specific topics such as worries/anxiousness, self-compassion, abundance, and so on. You also can create your own, making sure that they are present tense, personal to you, and positive! For me, I am a post-it girly, so I write them on post-its and stick them on my full-body mirror that I finish getting ready in front of in the mornings. There are also apps where you can get affirmation reminders, record yourself saying the affirmations to listen to later, and so on.

4. Asking for help/seeking professional assistance! I know that for many reasons different to each and every one of us, it can be a hard realization that you need to ask for help and/or seek out professional assistance with your mindset and mental health battle. But let me say this, the best investment I have ever made with my money and time was getting intensive mental health assistance this year. Whether it be a partial hospitalization program, a DBT program, weekly therapy, medication management, or whatever works best for you and your needs. Between what you learn and the accountability, it has been worth every penny!

5. Utilizing a planner and calendar. Let me tell you, when it came to scheduling things for each day, week, or month, I was DEFIANT. I had a misconception that using a planner and scheduling things was "boring" and that it would take out a lot of spontaneity in my life. However, my planner and calendars are like phoning a friend for what I need to do, want to do, "me time," dinner, chores, the whole 9 yards! It really helps to have initiative and helps me work towards not putting too much on my plate and being compassionate with myself on days when not every single thing gets done.

6. Focus on your foundations! Your mental, physical, and spiritual health. When one or more components of your foundations are cracking, the whole house starts to crumble. So, do your best to make sure you are getting movement in, going to routine appointments (and scheduling appointments for concerns you may have been putting off), hydrating, sleeping, and fulfilling your spiritual needs however that looks like for you. For me, that is through prayer, worship, attending church (online in the comfort of my own home, may I add), and Bible study. Making sure you are resting and relaxing when needed, and making time for leisure and fun so you don't burnout! Basically, keep your bases covered as much as possible. It may take some time to figure out what works best for you. However, sometimes our greatest teacher is trial and error. Plus, we are always and forever changing, so don't be afraid to mix things up and/or try something new!

In real "Mia fashion," I will leave you will these reminders:

- You are worth fighting for, both the current you and the future version of you. Most importantly, though, don't neglect your current self of love, compassion, and grace for a version of you you haven't met or fully culminated to yet!

- Hardships will come, they are a part of life! Don't get hung up in the false ideology that life is supposed to be easy each and every day. Free yourself of the chains of the "peaches and rainbows mentality." Trust me, you will thank yourself later for it!

- Both joy and sorrow can coexist! Sorrow should not deprive you of or steal your joy! After all, each and every moment of the day, our brains will naturally look for (and find) the negatives. Let's try to look for more positives, instead!

- You are loved and needed more than you will ever know! And if anyone hasn't told you today, I am glad to have been on earth at this same moment in time as you!

And with that, I will leave you with this:

"The most beautiful people we have known are those who have known defeat, known suffering, known struggle, known loss, and have found their way out of the depths. These persons have an appreciation, a sensitivity, and an understanding of life that fills them with compassion, gentleness, and a deep loving concern. Beautiful people do not just happen."

—Elisabeth Kubler-Ross

WILDFLOWER ALLERGY AND HERBS
Kerri Ballinger
Owner

My Journey into Holistic Health started with my son. He was misdiagnosed with Autism, ADHD, Dyslexia and Behavioral Issues. They did every allergy test available to western medicine, they biopsied his bumps and taught me hold to hold my son down during his head banging episodes. They prescribed medications that made my son a walking zombie. Fortunately, a person who saw both myself and my son crying, outside the pet store after having to give away his beloved Guinea pig due to his "allergies", gave me a business card for a woman who she said saved her daughter's life. We discovered NAET and the undiagnosed 85 food allergies that my son had. After several treatments, my son is now not allergic to anything and has a new lease on life. He became the healthy child that I prayed for. Afterwards, I knew that's what I wanted to do for others

https://www.linkedin.com/in/kerri-ballinger-41437530/
https://www.facebook.com/profile.php?id=61551905116530
https://wildflowerallergyandherbs.com/

FIGHTER

By Kerri Ballinger

Have you ever felt like you were drowning? Constantly, trying to reach the surface for air, prosperity, or growth? Your entire body seething in pain just from trying to stay afloat. If you have felt this way at one time or another in your life, know that the endless search for a long deep breath can be found.

My struggles for air started very early, around seven years old, when I could not find enough air to breathe at least two to three times a week. I was severely asthmatic and went to many doctors for breathing treatments and ways to avoid being out of breath. Every normal Western medicine test was given, and every medicine tested on me, but I still ended up being rushed to the hospital for adrenaline a few times a month. I would spend countless nights bent over a pillow in my lap, gasping for air and praying that I would just "be normal." According to the doctors that I encountered, I was not supposed to run, play too hard, and always carry my emergency inhaler. Along with the struggle to breathe, I was also diagnosed with extreme eczema. I remember sitting in oatmeal baths and constantly putting what seemed like gallons of lotion on me. It seemed like a never-ending struggle to find air and to stop itching. Because of my medical issues, I started to feel isolated. I could not play like the other kids did and spent a lot of time out of school. Unfortunately, at that time, the doctors never linked the two symptoms together and never researched the causes of my ailments.

As I grew, the asthma became a bit more bearable, and the eczema seemed to partially fade. My parents thought that I just "grew out of" my illnesses. Even though some days I still couldn't do all of the things the other kids were doing, I decided that I wasn't going to let myself be left behind and left out because of my health. I was an adventurous kid, I played outside, built forts, and raced my neighbors on my bike. It didn't matter how much time I was going to have to spend on my breathing machine, I wasn't going to let this beat me, and I think that's when I learned to be a fighter—a fighter for my health.

During my teenage years, my health fluctuated. Some days, I felt really healthy, and other days, I struggled to keep up. I had strange bouts with common colds, flu, and my gut health, which were commonly labeled as stomach aches. Through the ups and downs of my teenage years, I decided that this was just going to be the way I lived, but I wasn't going to let my health issues win. I fought to be healthy. I started running, short sprints at first, then longer runs. I ate well, I didn't drink or smoke. I got eight hours or more of sleep and drank lots of water. I worked and studied hard. I decided that if my health wasn't going to be the best, I had to be the best at everything else. I was stubborn, determined, and strong.

At the age of 19, my life was turned upside down. I was working my way through college, bartending, and had set my sights on a nursing degree. Late one evening, I was turning off the neon lights at the outdoor venue where I worked, and something crawled up my sweatshirt. I immediately took the sweatshirt off and didn't see anything that could bite me, but I saw a small spot that was red and swollen on my arm. Not thinking much about it, I went on my way and finished off my day. After a close examination of myself when I got home from work, I noticed that I had been bitten twice, once on my arm and once on my back. Still thinking nothing of it, I took an allergy pill and went to bed. Within the next two days, both bites had become ulcerated, and I decided that I better get to the doctor. My doctor immediately sent me to the emergency room, where they concluded that I had been bitten twice by a brown recluse spider. After some antibiotics and rest, the bites began to fade, but so did my health. I was tired all the time, I felt very weak, I felt like I couldn't get enough to eat, and I was dropping a lot of weight very quickly.

One morning, after being out of work and school for a few days, the phone rang. I was still in bed. I tried to reach for the phone but couldn't. My arms felt like I had elephants sitting on them, and the rest of my body was not responding to the commands that my brain was telling my body to do. I felt alone and very scared. I started to scream for help. My roommate found me and helped me call my parents. They took me to the hospital, where they gave me more antibiotics and sent me home since the preliminary tests only showed that my body had major inflammation. I lay in bed for several days but soon regained my strength and plotted on with my normal everyday activities.

In the following weeks, I noticed that I was always thirsty, still dropping weight, and feeling very spaced out. I had revisited many doctors, who said that I should eat better and get more sleep. What they didn't know was that I always monitored my food intake. I never ate sweets and led a pretty active and healthy lifestyle. Their diagnoses did not make much sense to me. Again, I chose to ignore what was happening to me and move through life without questioning the doctors or my results.

A few months went by and by this time, I had dropped almost 30lbs of my original weight since being bitten. My family was very concerned, so my mother made an appointment for me at her OBGYN, hoping for some insight into what was happening with my body. A few minutes after submitting my urine for testing, the doctor. flung open the door. I can still vividly see her face. She said, "I don't know how you are standing in front of me right now." My blood sugar was over 1000, and I was in severe diabetic ketoacidosis. Normal blood sugar is between 70 and 130. She called an endocrinologist and sent me to see him the same day. I still credit her for saving my life!

At the time, adult onset of juvenile diabetes was rare. Most juvenile diabetics were diagnosed within 5 years of being born. In 1990, 4.9% of the population was considered diabetic (both type 1 and type 2). Today diabetes, both type 1 and type 2, affects over 10% of the population.

You would think that that would be the end of my story, that I got the treatment that I needed, and I became healthy once again. Unfortunately, that is only the beginning of my story. After being put on meds to control my sugar levels, I continued to lose weight, so the doctors recommended that I go on an insulin pump. This contributed to a deep depression of unworthiness and hate for my own body. I thought that no one would love me with the contraption that I now had to wear. I battled that insulin pump. It was the enemy. A lot of times, I decided not to wear it, I was ashamed and disgraced by the effort I had to make to be healthy while others who led less healthy lives lived easily and prosperously. I was embarrassed when people asked me what that was, or why I was still carrying around a beeper. Explaining my illness to others was not easy, and most people would make comments like, "I feel bad for you, or "I am so sorry," or what my grandmother used to say, "That's a shame." The last thing I wanted was to be pitied. It angered me and still does to this day.

Getting used to wearing a pump came with its own complications. My body had been used to running with a blood sugar of 1000, so when I started wearing my pump consistently, my health declined very rapidly. My now-husband asked me to marry him in February, and by May, I had lost most of my hair and most of my muscle mass and could barely stand. I thought I was dying and going to lose the love of my life all at the same time. I was misdiagnosed with fibromyalgia, rheumatoid arthritis, and neuropathy.

I was put on many meds that only made me more ill, to the extent of wanting to take my own life. I had just started teaching and couldn't go to work and almost lost my job. I cried often, some from depression, some from the endless pain that engulfed my entirety. I ended up back in the hospital. This time for two weeks. The doctors were baffled. They had no answers for me, so I checked myself out and tried to go back to some kind of life. At this time, my coworkers were concerned, and one of them called me. She said, "Please try my holistic doctor. He has healed me, and I think he could help you too." I was desperate and willing to try anything. Within a few days, I had gotten an appointment and was shocked at what I learned.

I had never encountered a doctor like this. His methodology was something I had never experienced. I thought his diagnosis had to be fabricated because in only minutes, without blood work or other normalized tests, he knew what was wrong with me. He examined my eyes and my tongue and did MRT (muscle testing) of allergens and my organs. He had traced my illnesses (including diabetes) back to my allergies in childhood, the spider bites, and an overgrowth of candida in my body. After following the natural remedies he recommended, within two weeks, my hair started to grow back, my energy returned, and my depression disappeared. By my wedding, in November, I was healthy and happier than I had been in a long time!

Even though the other ailments (hair loss, weight loss, depression, and fatigue) had been cured, I still had to battle my diabetes. I was just so incredibly happy to be able to function again, I just went on managing my diabetes as best I could, which was and is still not very easy. My blood sugar continued to be inconsistent, and I would have drastic changes in my levels depending on mood, stress, activity, and food intake. I have had many low-blood glucose episodes and seizures. When the brain is deprived of sugar, or your sugar levels fall quickly, the brain can react in many ways. Over the years, I have lost the use of my legs, screamed and yelled, spoken and acted like I am intoxicated, bitten my husband, and even run around my home with my newborn in my arms. Sometimes an ambulance must be called to give me an IV full of glucose, sometimes, I can get enough glucose in me before I get worse. I have a fight-or flight instinct deeply engraved in me even when my conscious state is abnormal and lacks the sugar to maintain homeostatic responses. I can go unconscious if my sugar drops while I am sleeping, and if left too long in that state, I could die. My husband has saved my life too many times to count. I am very grateful for him, because I know that this journey has not been easy on him either, but yet we persist and thrive together no matter what.

A few years into our marriage, we decided to try to have children. I was told back in my twenties that it would be very hard for me to get pregnant. Again, fooling the doctors, I got pregnant on the first try. Even though we lost our first child, we persisted and got pregnant again soon after. Pregnancy came with a bunch of challenges, as the seizures increased and the dramatic plunges in blood sugar happened way too often. We fought through those challenges and gave birth to a beautiful son, named Logan.

I knew that maintaining a healthy hemoglobin A1C (which is a test that measures your average blood sugar over the past three months) was dire to having a healthy child. Four years after having my first child, I got pregnant again. This time, it was a bit of a surprise, and I was very worried about the health of my child because I knew that my Hemoglobin A1C was running significantly higher than it should be. I experienced a few seizures and some extra testing that had to be done due to the slow development of his lungs, but again successfully gave birth to a healthy baby boy, named Luke.

After bringing him to the doctor for the normal check-ups, we followed up with his immunizations. The nurse administered three shots that same day. We left, and I thought nothing of it. When getting back to the house, Luke had a severe reaction to one of the shots causing his leg to swell to three times the normal size. The nurse kept saying, "I'm sorry, I'm sorry." They gave him something to suppress the reaction to the immunization, and I was told to keep ice on the leg when I got home. After several weeks, I noticed that Luke had dark circles and redness around his eyes. He also did not sleep for the first eight months of being on this earth. If he did sleep, it was only a few minutes at a time. I wished I had asked more questions or knew what I know now. I was told to change his formula, which I did, and I had to do an additional three times until I finally found a formula that seemed to make him content.

The redness and dark circles persisted around his eyes, but I was told that he just had allergies. I decided to make sure that he ate healthy and enjoyed his fruits and vegetables on a consistent basis. For the next couple of years, both of my children seemed to be growing and developing into healthy and happy little boys.

At about the age of five Luke's kindergarten teacher called me in for a conference. She said that she saw Luke having trouble keeping up with the other kids. I dismissed the teacher's findings and chalked it up to him being a little bit behind and was determined to help him "catch up." I read to him every night, we played learning games, and he listened to songs that taught him the alphabet and rhyming. I implemented white noise to help him sleep. Over the next couple of years, we danced out problems, sang songs, and worked on coloring inside the lines. He progressed, but at a much slower pace than other children. I started to see his happy, infectious smile turn to sadness and frustration. My son started banging his head, screaming and yelling, ripping off his clothes, and all anyone showed me to do was to hold him down so he didn't hit his head too hard. I brought him to see several different allergists, internists, and even a behavior specialist. All these doctors gave to me for solutions were labels. They labeled Luke as autistic, dyslexic, ADHD, and behaviorally impaired. They heavily medicated him, so he was more like a zombie than my little boy. I was desperate for something to help my son.

Finally, about a year later, we got the help that I prayed for. We were exhausted, standing outside a pet store returning my son's guinea pig, crying, because we thought that the guinea pig may be playing a role in his allergies. Suddenly, an elderly lady asked me what was wrong. I explained the circumstances that led us to the pet store. Immediately, she said, "Oh honey, I got you." She then went to her truck, pulled out a card, and handed it to me. It was the location and phone number of a NAET (Dr. Nambudripad's Allergy Elimination Technique) practitioner. She then told me the story of her daughter, who, at one time, could not leave her home due to the extensive allergies, illnesses, and sensitivities that she once had. She said that this holistic approach would cure my son's allergies and ailments. I was again skeptical, but we went anyway.

On our first encounter with the NAET practitioner, she asked a lot of questions that were never asked before and concluded that the allergies and behavioral issues most likely stemmed from the vaccinations and my higher-than-normal hemoglobin A1C when Luke was conceived. EVERYTHING has a cause, and she was like a detective putting together the symptoms and the causes. She used the same MRT (muscle response testing) that was used on me when I was ill. She discovered that his stomach was not digesting the nutrients for the body's homeostasis and also discovered 85 food allergies that Western allergy tests did not detect. After several treatments, my son no longer suffered from any allergies, including sadness, frustration, and head-banging. He once again became a bright and happy child. He now eats whatever he wants and lives as a very successful athlete and 11th grade student. The labels are gone because there are no ailments to label.

It took me many years of illness and frustration to fully grasp holistic health. It is often overlooked and mislabeled. My experience and my son's experiences have truly opened my eyes to what perseverance, healing, and treatment should look like. That's why I became who I am today, a NAET practitioner, Holistic Health Practitioner, Acupoint Medicine Practitioner, Functional Nutrition Practitioner, and Herbalist. I am also the owner of Wildflower Allergy and Herbs. I am able to treat a person's physical, physiological, and emotional imbalances, allergies, and ailments. I treat the body as a whole, not just the symptoms. From my own personal experiences, I can relate to the frustrations and roadblocks that others may have encountered with their own health struggles. I believe that my purpose in life is to support and help others the way both myself and my son were helped. I will fight for your health, the same way I fought for my health and the health of my son. Are you ready to join me?

Thank you,
Kerri Ballinger

Wildflower Allergy and Herbs
100 Linton Blvd Suite 206 A2
Delray Beach, FL 33483
561-706-4772
Wildflowerallergyandherbs.com

FOREVER AND A DAY PUBLISHING LLC

Antoinette McDonald

CEO

Antoinette is the CEO of Forever and a Day Publishing LLC providing services of self-publishing, financial literacy, proper protection, and education coaching. The tenets of the business; God – Family – Career – Finances are woven throughout all business interactions. Antoinette is a retired elementary school principal and has over 22 years of experience in the education field as a teacher and building administrator.

She is a fighter of Multiple Sclerosis, with a diagnosis in 1997 at the age of 18 and is determined to educate others about how to be prepared for life's changes through prayer, mindfulness, and a blessed mindset.

She welcomes difficult conversations with love, patience, and attention.

Antoinette is originally from Pittsburgh, Pennsylvania and has been in Virginia since 2001. She married her husband Sean and they are parents to Seani and Sean II.

In her spare time, Antoinette enjoys traveling, spending time with family, and writing.

https://www.linkedin.com/in/seanantoinette-mcdonald-77255b1a8/
https://www.facebook.com/FAADLLC/
https://www.instagram.com/faadllc/
https://faadpublishingllc.com/

ANTOINETTE:
1 MULTIPLE SCLEROSIS: 0

By Antoinette McDonald

It's 1994. The Pittsburgh sun was high in the sky, casting long shadows across the field where the band practiced. It was the summer of my sophomore year, and I was living the life of a typical active teenager. As a new pom pom member of our school band, my days were filled with practices, performances, and the exhilarating rush of being a part of something bigger than me. *Oliver Bears High Stepping March Band. Huh!*

On that particular summer day, I was out in the field, participating in another rigorous practice session. The heat was intense, but we were used to pushing through it. However, something felt different that day. As I high-stepped on the grass, my vision started to blur, and my head felt like it was spinning. I tried to shake it off, but it became harder and harder to focus.

I barely made it to the outside bathroom before my legs gave out. The world went dark as I collapsed on the dirty, cold, hard floor. Unsure of how long I was unconscious, I drifted in and out of consciousness, feeling my body rock as the ambulance raced to the hospital. The paramedics' voices were muffled, but I caught fragments of their urgent conversation. "Her body temperature is so high, we have to cool her down," one of them said, and I remember thinking, "What's happening to me?"

That summer marked the beginning of a journey I never anticipated. It was a journey filled with uncertainty, fear, and ultimately, resilience. My name is Antoinette McDonald, and I was diagnosed with multiple sclerosis at the age of 18. This is my story of navigating life with a chronic illness, finding strength in the face of adversity, and learning to thrive despite the challenges that came my way.

The sudden onset of symptoms that day was the first sign that something was seriously wrong. Over the next few years, my life would be turned upside down as I faced a series of medical tests, doctor visits, and the eventual diagnosis that would change everything.

Living with multiple sclerosis has been an ongoing battle, one that has tested my limits and reshaped my perspective on life. But through it all, I've discovered a well of inner strength and resilience I never knew I had. My journey is one of learning to cope, finding support, and embracing the ups and downs that come with a chronic illness. It's about finding hope in the darkest moments and celebrating the small victories along the way.

In this chapter, I will share my story, from the early days of my diagnosis to the strategies I've developed to manage my symptoms and maintain a fulfilling life. I hope that my experiences can provide comfort, encouragement, and practical advice to others facing similar challenges. This is my unseen battle, and these are the lessons I've learned along the way.

Part I: The Diagnosis

In 1997, the symptoms that had subtly crept into my life became impossible to ignore. I had always been active and energetic, but I began experiencing a strange numbness in my legs that wouldn't go away. At first, it was easy to dismiss these feelings as the result of sitting in one position for too long, but the numbness persisted and grew worse. It spread to my hands and feet, and the sensation was unlike anything I had ever felt before. It was as if my extremities were constantly asleep, yet there was no obvious reason for it.

Walking even short distances became a challenge. My legs would go numb and feel cold to the touch, making it difficult to move around. These symptoms were alarming and confusing, and I knew something was seriously wrong. The lack of focus and persistent neuropathy were affecting my daily life, and I needed answers.

I begged my mom to allow me to see a doctor. My PCP referred me to a neurologist, hoping to find some clarity. The neurologist conducted a series of tests, including an MRI, to determine the cause of my symptoms. The MRI revealed lesions on my brain and spinal cord, indicative of multiple sclerosis. Hearing the diagnosis was a shock. I had never heard of multiple sclerosis, not only were there few resources to provide insight, I was unprepared for the impact it would have on my life. Some nine years later, I was diagnosed with Relapsing-Remitting Multiple Sclerosis (RRMS).

Receiving the diagnosis felt like the ground had been pulled from under me. I was overwhelmed with fear, uncertainty, and sadness. I had so many questions: How would this affect my life? Would I ever feel normal again? What kind of treatments were available? The neurologist provided minimal answers, but many aspects of MS remained a mystery to me.

I struggled to come to terms with the diagnosis, oscillating between hope during remissions and despair during relapses. The unpredictable nature of RRMS made it difficult to plan for the future, and I often felt like I was living on borrowed time during the periods when my symptoms subsided. It took a while for me to grasp the chronic nature of MS and to understand that remission didn't mean the disease was gone; it was merely dormant, waiting to flare up again.

A significant adjustment had to happen. I had to learn to listen to my body and to recognize the signs of an impending relapse. This meant adopting new habits and strategies to manage my symptoms and maintain as much normalcy as possible. I began to educate myself about multiple sclerosis, learning about potential triggers for relapses and ways to manage my condition. Over time, I developed a routine that helped me cope with the daily challenges of living with MS, and I started to find a sense of balance amidst the uncertainty.

Part II: Navigating Life with MS

As the years passed, the progression of multiple sclerosis brought a host of daily challenges. One of the most visible signs of my condition was the increasing difficulty I had with walking. There were times when I needed to use a cane to support myself, particularly during relapses when my legs felt weak and unsteady. Navigating simple tasks, such as stepping onto or down from a curb, became daunting due to my impaired depth perception.

My relapsing-remitting MS was pretty much stable throughout my career, but the stress of my role as an elementary school principal exacerbated my symptoms. Managing the responsibilities of the job often led to bouts of double vision, making it hard to focus on paperwork or even recognize faces clearly. I experienced difficulty using my hands, which would sometimes go numb or lose coordination, complicating tasks that required fine motor skills. My gait changed, becoming more labored and unbalanced, and the persistent neuropathy made walking feel like trudging through thick mud. I often battled unexpected bouts of fatigue, sudden symptomatic flare-ups, and other conditions that presented temporary impediments to my job. After year three, my MS began to take center stage. It was tedious to pull all-night data crunch sessions, review curriculum, and plan out lessons to model for probationary teachers or review and respond to emails. Numbness began to move from my feet and hands to my legs and arms, even sometimes the right side of my face. During Principal Meetings, grade-level planning, and Parent Advisories—these sensations became an everyday occurrence. After visiting with my neurologist, we agreed to begin a disease-modifying therapy (DMT), Ocrevus.

Despite these physical limitations, I was determined to continue my work and maintain as much independence as possible. With the addition of the DMT, I learned to adapt to my new reality, finding ways to cope with the challenges that MS presented each day. This often meant being creative in finding solutions and not being afraid to ask for help when needed.

One of the most challenging aspects of living with multiple sclerosis is that it is an invisible disease. To the outside world, I may not look like I have a chronic illness. This invisibility can be both a blessing and a curse. While it allows me to move through the world without constant pity or questions, it also means that people often don't understand the severity of what I'm experiencing.

You cannot see neuropathy, but during flare-ups, it feels as though my limbs are amputated, I cannot feel them. I have to, oftentimes, look at my limb to ensure it is still there. I have to speak out loud to my feet, "Left foot, right foot," in order to walk. The misfires of the nerves and the damaged myelin sheaths act like frayed wires sending erratic sparks throughout my central nervous system. Neuropathy is like having a million red fire ants marching up and down my legs, following the misfired commands of "Lieutenant Brain Lesion." These sensations are incredibly painful and debilitating, yet they remain hidden from view. Invisible.

I was an educator for 22 years, with 14 of those years spent as a school administrator. I maintained a high-level position with grace and dedication. However, as MS progressed and took center stage in my life, I had to make the difficult decision to retire at the age of 45. This decision was not easy, but it was necessary for my health and well-being.

Throughout this journey, my support system became my foundation and inspiration. My family, my nucleus, stood by me with unwavering love and encouragement. At the time of my diagnosis, my boyfriend was a steady source of support, and in 2000, he became my husband. He has been my ultimate advocate and cheerleader, providing both emotional and practical support.

My husband immersed himself in understanding multiple sclerosis. He educated himself thoroughly about the condition, attending all my medical appointments and conferences to learn more about how to support me effectively. His dedication and willingness to stand by me in this battle have been invaluable. He has taken on roles that go beyond those of a typical spouse, ensuring I have the care and support needed to navigate the ups and downs of living with MS.

Additionally, my colleagues and school staff played a crucial role in my support system. Over the last three years, they embraced my accommodations with kindness and understanding. Their words of encouragement and willingness to adapt to my needs made a significant difference in my ability to continue working.

The sense of community and solidarity from my family and colleagues has been a cornerstone of my resilience. Their belief in me and readiness to assist in any way possible have been instrumental in helping me manage the daily challenges of MS. They remind me that I am not alone in this journey, and their support fuels my determination to keep pushing forward.

Navigating life with MS has been a continuous learning process. Finding balance in the face of uncertainty and physical limitations requires patience and perseverance. I had to learn to listen to my body and respect its boundaries, even when it meant slowing down or taking breaks. Self-care became a priority, as did finding strategies to manage stress, which often triggered flare-ups.

I lean on the adage, "It's better to have it and not need it than to need it and not have it!" This philosophy has guided me through many challenging moments. I use a cane when needed, not as a sign of weakness but as a tool that allows me to maintain my independence and mobility.

Staying in the moment and not dwelling on the past has been crucial. I focus on what I can do now rather than what I was able to do before my diagnosis. This mindset shift has helped me accept my limitations and find new ways to achieve my goals. I break my work into smaller tasks and manage their completion, over time.

Listening to my body is a daily practice. I take breaks and pace myself to avoid overexertion. Conserving energy is vital, so I move slowly and deliberately, avoiding the risk of running into "low battery mode" or completely shutting down. Rest has become an essential part of my routine; I make sure to rest, allowing my body the recovery time it needs.

Part III: Finding Strength and Resilience

Living with multiple sclerosis has profoundly transformed me, teaching me that all things are possible to those who believe in Christ. Each morning, I wake up with a renewed sense of purpose, knowing that God has not forsaken me and that there is work to be done. This spiritual realization has been the foundation of my strength and resilience.

My daily motivation comes from the Bible and what God says about me, as His daughter. I draw strength and inspiration from scripture, turning bible verses into empowering affirmations that guide me through my day. These verses/affirmations remind me of my inherent strength and the support I have from a higher power, providing the motivation I need to face each day with confidence and hope. I pray away my worries about the future and clothe myself in God's blessings. My journey with MS is bolstered by the wisdom and comfort I find in scripture. I start with The Beatitudes from Matthew 5:1-12 and then meditate on Bible devotionals to transform these sacred texts into empowering motivations. Some of my most cherished motivations include:

- "Jesus' grace is sufficient, His power is made perfect in my weakness." (2 Corinthians 12:9-10)
- "God's plans are to prosper me and not harm me, plans to give me hope and a future." (Jeremiah 29:11)
- "I praise You because I am fearfully and wonderfully made." (Psalms 139:14)
- "Be strong and courageous, Antoinette and do the work for God is with you!" (1 Chronicles 28:20)
- "You will never leave me or forsake!" (Hebrews 13:5)

Affirmations have been an integral part of my lifeline, guiding me through the toughest days, so daily, I remind myself:

- I am stronger than my challenges.
- I am resilient.
- I am capable of overcoming anything that comes my way.
- I will never allow my circumstances to determine my destiny.
- I AM the dream of the slaves!

Despite the challenges of living with MS, I have reached several significant milestones and achievements:

- **Wife and Mother**: My greatest accomplishment is being happily married to my husband, Sean, of 23+ years and stewarding over Seani and Sean II.
- **Elementary School Principal**: Leading as a servant leader in a Title I School, I initiated the first and only Global School and Dual Language Spanish Immersion Program in our school division.
- **Co-Founder and CEO of Forever and a Day Publishing LLC**: Our mission focuses on God, Family, Career, and Finances. It allows me to use my expertise to help others put pen to paper to share their life's struggles and triumphs, dreams, and experiences. I firmly believe in the principle that "It's not ours to keep!" and strive to give back in every way I can.
- **Educational Consulting**: Leveraging my 22 years of experience in education, I provide resume writing and interviewing services to clients.
- **Life Insurance Agent**: By offering life insurance services, I help families become properly protected, debt-free, and financially independent.
- **Community Involvement**: I actively participate in community events and support groups, sharing my MS journey and encouraging others facing similar battles.

These accomplishments are a testament to my resilience and determination. They demonstrate that, despite the limitations imposed by MS, it is possible to lead a fulfilling and impactful life.

Part IV: Practical Tips for Others

One of the most important aspects of managing multiple sclerosis is being your own advocate. You know your body, so it's crucial to listen when it speaks. As a Black woman, I am acutely aware of the health disparities that exist and the need to voice concerns surrounding healthcare. If one doctor fails to attend to your concerns, don't hesitate to seek another opinion. Treatment knows no discrimination, and there are health professionals whose life's work is to help with accurate diagnoses and effective treatments.

Before any appointment, brainstorm questions to ask, document your symptoms and experiences, and be prepared to advocate for the treatment you need. When seeking medical attention, bring someone with you to take notes while you talk with the health professionals. This will allow you time to share and reflect on the responses without being overwhelmed by emotions.

I encourage others living with an illness to research support groups in their area and connect with groups on social media platforms. Also, subscribe to mailings for updates on care, research, conferences, and healthy lifestyle options. Building a network of support and staying informed about the latest developments can make a significant difference in managing your condition and maintaining a positive outlook.

My relationship with God is impenetrable, and it has been a heart of my strength. In addition to my faith, I have a psychotherapist who has helped me deal with childhood trauma. She functions more like a life coach, redirecting me to the greatness within and reminding me of what I have overcome.

Living with an illness such as MS can cause anxiety and depression, or you may also battle conditions like ADHD. Seeking a collaborative team of medical professionals can ensure that not only your physical health is managed but also your spiritual, mental, and emotional well-being. It's essential to address all aspects of health to maintain balance and resilience in the face of chronic illness.

My journey with multiple sclerosis has been filled with challenges, but it has also been a journey of immense personal growth, faith, and resilience. Through my faith in God, the support of my family, and my health team, I have found the strength to overcome obstacles. I hope that my story can inspire others to find their own strength and resilience, reminding them that they are not alone in their unseen battles. I see you!

****

Have you dreamed of seeing your book on the shelves, in readers' hands, or available online? At Forever and a Day Publishing, we specialize in transforming your writing dreams into reality. Whether it's fiction, nonfiction, or memoirs, we are here to guide you through every step of the publishing process. Your story matters, and the world needs to hear it! Let us help you bring it to life. Contact us today to get started on your journey to becoming a published author with a free consultation and to access all of our published books at https://faadpublishingllc.com. Join us a @faadllc on Facebook and Instagram social media platforms to link with others about overcoming obstacles, perseverance, and faith.

.

SENSITIVE BUT UNSTOPPABLE

Maggie Kelly

CEO & Coach

Maggie Kelly is the CEO of Sensitive But Unstoppable Coaching Services which helps highly sensitive people rise from their shadows into their strengths. With over 5 years of experience in helping others recognize their hidden gifts/talents, she previously worked as a medical administrator in the field of psychiatry specializing in schizophrenia and bipolar depression. . Maggie holds certificates from the Nickerson Institute and the Highly Sensitive Human Academy as a Certified Highly Sensitive Person Coach. Maggie is passionate in educating others about this unique character trait that 15-20% of the population are born with. Many people don't even know they are highly sensitive subsequently, they are not realizing their full potential as a human being. Highly sensitive people are a benefit in the workplace, home environments, etc because of their leadership, empathy & understanding skills they bring to the table. In her spare time, Maggie loves reading, cooking, writing and needlework.

https://www.linkedin.com/in/magk/
https://www.facebook.com/MaggieKEssentialoil
https://www.instagram.com/sensitive_but_unstoppable/
https://sensitivebutunstoppable.com/

A HEART OF FAITH: FINDING STRENGTH IN SENSITIVITY AND GOD

Navigating Life as a Highly Sensitive Person with Unshakable Faith

By Maggie Kelly

When we depend on God, and turn to Him, we have no idea how our needs will be answered. That's where trust and faith come in.

I was the oldest of 5 born into a very traditional Irish Catholic family. At the time of my birth, the doctor said, "This is the longest, bonniest baby I ever delivered." When I was baptized, the Irish priest said, "This lass will be the bell of Ottawa East." My parents even fought over my name. My mother wanted to call me Maggie, and my dad said, no, it is Peggy, or I am out of here. If I had my way, I would have chosen Mary Margaret. So, can you see why I can say, I was always causing a stir? People have always had a lot to say about me. Dad always said, "I made life more difficult for myself than necessary, or "Peggy, you are too tense, just relax." Yes, and there was a reason why I was tense and unrelaxed. Then again, my aunt would say, I was the only one she knew who put the cart before the horse. Obviously, my thinking pattern was definitely very different.

Both parents had very deep Irish roots, along with that deep Irish Catholic faith, which was passed onto me. Dad was 5th generation on his Dad's side and 2nd on his mom's side. My recent DNA results showed I am 98% Irish and 2% Scottish. Strange indeed! Dad, the oldest of 13, 6 boys and 7 girls, had trouble saying any word that started with letters like th. It would appear as though he just got off the boat. Mom, second youngest of 7, 6 girls and 1 boy, was just as Irish, but that picture of the Irish always laughing and joking did not prevail with my mother. Dad was a very handsome, friendly-looking man, though you had to approach him very delicately, as you just never knew whether he would erupt or not. Something I couldn't figure out at the time, but I now know why. Mom was absolutely beautiful. She had a beautiful smile, could be so kind, quite funny but... but...!

It was fun going out to Dad's homestead when we were kids. Jumping in the haystack, playing with the other Kelly cousins, tantalizing my male cousins to go where no one else would go- those were the days. There was always lots of laughter, banging the table at a game of euchre, teasing, and joking. It really was very refreshing because one could smell the love in Granny's home and in the air. Dad came from such a positive, loving family. I treasured and held these special memories very close to my heart, which would serve me well as they played a huge factor in how I managed the horrendous events that were to come.

I always knew I was different and always felt as though I didn't fit in anywhere, yet I didn't know why. I knew I was unhappy inside, even though the world saw me as a cheerful, upbeat, and friendly person. I made friends easily, but couldn't keep them. Personally, I felt like a clown. I am sure my low self-esteem and lack of confidence were very obvious. Yet, I always sensed something was just not right. Even as a young 3-year-old, I sensed deep anger in my mom, which made me nervous, tense, and most uncomfortable. I even sensed her lack of love. Why I felt this, I have no idea. I just knew.

She was very critical, judgmental, and much more opinionated than Dad. I was very young when I picked up on this constant criticism, putting people down. It not only made me feel sad and upset, but it also angered me. Not only that, of all my siblings, only Dad and I were the primary recipients of being constantly put down, minimized, or even set up for a fight. It made both of us look bad and equally did an awful lot of damage, as we always reacted. I made up my mind to be more like my father, non-critical, and non-judgmental, even though I always felt a huge backlash from Mom as I was constantly standing up to her. Somehow, I can't say how, but at a very young age, I just knew her way of looking at life was just not right; As a matter of fact, downright wrong. Hence, the table has been set! I started to dig in my heels.

All my life, Mom told me, I can't do this, I can't do that, no one would ever want me, I won't amount to anything, everything was just in my head that sort of thing. Even when it came to my second marriage, she said to my future husband, "Why would you want to marry her? She has no money." My intuition was compromised. Whenever I would sense something, I was always told I was just imagining things. Gaslighting! Every friend I made was taken away from me. I was unable to have a relationship with my siblings. My relationship with my dad was compromised. If I tried to have a relationship with my aunts, I faced consequences. I felt robbed of my intuition, insight, and identity. The roots of depression/anger, which started to set in and control me, manifested in my ability to learn in school. Thus, anger and depression were becoming more evident.

Yet something else was emerging within me. My grade 1 teacher had a huge influence on me. She seemed to understand me, and the way she presented the Life of Christ, First Holy Communion, etc., was the beginning of what would eventually sustain me through some really horrendous times.

It was just too much to bear. I was struggling with the same negative, critical judgemental attitude in my marriage as I did growing up. I was beginning to think I never left home. I was also experiencing the same struggles at work as I had in school. I was wrought with anxiety/depression. I had gut issues, a spending problem, and relationship issues. Two doctors and two priests told me to leave the marriage, but I couldn't. I just couldn't put my oldest daughter through more trauma. Hindsight is a great virtue, as I should have left. I actually put her through more trauma by staying. She was never the same after I spent 10 weeks in the hospital due to a pregnancy. Even though I was very ill and almost died, I did deliver triplets who did not survive. One died nine hours after birth; the other, 24 days after birth; and the last one came home and died in my arms 7 months later. This was a huge tragedy as I always wanted a huge family. But it was my 3-year-old daughter who was really traumatized as she never bonded with me again.

I did not have the confidence or self-esteem to leave. But at the same time, my anger/depression was growing exponentially. I was in a bad marriage. I didn't know it at the time, but I was actually married to a dry drunk. Insidious, actually, as that is worse than one who drinks. The medical professionals said I was bipolar or had ADHD. I knew this was not true. But of course, that good old stand-by medication is the only answer. Something was really wrong.

I had a choice. I could become a victim of the situation or use my God-given intelligence and find an answer knowing that God helps those who help themselves. What am I going to do?

I turned to God. The only area I was relatively free of issues was my spiritual life. "Thank you, Lord, for that, " as no one else understood. God knew "that:"

- An aunt would leave me some money, and some cousins would accuse me of taking that money. That's another story.
- A doctor would try to violate the essence of my very being as a woman by challenging my moral and ethical beliefs.
- My husband would not support me.
- My dad would die when I was facing a divorce, and job loss.
- I would hear his voice 3 days following his death, telling me, "Don't try to figure your mother out, I couldn't, and you won't." I was sitting quietly by myself in church when I heard that – I shook like a leaf after.
- I would go bankrupt, lose my marriage, my home, my 2 girls, my job, and literally be left on the street.
- Another aunt would help me to get a new lease on life, but we would get ripped off by the home builder for thousands and the next morning find her dead in bed.
- I would be accused of manipulating my aunt for her money, which was not true. She wanted to give me a chance. She said, "Anyone who had been put down as much as I needed help."
- Every time I would get a job, I would get fired.
- My mom would help others but made it extremely difficult for me to expect help from her as her anger came through, meaning she really didn't want to help me.
- My husband, who was a deacon in the church, would say nasty things about me. Thus, priests turned away from me.
- I would get the answers to all my "whys."
- I would continue to trust in Jesus, cling to Him intensely as a child clings to his/her mother as well as, stay close to my faith. Because He knew I knew He allows people to use their free will.
- My girls would never make an effort to reach out to me, talk to me, hear my side of the story.

- I would hear something terrible about my oldest while sitting in a restaurant. I went absolutely ballistic.

It was during this time that Pope John Paul II, through his writings and homilies, described Divine Mercy as an answer to the world's problems. I made the decision. I turned to Divine Mercy to help me as I felt totally abandoned. It was just too much to bear. That's when things slowly started to change. This total dependence on Divine Mercy brought me relief as I realized my mother rejected me even before I was born. What an epiphany that was. It released me from a lot of hurt and anger.

God does work in mysterious ways, and He really does have a sense of humour. I was stuck in a ditch in front of my house when a gentleman walked by and started to chat with me and pulled me out of that ditch. His wife had passed, and we instantly connected. I found the man who understood me, accepted, and loved me for who I am. After we got married, he said to me, you know you should be on our police force because you miss nothing. I said, "Are you kidding me?" I am the last person for that job. I can't stand the suspense around police work, let alone what could happen. But he got me thinking. One day, while browsing in a bookstore, I discovered the book *The Highly Sensitive Person: How To Survive When The World Overwhelms You*, by Elaine Aaron.

I wanted to jump off the mountain tops. I wanted to scream from the bottom of my lungs – because I realized for the first time in my life I didn't have a disorder or a disease. I wept bitterly. I am a normal, healthy, functioning human being. I am just a woman who has been given a unique gift, that of being a highly sensitive person. What a breakthrough. Finally, I understood. My life took a 180% turn. I have never looked back as I not only felt I got my life back, but I realized my full potential as a human being. I have a purpose in this world. Because I have been given this gift, I feel I have a moral responsibility to use it for the betterment of mankind.

I am now on a mission. Many people, like myself, don't realize they may also be highly sensitive. Since I have always had a huge desire to help others, and being led by my intuition, I decided to set up my own coaching business specializing in the highly sensitive person. My coaching is based on the holistic approach to healing in that it is broken down into body, emotions, spiritual, relationships, and financial. When one of these is out of order, it can really affect every other part of us. When we harness our unique sensitivity as a source of strength, we can navigate our lives with confidence and clarity.

Even though being highly sensitive doesn't make me any better than anyone else, it is a gift that 15–30% of the population is born with. Again, going back to my spiritual life, because I have been given this gift, I have a moral responsibility to use it for the betterment of mankind.

Since I didn't know who I really was, I was actually living in the shadows, allowing my faults and weaknesses to control my life and not permitting my strengths to shine through. I was also living in my woundedness. No doubt, I was badly wounded and badly traumatized, but I was determined not to allow myself to become a victim.

So, as I continue my personal growth and development, it is becoming more and more obvious to me that my unique character trait actually saved me in the long run. One of the gifts of being highly sensitive is our ability to experience a deep inner life. As a highly sensitive person (HSP) we can tend to chew over things, events, etc., like a dog is chewing over a bone. However, this tendency actually coupled with the spiritual side of me, helped me to go far deep into myself to come up with the answers so that I was able to put things into perspective. While it didn't save me from all the bad things that happened to me, I did get and still do get peace.

It was Good Friday, April 7, 2023, when I heard a huge pounding on the basement window. What is that, I thought, hitting our basement window? A bird! How strange is that? It's only a bird. Weird, I thought. The next morning, again, a bird hit our bedroom window, which awakened me from a deep sleep. I went to the kitchen to make coffee, and yet again, that darn bird hit the window with its peak. I pulled the blind down as I couldn't stand seeing the bird hurting itself, and yes, I was a tad upset, to say the least. Two hours later, on Holy Saturday, I got a text, not a phone call but a text saying, "Mom had passed." She was born on a Good Friday and died on Holy Saturday.

Finally, by her death, I was released from the clutches that had encompassed me since birth.

There really is truth in the saying, "Highly sensitive people process things differently."It has been just over a year now since my mom died. And to be so honest with myself and others, I didn't shed one tear. This disturbed me a lot, and being who I am, I had to find out the WHY! Why didn't I cry? I am highly sensitive. I feel for others, I have empathy, I care. I confided my thoughts to a very close friend, but still, I couldn't get an answer. Then after a year, it hit me like a ton of bricks. Let me explain. The bond between a mom/daughter/child is very strong. We feed off that person for 9 months till we are allowed to enter society. There is nothing stronger than a mother/child relationship. But in some cases, some mothers, for whatever reason, have trouble with such a bond. And while I loved my mother deeply, the hurts, the rejections, and the pushing me away all the time closed down one side of my heart. I had to protect my heart as I just couldn't take more pain.

God also knew I knew when we are nice to people, it makes a difference; when we are mean to people, it makes a difference; so we have a choice "in" how we treat others.

God also knew I knew He would never send me anything I couldn't handle. He knew when He created me, I would be given the gift of being highly sensitive. He knew I was strong and resilient, being highly sensitive.

God knew I would get my answer. He knew why I couldn't cry for "my" mom, even though I loved her. He knew my heart was totally broken. He knew I would figure it all out as it is important for a highly sensitive person to get answers. He also knew I had deep empathy, cared a lot for her, and wanted to make her happy. No matter what I tried to do for her, she was never happy, never satisfied.

He knew her death set me FREE! I cried bitterly. God knew.

God knew that gentleman, a police officer, who got me out of the ditch, also helped me to discover my full potential by saying just one thing, "You notice everything." His love, his support, and his caring pulled me out of an emotional ditch and gave me a new lease on life. Life is strange with its twists and turns, but without knowing that someone loves you, feels for you, and cares for you, our chances of fulfilling our purpose in life can definitely be compromised.

I depended on God, I Trusted Him, and I found love.

BRUNSWICK ORGANIZING SOLUTIONS

Karen Wrenn

Professional Organizer

Karen was born in a small town in Western Maryland. After high school, Karen attended Hagerstown Community College, received her BS degree in Elem Ed/Special Ed from University of Maryland, and her Masters in Human Development from George Washington University in Washington DC. Karen taught children with special needs for 35 years, retiring in 2012. Karen was married to her husband, Gary, for 37 years until his passing in 2021. They moved to Wilmington, NC after both of them retired from the school system. Karen has two grown children and three grandchildren. Karen started her professional organizing service, Brunswick Organizing Solutions in 2018. She credits her success to God and to her strong faith. In her spare time, Karen enjoys volunteering at 2 local theatres, swimming, going to the beach and spending time with her family and friends. She loves to plan adventurous trips with her friends and family!

https://www.linkedin.com/in/karen-wrenn-6b1836207/
https://www.facebook.com/karen.wrenn.79
https://www.instagram.com/Karenwrenn/
https://www.getorganizednc.com/

RISING ABOVE YOUR RAISING

By Karen Wrenn

I was born and raised in a small town in western Maryland called Hagerstown, surrounded by the beauty of the mountains. I lived there until I left for college at the University of Maryland. My memories of growing up in Hagerstown date back to when I was five years old, and my upbringing there has profoundly shaped my life and influenced who I am today.

I lived with my family—my mom, dad, and two sisters—in a duplex in the southern part of Hagerstown. My extended family included my maternal grandmother, two uncles, one aunt, two aunts by marriage, and three first cousins, along with other relatives spread across Maryland and Pennsylvania. My maternal grandfather passed away before I was born, and I had little exposure to my father's side of the family, so I know very little about them.

My extended family played an integral role in my childhood. Sundays were special, filled with family gatherings, games, and cookouts that brought us all closer together. I cherished these moments, as they were filled with joy, warmth, and a sense of belonging. However, the comfort I found in my extended family contrasted sharply with the reality at home. My father was an alcoholic, and his violent tendencies often cast a shadow over our lives. I have vivid memories of him pushing my mom down the stairs and getting physical with her, incidents that left me feeling helpless yet determined to protect her. I would often find myself standing between them, yelling at my dad to stop. One night, when I was just five years old, my father came home drunk, ripped the phone off the wall, and nearly hit my sister with it. My mom told me to run next door and call the police, but my dad threatened me if I did. For a brief moment, I hesitated, paralyzed by fear. Then, summoning all my courage, I bolted for the door, ducking under his arm, and stayed with our neighbors until the police arrived. As they took him away, he threatened me again, but my mom comforted me, reassuring me that I did the right thing and that she would protect me.

Over time, my father's drinking worsened. My dad eventually lost his job and spent more time at the local tavern. My mom, doing her best to hold everything together, would send me there to ask him for money to buy milk and bread. He usually gave it to me, likely because others were watching. Eventually, he left us for good, moving in with another woman. We lost our home to foreclosure, but with the help of my extended family, we found a small apartment. It was cramped, but to me, it was peaceful—the first sense of normalcy I had experienced.

With my father gone, I was able to focus more on school and other activities. I thrived in middle and high school, with little contact with my father. My mom worked hard, cleaning houses and at a furniture company, while my older sister and I got jobs at a local ice cream store called Hoovers. My grandmother moved nearby to help us, and I often visited her. One day, when I was 16, my grandma asked me to come help her clean. She had just recovered from the flu, but instead of cleaning, she asked me to sit and talk about school. Suddenly, she slumped over, unresponsive. I called 911, but she was pronounced dead at the scene. Her death triggered panic attacks and vivid dreams, which took nearly two years to subside.

In high school, I made many friends and was active in various activities, including the South High Rebelettes, a pom-pom squad. I was focused on my studies, earning good grades, and had my sights set on becoming a teacher. After graduation, I applied for grants and scholarships to attend community college, which helped me cover my tuition. To support myself further, I worked for spending money and took on several volunteer roles. My friends encouraged me to run for vice president of the Student Government Association, and I was thrilled to win. When the president resigned six months later, I stepped into the role, becoming the first female president at the college. I quickly learned parliamentary procedures, engaged with faculty, and even attended the National Student Congress Association in Miami, Florida—my first time on an airplane!

After two years, I applied to the University of Maryland, where I was accepted and awarded tuition, room, board, and a spot in the work-study program. I majored in Elementary Education and Special Education, completing student teaching in both fields. I graduated in two and a half years with a BS degree. My family, including my father, attended my graduation, and he helped me move into my apartment. Although I kept in touch with him, I limited our interactions due to his continued drinking, which brought back painful childhood memories.

I began interviewing for full-time teaching jobs and was hired on the spot by the principal of a brand-new special education center, starting my 35-year teaching career. That principal became a father figure to me, and many other young teachers, and our bond grew into a lifelong friendship. To this day, he calls me every Friday morning to check in. Recently, I had the honor of organizing his 90th birthday party, reuniting many of the teachers who had started their careers with him, all coming together to celebrate this remarkable man.

I met my husband at a state's Special Olympics event, where we were both actively involved at the state level. A year later, we were married.

At the time, I was teaching and pursuing my Master's degree at George Washington University in Washington, DC. My days were long—I'd teach, take the metro into the city for classes, return home around 10 p.m., and start all over again the next day. Three years into our marriage, we decided to start a family. We had a son first, followed by a daughter three years later. Now, both of our children are grown with families of their own.

I became a caregiver for my husband when he became a type 1 diabetic with kidney disease and trigeminal neuralgia, a debilitating facial nerve issue that required narcotics to cope on a daily basis. Being a caregiver comes with its own share of challenges. It takes an emotional toll on the entire family, by having to juggle your personal life while balancing your career, raising children, and maintaining a husband/wife relationship. There is a commitment of time with frequent medical appointments, blood sugar checks, and medication management, to name a few. There are lifestyle adjustments like dietary changes and social planning changes centered around medication schedules. As a caregiver, you become the sole manager of your home. Financial decisions, health insurance management, household chores, and work, all require good time management. Establishing a work/life balance is essential for your own mental health. There are fears of complications. It was very important to me to maintain my husband's dignity as well as respect for his autonomy. This requires reaching out to a support system to help you, the caregiver, with self-care. Navigating the job of a caregiver is a journey that comes with challenges. It was important to me to be flexible, patient, and kind to my husband and myself.

My husband retired several years before I did, and I eventually retired after 35 years of teaching. Shortly after, we moved to Wilmington, NC. Despite retiring, I knew I wasn't ready to step away from working fully. I felt that I had more to contribute and decided to become a professional organizer.

My cousin and I started the business together, but sadly he passed away from battling cancer earlier this year. Although many people advised me to find another partner, primarily because of my limited business experience, I was determined to succeed on my own. I became a sole owner and built a successful company, Brunswick Organizing Solutions, which has now been thriving for six years. Recently, our county's Chamber of Commerce recognized my business with an excellence award for small businesses. I've developed a training program and led a team of 12 organizers, helping mostly seniors transition into the next stage of their lives.

So, how did I get here?

I made a decision early in life to make an impact and to continue helping others. I've always enjoyed helping others—whether it was assisting a blind woman with her mail when I was 10 or learning sign language to communicate with my deaf friend.

I've faced many challenges throughout my life, including the loss of both of my parents. My mother was a wonderful, patient, and loving woman who did her best despite difficult circumstances. My father, though he became sober through treatment and AA meetings, struggled with a gambling addiction and a pattern of self-centered behavior. I chose to limit my interactions with him.

We all have the power to make choices in life and choose a different path. I chose to remain strong, focused, and determined. I encourage others to pursue their dreams, make wise choices, and keep their faith. Most importantly, for those who have endured a difficult or traumatic childhood, I urge them to "rise above their raising."

ACTIVE INGREDIENTS INC.
Vandana Puranik
Founder & Owner

#THINKFLUENCER, BRAINSTORMER, BUILDER & BRANDER. Vandana Puranik has been a marketer, innovator, and strategist for 25+ years in a variety of complex industries. She has built businesses from the ground up and established ones by as much as 60% in ONE month!

A truly global citizen, Vandana's experience has led to a deep understanding of human insights – those that transform figments into creative & break-through ideas. She is a USA Today & Wall Street Journal bestselling co-author & international speaker who serves progressive, growth-minded individuals to solve impossible problems by figuring out where to go when nothing seems to work. She is often asked to mentor others.

She is a graduate of Duke University in the field of Comparative Area Studies. Her company is Active Ingredients Inc. And she just launched What She Said – a posse of bad bitched doing great things!
Join her in transforming the way we think.

https://www.linkedin.com/in/vandanapuranik
https://www.instagram.com/whatshesaid.next
https://thisiswhatshesaid.com/
https://www.activeingredientsinc.com/

RISING FROM THE BRINK

The Power of Choice, Curiosity, and Resilience

By Vandana Puranik

In the quiet moments between life and death, when the line between existing and slipping away blurs to near invisibility, I made a choice. I chose to rise—not just to survive but to confront the very essence of how we face our challenges. The journey isn't about the obstacles we see; it's about the outcomes we choose to pursue, the relentless curiosity that drives us forward, the deliberate actions we take, and even the humor we find along the way.

There are countless stories I could share, but the one that resonates most deeply right now is this: Earlier this year, I returned home after spending two months in the hospital, two weeks of which were lost to a coma. A coma hypothetically triggered by a rare and severe reaction to one of my chemotherapy medications. It was an unexpected and brutal twist—one that shocked not just my family and friends but also my entire medical team. According to the outside world, I had essentially fallen off the face of the earth. The condition I faced is known for its grim statistics, and its survival rate is anything but favorable. Yet here I am, writing these words, breathing, and living a life that is both fragile and fiercely resilient.

Defining Your Own Path

One thing I've learned in this process is that battles aren't won through sheer strength alone. They are won in all those little moments in between, the ones that lead you to decide to define your own path, no matter the odds or statistics stacked against you. We are all battling something—whether it's visible or unseen, whether it's medical, emotional, or mental. And in those moments of battle, you have two choices: surrender or fight. But not all fights are with swords raised; some are with quiet persistence and resilience.

For me, that choice began with a mindset shift. I had every reason to give up—my body felt broken, my spirit tested—but I made a conscious decision not to be a victim of my circumstances. I refused to allow breast cancer to define me. Instead, I became obsessed with the power of my thoughts. Here's the thing: Our mind is the most potent weapon we have. If we can harness its strength, if we can train it to focus on what we can control, then the battles we face become opportunities for growth, not defeat.

Practical Tip #1: Choose Your Outcome. Take a moment to reflect. What challenges are you facing today? Now, visualize the outcome you want—not the one you fear. Write it down. Keep it somewhere visible. Every day, take one small action toward that outcome, even if it's as simple as getting out of bed, moving your body, or reading something that lifts your spirit. The mind is powerful; when you focus it on what you want, rather than what you fear, the universe responds in kind.

The Power of Curiosity

There's a reason I talk about curiosity so often. Curiosity is the antidote to despair. When I found myself awake after two weeks in a coma, I didn't focus on why this happened to me or what I had lost in the process. Instead, I became intensely curious about what I could do next. How could I use this experience, this fight for survival, to not just rebuild myself but to help others? What could I learn from this? How could I push the boundaries of what I thought was possible?

This mindset of curiosity isn't about avoiding the pain. It's about leaning into it, asking the questions that feel uncomfortable, but doing so with childlike wonder or a scientist, and using the answers to propel yourself forward. I've often asked myself, "What would my life look like if I didn't have cancer?" But then I shifted the question: "What can my life look like because of this?" That shift—however small—has been life-changing.

Practical Tip #2: Ask the Hard Questions. In your own life, whether you're dealing with illness, career challenges, or personal struggles, try flipping the script. Ask yourself the questions you're afraid to answer. Don't just wonder, "Why me?" Instead, ask, "What now? What can I do with this experience that will serve me or others?" And keep asking. Curiosity keeps the mind open to possibility.

The Power of Deliberate Action

Alongside curiosity, another guiding principle for me has been being deliberate in all that I do. Being deliberate means making conscious, active decisions rather than letting life happen to us. It's about choosing how we respond, especially when things feel chaotic or uncertain.

When we're passive, we let circumstances, emotions, or others' expectations dictate our direction. But being deliberate is different—it's deciding to take control of what we can. It's an intentional choice to steer our actions, our mindset, and our approach to life's challenges.

When I woke up from that coma, I had every reason to feel defeated, to retreat into passivity. No one would have blamed me for it. But instead, I made a deliberate choice to take action. I chose to actively engage with my life, to pursue the things that matter to me, even if it felt like the hardest thing in the world. Three days after returning home, I was standing on a stage, delivering a TEDx talk. That didn't happen by accident. It happened because I made a deliberate decision to move forward. To take the next step, even when it felt daunting.

Practical Tip #3: Make One Deliberate Choice Every Day. Start small. Each day, take a moment to consciously make a deliberate choice. It could be as simple as deciding how you want to spend your morning or how you'll respond to a difficult situation. When you start making small, intentional choices, you begin to build the muscle of deliberateness. It's not about being perfect; it's about being present and aware of the power you hold in every moment.

The Role of Humor in Resilience

Curiosity and being deliberate have shaped my path, but there's another force that has carried me through some of the darkest moments—humor. It may seem strange to talk about laughter in the midst of a life-threatening battle, but humor has been one of the most powerful tools in my recovery. It's the light that cuts through the heaviness, the reminder that even in the most serious situations, we're still allowed to find joy, to laugh, to be human.

There's something about humor that can't be explained by science or logic. It just works. Whether it's cracking a joke about the absurdity of my situation, or finding humor in the mundane hospital routine, laughter became my lifeline. It broke the tension, softened the blow of reality, and gave me space to breathe. More importantly, it reminded me that I wasn't just a patient—I was still me.

Humor has a way of lifting the spirit, resetting the emotional clock, and giving us the strength to face what's next. It doesn't make the pain go away, but it gives us a break from it. It's like taking a breath in the middle of a storm. For me, laughter wasn't just a coping mechanism— it was an essential part of my recovery.

There's a misconception that if you're serious about your battle, you can't laugh about it. I reject that entirely. Humor doesn't diminish the seriousness of what I've been through; it's part of how I've dealt with it. It's how I've connected with the people around me—my family, my friends, even my medical team. It's also how I've stayed connected with myself.

Practical Tip #4: Find Humor in the Small Moments. When life gets heavy, allow yourself to laugh—especially at the small, ridiculous moments. Humor isn't a denial of pain, it's a celebration of life in the face of it. Whether it's sharing a funny story or laughing at the absurdity of a situation, let humor remind you that there's more to life than the battles you're fighting.

The Courage to Trust in What We Cannot See

I have an unshakeable faith in the energy that surrounds us, the unseen forces that guide our steps. It's this faith that keeps me strong, keeps me positive. When I woke up, alive and functioning, the medical teams couldn't contain their amazement. They were giddy with disbelief, witnessing a recovery that defied their expectations. I'm not just alive; I'm thriving. Just three days after returning home, I delivered a TEDx talk. Then, I spoke at an international summit. I've been interviewed on a few podcasts, with several more to come. And by the end of the year, I plan to publish a book that's been long in the making. On top of that, I've launched "What She Said"—www.ThisIsWhatSheSaid.com— a posse of Bad Bitches doing great things.

I'm often asked if I believe everything happens for a reason. I do not. What I do believe is that whatever happens, you have to make sure it has a purpose—otherwise, it would have happened in vain. Life's events don't always come with a neat explanation, but we have the power to shape meaning from them. In my case, this experience could have been a senseless trauma, but I made the choice to turn it into a catalyst for growth, for impact, and for lifting others up.

It's not enough to just thrive for the sake of it. I am energized—energized to keep moving forward, to embrace life with an intensity that honors the hundreds of hands that played a role in saving mine. I refuse to slow down because I believe so much of our experience, so much of our behavior, is shaped by the mind. Our thoughts and beliefs are powerful beyond measure. Through my work, I delve into creative problem-solving, and inevitably, the science of neuroplasticity comes up. It's nothing short of remarkable how we can train our brains, shape our thoughts, and, ultimately, steer our lives toward the outcomes we desire. All of this happens in the shadows, unseen, yet it's the driving force behind everything we do.

One of the hardest things to do is trust in the unknown. It's easy to have faith when everything is going according to plan, but it's in the moments of uncertainty that true trust is built. I've learned that trusting the unseen—whether it's faith, intuition, or the support of those around you—isn't about blindly hoping everything will work out. It's about making the deliberate choice to believe that even in the chaos, there is meaning. There is growth. There is a way forward.

This experience has deepened my trust in the unseen forces guiding my path. I may not always know what comes next, but I've learned to trust that I will find the strength, the people, and the purpose I need to move forward. It's a trust built not on guarantees, but on the belief that I've already made it through more than I thought possible. And if I can do that, there's nothing I can't face.

The Power of Now

As I reflect on this journey—one that continues to unfold—what stands out most is the strength that lies in how we choose to live. Life doesn't hand us reasons for the things that happen, but we make choices every step of the way. These decisions are where we find our true power.

Getting through something isn't enough. It's about making the most of every moment—the joy and the struggle alike. It means being curious and deliberate, finding humor, and trusting the unseen forces that guide us.

I've come to realize that life is about transformation. It's about taking what has happened—good or bad—and shaping it into something meaningful. For me, that has meant using my story, my experiences, to fuel the work I do with women, helping them reclaim their own power and navigate their battles. It's the choice to turn pain into something that serves a greater good, to leave a mark, to uplift others.

So, as you walk your own path, remember that life's meaning isn't handed to us—it's something we create every day. And the only time we have to do that is in this moment. Remember, all we have is NOW.

.

ALICIA FUENTES COACHING & CONSULTANCY SERVICES

Alicia Fuentes

Founder & Certified Coach

Alicia Fuentes is a Revalidation Coach with 28 years of corporate experience, offering deep insight into the challenges faced by professional women. Leveraging her expertise in leadership, personal development, change management, and human performance, she empowers high-performing women to rediscover their identity, reclaim their worth, and redefine their paths after redundancy or major life changes.

Through her signature program, *The Revalidation Revolution*, Alicia guides her clients to rise stronger by embracing their feminine energy. Her compassionate approach, paired with actionable strategies, helps women overcome self-doubt, break through limiting beliefs, and step confidently into their potential as impactful feminine leaders.

Alicia's coaching equips women with the tools to balance personal and professional demands while unlocking the confidence to thrive. She is dedicated to helping her clients transform their lives with purpose and power.

#EmbraceChange #BeUnstoppable

https://www.linkedin.com/in/alicia-fuentes-7040112a4/
https://www.facebook.com/aliciazfuentes/
https://www.instagram.com/alicia.zaida74

BREAKING BARRIERS

A Journey from Corporate Constraints to Personal Empowerment

By Alicia Fuentes

November 30, 2023, holds a significant place in my heart—a date that marks the anniversary of a turning point in my life. But to understand how I reached that moment, it's important to look back at where it all began. My childhood was a happy one. My parents were always there, taking care of me, and providing love and support. I don't recall being shouted at, belittled, or abused in any form. Instead, I have countless memories of being praised and rewarded, especially when I excelled in school. My parents believed in education and created an environment that allowed me to thrive academically.

As a young girl, I had a natural desire to support and develop others, dreaming of becoming a teacher, just like my dad. Teaching seemed like the right fit for a woman—simple 8 a.m.–3 p.m. days, lots of holidays, and the opportunity to nurture young minds. Throughout university, I tutored students, feeling immense fulfilment when they succeeded. After university, I applied for a teaching position and got accepted. But then, I also received an offer for a marketing role with a company that promised many perks, including the opportunity to travel for business. I found myself at a crossroads and ultimately chose the marketing job, leaving behind the path I initially thought was meant for me.

In my early career, I still found ways to fuel my passion for supporting and developing others through training responsibilities. Those initial roles were strong building blocks, helping me become more outgoing and financially independent. But nothing prepared me for the world I was about to enter: the high-stakes, fast-paced environment of the oil and gas industry.

The Early Days: Building Resilience

Navigating Corporate Life: A Shock to My System

My first role as a Health, Safety and Environmental (HSE) Officer was a baptism by fire. I was a timid young woman of 29, suddenly thrown into the thick of an industrial port, surrounded by cargo containers, cranes, and forklifts. My job was to ensure safety—a task that demanded respect and authority. I often found myself complaining to my boss about the poor behaviours, the lack of compliance, and the overall disregard for safety protocols. His response was a simple yet profound lesson: "Anyone can bring me problems; I hired you for solutions." That statement stuck with me and became a guiding principle throughout my career, teaching me to be a problem solver and to add value wherever I went.

Building rapport with workers, actively listening to their challenges, and following up on leaders' commitments slowly led to improved behaviours and safety culture. The corporate world was harsh and demanding, starkly different from my nurturing upbringing. It forced me to change, become more rigid, delivery-focused, and at times, put up a facade of strength to navigate male-dominated spaces. As I climbed the ladder, I realized how much I had moulded myself to fit this world at the expense of my empathetic and authentic self.

Climbing the Corporate Ladder: A Balancing Act

As I began working for an Oil and Gas major, my passion for HSE grew, but so did the demands of the job. I became well-versed in managing systems and crises, leading teams, and navigating the complex dynamics of the corporate world. As I moved up the ranks, the years were a blur of meetings, project deadlines, and corporate events. My personal life often took a backseat to my career, and I found myself embodying a dominant masculine energy to succeed in a male-dominated industry.

Egypt: A Turning Point

The Egypt Experience: Breaking and Rebuilding

In 2015, when I was offered the opportunity to work in Egypt, I seized it without hesitation. It was a chance to challenge myself in a new environment, to test my leadership skills, and to make a meaningful impact. My time in Egypt presented both challenges and opportunities. Initially, it was tough; getting around was dangerous due to the driving challenges, finding familiar foods was a struggle, and language barriers made simple tasks feel insurmountable. At work, I felt unheard and unappreciated. I questioned whether I was failing to communicate effectively or if it was simply that no one cared about the safety messages I was trying to deliver. My quiet disposition was a challenge in Egypt. There were many days when I wanted to give up and return home.

But with my husband's unwavering support and the kind guidance of Egyptian friends, I began to navigate the unique cultural landscape. I learned that to be taken seriously, I needed to step out of my comfort zone. I also learned that relationships mattered deeply; building trust meant leaving my desk, engaging in face-to-face conversations, and genuinely connecting with others. I began to realize that to be taken seriously, I had to adapt and engage in ways that resonated with the local culture.

As a female in a male-dominated environment, special arrangements were often made for me—like having a dedicated washroom at the onshore gas facility or a separate villa when I was overnighting on-site.

Leading HSE initiatives in Egypt was not just about enforcing standards and practices; it was about inspiring others, igniting a passion for safety, and developing aspiring professionals in the field. My greatest accomplishment was not just in the results we achieved but in the relationships I built and the lives I touched.

It was not all challenges; my time in Egypt was also filled with immense joy and unforgettable experiences. The warmth and hospitality of the Egyptian people were truly heartwarming; their kindness made me feel at home in a foreign land. The vibrant culture was a daily celebration of life, with its colourful markets, rich history, and lively festivals. I delighted in the delectable local cuisine, from aish (bread) and koshary to savoury kebabs to Omm ali, Kunafa and sweet, fragrant pastries, which offered a culinary adventure unlike any other. Exploring the ancient wonders of Egypt, like the majestic pyramids and the serene Nile, was a dream come true. The beauty of the landscapes and the depth of the cultural heritage enriched my life profoundly, creating memories that I will cherish forever. But above all, were the magnificent friends my husband and I made; people we now consider our family.

These experiences, while initially daunting, helped me grow in resilience, courage, and humility.

Personal Growth and New Beginnings

Living in Egypt for five years transformed me in ways I never imagined. I gained:

- **Confidence as a Female Leader**: I learned to embrace my leadership style, balancing strength with empathy.

- **A Profound Appreciation for Diverse Cultures**: Immersing myself in a new culture broadened my perspective and deepened my understanding of global dynamics.
- **A Deeper Understanding of My Life's Purpose**: I realized that my true calling was not just in corporate success but in making a meaningful impact on others.
- **A True Desire to Serve Others Authentically**: I developed a passion for helping others
- **The Realization That Family Extends Beyond Blood Relations**: The bonds I formed with my Egyptian friends became a new kind of family.
- **An Eternal Love for Egypt**: My beloved fur-baby Buffy passed away there, and Egypt will always hold a special place in my heart, along with the beautiful friendships fostered.

Achieving international work experience had been a long-held dream, but what I received was far more than a career milestone—it was a life-changing journey that reshaped me.

Facing the Unexpected: A New Chapter

I returned home from Egypt feeling transformed and equipped with a renewed sense of purpose.

However, it was during the COVID-19 pandemic, and working from home made it difficult to engage with others and feel part of a team. These years were challenging, with long working hours and endless meetings. I began to question my purpose. Even as I excelled in my corporate role, something felt off. The work that once filled me with pride now felt hollow. The back-to-back meetings, the challenges with leaders, and the pressure to conform to corporate norms drained my energy. I quickly lost my spark. God and my family became my support, but leaving a high-paying management-level job seemed unthinkable. I continued to show up and serve, but the signs of change were undeniable. My decisions were questioned, I was increasingly sidelined, and I felt a growing sense of alienation.

Then came November 30th—the day I was made redundant. It was Thanksgiving Day in the US, I was on vacation in Florida when I received the news that my job was no longer mine. It felt like divine intervention—the end of one chapter and the beginning of another.

Initially, I was in a state of euphoria, feeling a newfound sense of freedom. But reality soon set in, and panic kicked in. At 50, full of energy and purpose, early retirement was not an option for me. I applied for numerous jobs, sending out applications week after week on LinkedIn. After several rejections, including one with a renowned organization where I endured seven interviews over two months only to be rejected without feedback, I hit a turning point. I realized that I did not want to return to the corporate world. I needed a new path, one that aligned with my values and passions.

Embracing Personal Development and Coaching

Instead of continuing the job hunt, I redirected my energy toward personal development. My first course, Ultimate Success Mastery with Mind Movies, reignited my passion. It helped me revisit my core values, confront limiting beliefs about money and productivity, and embrace the power of visualization. This period of rediscovery sparked my desire to explore coaching as a new career path.

Transitioning to Entrepreneurship: Embracing the Unknown

After 28 years in the corporate world, I turned to entrepreneurship and coaching. Transitioning to this new space hasn't been easy. It required me to unlearn years of rigid corporate conditioning. There have been days when I considered going back; days when it seemed simpler to follow instructions and receive a guaranteed salary. But each client testimonial, each transformation I witness, brings a smile to my face, reminding me why I chose this path and that I am exactly where I am meant to be. Coaching allows me to be empathetic yet empowering, nurturing yet strong. I have the opportunity to guide career-driven women who struggle with self-doubt, burnout, overwhelm, and lack of confidence.

When challenging days arise, I remind myself of the blessings I've received and my purpose for being a coach. It's not just about business—it's about making a difference, one conversation at a time.

I recognize that there are many coaches out there, and people are cautious about how they invest their money. Yet, I chose to move ahead with faith, not fear. I get to engage in meaningful conversations, hold space for vulnerability, and help working professional women rediscover their strength and confidence while creating work-life harmony.

Today, my new career is thriving, and I wake up excited and motivated. I've embraced my feminine energy and discovered a path that aligns with my true self. I've broken through the barriers that once held me back, and now I confidently pursue opportunities that ignite my passion and purpose. My professional life is not just a job; it's a fulfilling journey that energizes and empowers me.

Key Lessons Learned and Insights

1. **Embrace Your Feminine Energy**: For years, I tried to conform to a masculine approach to success, which left me drained and unfulfilled. Embracing my feminine energy has allowed me to tap into my intuition, creativity, and compassion, leading to a more authentic and satisfying career path.

2. **Challenge Limiting Beliefs**: I realized that many of my career limitations were self-imposed. By identifying and challenging these limiting beliefs, I was able to break free from the constraints that held me back and open new opportunities for growth.

3. **Prioritize Self-Care**: Burnout was a constant companion until I learned to prioritize self-care. Taking care of my physical, emotional, and mental well-being gave me the energy and clarity to pursue my career goals with renewed vigour.

Practical Steps for Your Journey

1. **Embrace Continuous Learning**: Invest in personal development courses, workshops, or coaching sessions that align with your career goals. For example, I took the "Mind Movies Ultimate Success Mastery" course, which helped me rediscover my purpose and set new directions.

2. **Cultivate a Growth Mindset**: Reframe challenges as opportunities for growth. When faced with setbacks, ask yourself, "What can I learn from this?" This mindset shift helped me navigate job rejections and ultimately led me to find my true calling in coaching.

3. **Network with Intention**: Build meaningful connections by reaching out to like-minded individuals who share your passions. For me, this meant stepping out of my comfort zone in Egypt and building relationships with colleagues. These relationships were vital to my growth and success.

4. **Set Clear Intentions and Goals**: Whether you're transitioning to a new career or navigating a difficult period,

setting clear intentions is crucial. Define what success looks like for you and break down your goals into actionable steps. This clarity will keep you focused and motivated.

5. **Stay True to Your Values**: In moments of doubt, return to your core values. Staying true to myself and my purpose guided me through my transition from the corporate world to entrepreneurship. Aligning with your values will keep you grounded and ensure your actions are authentic.

6. **Create a Support System**: Surround yourself with a community that uplifts and supports you. For me, it was connecting with other coaches and mentors who shared my vision of serving others. Find your tribe, and don't be afraid to lean on them for support.

Actionable Steps:

- **Define Your Vision:** Write down your long-term goals and create a vision board. Visualizing your desired future helps keep you focused and motivated.
- **Develop a Daily Routine:** Establish a routine that includes meditation, journaling, and self-care. Consistency in these practices can significantly impact your well-being and progress.
- **Seek Support:** Join a Mastermind group or find a mentor or coach for guidance and accountability. Surrounding yourself with a supportive community can accelerate your growth.
- **Set SMART Goals:** Use the SMART framework (Specific, Measurable, Achievable, Relevant, Time-bound) to set clear, actionable goals. Regularly review and adjust as needed.
- **Track Progress:** Keep a journal or use an app to monitor your progress. Reflect on your achievements and areas for improvement to stay motivated.

Affirmations to Fuel Your Journey:

1. *"I am resilient and capable of overcoming any challenge that comes my way."*
   This affirmation helped me through the uncertain days after redundancy, reminding me that every setback was a setup for a greater comeback.

2. *"I choose to embrace change and see it as an opportunity for growth."*
   Embracing change is what allowed me to transition from a structured corporate environment to the fluid and unpredictable world of coaching. Change can be scary, but it can also be exhilarating.

3. *"I am deserving of success and will take aligned action toward my goals."*
   This affirmation empowered me to keep pushing forward, even on days when the path seemed unclear. It reminded me that I deserved to succeed and had the power to make it happen.

4. *"I embrace my authentic self, and I am enough just as I am."*
   For years, I tried to fit into corporate moulds that were never meant for me. This affirmation grounds me in my truth.

5. *"I am a creator of solutions, and my voice matters."*
   My boss's advice to focus on solutions over problems shaped my career. Now, it's a guiding light for my clients and me.

Conclusion: A Journey to Purpose and Fulfilment

Transitioning from a long-standing corporate career to becoming a coach has been a challenging yet rewarding journey. I am grateful for every experience that shaped me—from the industrial port, where I learned to be a problem solver, to Egypt, where I found my confidence and courage, to the post-redundancy period, where I discovered my passion for coaching.

Today, as a Revalidation Coach, I am dedicated to empowering high performing women to rediscover their strengths, reignite their passions, and redefine their future paths. My mission is to help them embrace their feminine energy and step confidently into roles as courageous leaders in any environment they choose.

I have learned that every step of the journey, whether filled with joy or struggle, is necessary. Each step brings growth, resilience, and an opportunity to live authentically and purposefully.

DIRECTION FINDERS
Anne Chapple
Coach & AI Expert

I am both an experienced educator and a versatile writer with a diverse history. My doctoral degree is in English Literature (University of Chicago), but I also hold Masters degrees in Biology (environmental science), and Higher Education from the University of Michigan. For over a decade, I have been doing commercial writing for websites, blogs, academic articles, non-academic articles, e-books, white papers, etc. for clients. I can write knowledgeably about a range of academic subjects: health and nutrition, English literature, world literature, psychology, art, biology, botany, and environmental science. Recently, I have added coaching to my repertoire: I coach women who are trying to excavate their personal authenticity. I support my coaching work with online courses that offer step-by-step exercises and meditative work to facilitate self-discovery and identification of work that draws on their unique personal strengths.

https://www.linkedin.com/in/anne-s-chapple-ph-d-3812a73b/
https://www.facebook.com/anne.chapple.7/

HOW TO RECOVER YOUR AUTHENTIC SELF AND CHOOSE WORK THAT SUITS YOU

By Anne Chapple

I think most women would like the chance to live their lives according to the promptings of their inner self. We struggle with choosing lifestyles (married, single, etc.) and meaningful work that suits who we are as unique individuals. All too often, well-meaning parents, friends, and other authorities in our lives block our attempts to live authentically. Centuries of indoctrination of women leave many of us trapped in layers of false beliefs and myths about who we really are ... and seemingly powerless to get out from under all of it.

But we are more resilient than we may realize! We CAN rise out of our mental enslavement to build authentic lives for ourselves. We CAN empower ourselves by committing to a careful process of self-examination, staying attuned to our inner promptings, and striving to stay honest with ourselves. This struggle to be ourselves is largely an "unseen battle," but a battle of the utmost importance.

There is far more at stake than we may realize in living an authentic life and charting a direction for our work in the future. If we choose a direction that is wrong for us, we may have to assume a false identity, live our life with people who don't share our passions, or who can't appreciate us for who we really are. Alternatively, a good choice will allow us to use our natural gifts and talents, pursue work that we love, contribute meaningfully to the world, and meet people who share our joys and our values! The personal costs of assuming a false identity – a "mask" – are enormous! We risk feeling deeply disconnected from our authentic selves , unable to connect with others at the deepest level, and lonely for kindred spirits.

Let's start by defining what we mean by your "authentic self." Your "authentic self" is who you truly are as a person, regardless of the situation in which you presently find yourself. It is the most honest version of yourself. To be authentic means not spending much time worrying about what others think about you. To be authentic means to be true to yourself in your thoughts, words, and actions. To be authentic, the actions of your life must come from within you and flow from your heart. Your authenticity is built on your strongest talents, values, and beliefs. To live an authentic life, you need to choose a direction that does not require you to construct a false self that hides the genuine person that you are. Your direction must enable you to be uniquely yourself! For that reason, my focus here is on BOTH authentic selfhood AND heart-led life's work. They are inextricably related!

I have decades of experience trying to figure out what it means to be my authentic self and how that relates to choosing my life's work: I have tried and failed many times. So how can I teach you to find your own authentic self without wasting as much time as I did spinning my wheels? First, you need to turn inward to discover (or recover) your own authenticity. There is just no substitute for your own inner voice. We all have an innate guidance system if we will only listen to it! Let's start by considering WHAT NOT TO DO as you strive to identify your own authenticity. Then, you'll be in a better position to know WHAT TO DO to find your own authenticity.

WHAT NOT TO DO

Don't Let Your Parents Make Your Choices for You

Parents, often with the best intentions in the world, too often attempt to tell their child who she is and, worse, choose a direction for her, one that does not – and cannot – fit because the choice did not come from within the child herself. In my opinion, parents should not interfere with their children's choices! It's important that children be given free rein so that they can experiment and slowly learn what works for them. Further, parents should not be an obstacle to their child's goals for a long-term career or life's work. If a child wants to play the piano or do a job that the parents themselves would hate, they should let the child do it! In short, parents should try very hard to resist the temptation to interfere with the choices their child makes! Easier to say than to do for many parents…

In the same context, parents should never hold their children hostage financially in the hope of forcing them to adopt a career that they themselves would make. Even more important, parents should never work out their own unfulfilled desires by attempting to live through their children. Instead, they should leave plenty of room for the child's own authentic interests to develop. Sadly, few parents seem to be able to resist the temptation to influence their children in one way or another. There are ever-growing financial considerations to take into account with a college education, and that in itself seems to be a major justification some parents use to choose a career for their children.

If you find yourself in such a situation with your parents – or as parents yourselves – dear reader, my message to you is to resist!!! It's critically important for you to be free to be who you really are – to be your authentic self – and to choose a direction for your work that suits you! That direction must take into consideration your strongest talents, values, interests, and inclinations. BE WHO YOU ARE and make your choices accordingly!

Avoid Choosing Work That is Socially Prestigious but Not a Good Fit for You

Many of us define ourselves by the work that we choose to do traditional work as mothers and wives, or as working women in the marketplace. My focus here is on women in the workplace because that is where my own experience lies. One of the most common mistakes that women make in choosing a career direction – especially women of college age – is to opt for careers with high social status and high pay, without first considering whether those careers are a good fit for their authentic selfhood. You know the high-status careers that I mean: in medicine, law, and upper-level business positions. Those careers buy instant social status and high pay or at least the general public believes that they do.

Let's take the law as an example. As a college teacher, I witnessed many women students (and male students too!) make an instant decision to become lawyers when they discovered what the starting salaries are for law graduates who are hired into prestigious law firms. They gave no thought at all to the real costs – personal, emotional, financial – that would result from their decision, or to whether or not that career suited them.

I had to make the decision about whether to become a lawyer myself at one time. I asked myself whether I had a genuine interest in law, whether I followed landmark legal cases in the news, and whether my personal values were aligned with the kinds of legal maneuvering I saw on television. I had to listen hard to my inner voice! Then, I decided to talk to several practicing lawyers. Think hard about your decision, they told me. Think about the long hours you're going to have to put in, they said, at least 60 hours a week! And don't even think about getting married if you're just starting out in law, they added, because you won't have time for a relationship! More: don't believe the hype about the high starting salaries, they said. That may be true for a few people graduating at the top of their law school class, but not for everyone. Worse: too many people are going to law school now, and there is a glut of lawyers in the market! Average lawyers don't make big bucks at all! Those revelations felt like pointed messages from some higher power! Maybe law wasn't such a good idea, I thought. You guessed it, I decided against it.

If you were like me when I was young, you might think that you are almost infinitely flexible, that you can twist and contort yourself into almost any shape that you like. You may think that you can put a mask over your authentic self and live comfortably in disguise ... But that is just not the case. Your authentic self is WHO YOU ARE, and it's not going to change fundamentally! If you have to put on a mask to function in your chosen profession – whether that's law or business or medicine – you are going to face unpleasant, and sometimes catastrophic, consequences down the road.

When you find a direction for yourself that is a good match for your authentic selfhood, it may not be one of the prestigious choices that our culture presents you with. If that happens, remind yourself that the fit is more important!! The key take-home message here is this: as you choose your all-important work path for yourself, think very hard about whether you are pursuing the right goal, in the right way, *for you*. If not, you'll likely have a hard time enjoying either the process or the outcome.

By the way, I am not saying that law is a bad profession or that some women are not perfectly suited for a legal career. Indeed, some are. But *not everyone* is, and that is the point I am trying to make! The same is true for the medical profession, or for CEO positions in big businesses, or any other prestigious profession that you might be tempted to choose. Those careers may be right for some women, but they are definitely *not* right for all women! The big question for us here is, *are they right for you*?

What is "a good fit," and how do we know when we've found one? For our purposes here, I am going to define "a good fit" as a life's work that is comfortably in alignment with your authentic self. When you "try it on," so to speak, there are no conflicts between the work you would be doing and your most cherished values and beliefs. If you choose this work as your path in life, you can apply your strongest talents in the service of other people and feel good about what you're doing. Can you make a meaningful contribution to the world? There should be no hint of shame that comes with trying to force a personal congruity with highly paid, prestigious work that is just not there. There should be no obvious misalignments and no nagging doubts about your choice. Chances are, if you've chosen a good career direction for yourself, you will know without having to be told.

Emulating Other People

There are a couple of key points to be made here. The first is the importance of finding your own unique path – a direction that suits you – instead of succumbing to the temptation to copy someone else's life. We all know people whose lives we would like to live … people who seem to have it all, know exactly who they are and what they want, etc. At least, it looks that way from a distance … But trying to be someone you are not is a betrayal of yourself! The second critical point is never to compare yourself to other people. We are all completely unique.

However, other people that you admire CAN teach you valuable things that can strengthen your grip on your own authenticity. But be sure to protect your feelings carefully when you work with mentors and resist the temptation to compare yourself negatively to them! There will always be people who know more than you do! Remember that they may have had advantages you did not have, or that they may have had more time to develop their abilities than you have had. We all move at our own pace and with our own unique sets of experiences and influences behind us. No two people are closely comparable, so comparing yourself to anyone else is a meaningless exercise in frustration. By trying to be someone you are not, you are, in effect, telling yourself that who you really are isn't okay. So trying to copy someone else, or ignoring who you really are, can leave you feeling alone, cut off from other people, and lost. In summary, honor your own precious uniqueness, and don't waste time trying to emulate others with totally different life paths ahead of them!

WHAT WE *DO* NEED TO DO

Reclaiming Yourself

To reclaim your authenticity, you need to reconnect with your "authentic self" – the self that puts a priority on living according to your values, pursuing your own unique purpose, and fighting for the causes you care about. If you want to put an end to the exhausting and mostly unconscious habit of placating others to either "fit in" with everyone else or "get ahead," you can do that by changing just one key thing: stop looking outside yourself for guidance, and start looking inside yourself instead.

To do that, you will need to summon the courage to face your fears and do a fearless self-exploration! As human beings, we tend to be most comfortable with what is familiar. The unfamiliar is often challenging, or even frightening, at first. Examining your inner self can be like exploring foreign terrain that we have largely forgotten. What you are looking for are "disconnects" between what we call your "adaptive self" and your authentic self. There may be many, and you may experience some anxiety when you spot them. But don't let fear deter you from an honest self-survey!

How do you begin to reclaim yourself? Here are a couple of tips to get you started identifying disconnects and working toward unmasking yourself.

Tip #1: Spend quiet time alone in blocks of several hours. Don't schedule any activities during that period. This is your time just to feel your feelings, to look back on the things that caused you pain or may have changed your willingness to show yourself to others as you really are. Cast your mind back to times when experiences you had caused you to begin to hide yourself. Don't censor any memories that bubble up! Let yourself fully feel any emotions that appear. How did you adapt to cope with the pain you felt? In other words, how did your adaptive self begin to take over? Write down your observations.

Prepare yourself for some unpleasant realities. Your authentic self will probably harbor a lot of fear, sadness, and anger. In the past, when your genuine self was hurt, it was your adaptive self that took over. However, the painful incidents from your past and how they made you feel are an important part of who you really are. So, as much as possible, and as slowly as you need to, courageously explore the truth of what makes you who you are. When you start to take a deeper look at yourself, you begin your journey toward reclaiming your authenticity. It's an important step to identify, experience, and accept the pain and disappointment in your past.

Tip #2: Take out a pen and record what it feels like when you are being more authentic versus when you are "acting. " For instance, under what circumstances do you merely "act?" In stressful social situations? At work? Alternatively, in what situations are you most authentic? At home? When you are alone? With very close friends? When do you feel best, when you are acting or when you are being authentic?

Monitor yourself when you are in adaptive mode versus authentic mode. Under what circumstances do you feel the onset of any fatigue or panic? Does your breathing change at all? Do you notice any tension in your body? Are your thoughts more positive or negative? There will be differences, so you just have to practice your awareness in identifying them. Write them down.

Tip #3: The next time you have to make a difficult decision, try to refrain from picking up the phone to call a friend. Also avoid reading horoscopes or tarot cards to make your decisions for you! Instead, turn inward and try to find your way through the difficulty on your own. No one knows better what you need than you do! One of the goals of becoming more authentic is to be more self-reliant. The more you can rely on yourself to make difficult choices, the more confident and grounded you will feel. Learning to go inside yourself and listen to your own inner guide is a critical step in becoming the captain of your own ship!

Tip #4: Keeping a daily journal is a good way to begin excavating your authentic self. In your everyday life, monitor your energy level as you engage in different activities. Pay attention to what energizes you, stimulates you, and makes you feel connected. Write down your observations. What implications do your findings have for what you should seek out or avoid? What do your findings suggest for your work life?

Not all of your inner work will be painful! Ground yourself by getting in touch with the "bedrock" in your life. What are the strongest talents with which you have been gifted? What do you most enjoy doing, both for work and for leisure? (What you most enjoy doing often points to your strongest talents because most of us enjoy doing what we are good at!) What kinds of things interest you so deeply that you lose track of time when you are immersed in them? Chances are that they hold a key to one or more of your strongest talents or values!

Also, explore your most deeply held values. Ask yourself what you truly believe. Living your **personal values, following your ethical convictions, and honoring your integrity** are effective ways to live more authentically. Ask yourself what you are willing to stand for. That question is going to follow you throughout your life...Pick a problem, any problem that matters to you. Think about the ways you could do something about it. Remember, that to somebody who is hurting, your "something" could be everything.

Ask yourself about the issues that you care most about, and for which you would make sacrifices. That is, what are your values? What issues or problems in your world move you to want to do something about them? Keep a written record of them as you survey your inner landscape.

WAYS TO FIND AN AUTHENTIC DIRECTION FOR YOUR WORK

There are many strategies for finding your life's work, or direction, in life. We are going to focus on two here. The first is to look to your past and what made you who you are. Resurrect your core self by revisiting the past. That's important because past events may hold the key to your work in the future.

The second takes a less personal approach. You may want to consider adopting a service orientation in your work to provide you with a direction. This approach begins by asking you to reflect on the problems in the world and to choose the ones that most powerfully affect you! Which problems tug at your heartstrings? They may be the ones you'll want to work toward solving.

Note that these two approaches are not mutually exclusive! Chances are that things that impacted you in the past are still relevant today and that they exert powerful influences on the world problems that speak to you now. Note that any meaningful life's work that you choose is likely to have a service component in it!

Revisit Your Past

Everything that makes us who we are, everything that has contributed to forming our values and our beliefs, is housed in our memory. None of us ever really leaves anything behind. It's all still there. To quote William Faulkner in this context, "The past is never dead. It's not even past." While we may tell ourselves that we have forgotten certain painful events in our past, or certain landmark events that have given shape to our identity, they remain as the bedrock of our identity. Those facts cannot be changed! Our *beliefs* about those facts can change, especially the limiting beliefs that may hold us back, but the truth of who we are is what it is. That's a good thing! Too much about our lives changes constantly, like shifting sands, and we need bedrock on which to build our lives. That's why we need to reacquaint ourselves with that bedrock in ourselves.

You can help yourself in your excavation of the past by pulling out any records you used to keep. Did you record your thoughts in a diary? Did you put together photo albums? Do you still have your old yearbooks from school? Did you have close friends who might have kept their own records? Any or all of those sources may help to recover your memories about your life in the past, how you felt about yourself, the problems that concerned you, etc. Take careful note of any patterns you recognize in your search of your records. Can you remember the origin of any such patterns? What were some of the most memorable events? What do your answers suggest about the potential for life's work, if anything?

If, after reviewing your past, you find nothing that speaks to you as potential for a life's work, don't despair! One promising place to start is with ways to help others (both human and non-human!). As I have mentioned, numerous studies show that people who engage in service work of various kinds experience heightened self-esteem and a strong sense of empowerment. Helping others is a root activity in a fulfilling life's work. How might you put your gifts to work in service to others?

Adopt a Service Orientation

We live in difficult times, and the world grows more troubled every day! Here in the U.S., we are aware that our culture is threatened on many fronts, including worsening environmental problems, contamination of water resources and food, inequitable distribution of basic human necessities, social injustices like racism and sexism, animal rights abuses, and so much more. So, the question becomes, are you interested in making a difference? Which of the many pressing problems in the wider world today has special meaning for you? How might you contribute your best talents and abilities to make a change for the better? The possibilities are endless!

You may want to consider doing humanitarian aid either here in the US or abroad. That kind of work offers exciting opportunities to travel the world and meet many kinds of people you might otherwise never meet. The work ranges widely, from work on behalf of women and children, work to support environmental initiatives, work to prevent hunger and famine, work to support healthcare, work on sustainable farming, work on economic development, work on human rights, etc. You can find a niche that is perfect for you!

Call to Action!

It was my goal here to help you begin the process of self-study that you'll need to recover your authentic selfhood and choose a suitable life's work for yourself. I hope this chapter was helpful. Of course, that journey is far more complicated than what I've touched on in this chapter! We've barely scratched the surface. But I can guide you much further in your journey if you are up for the challenge!

I offer a reasonably priced, eight-week online course that offers in-depth guidance on authentic selfhood. There are a number of guided exercises in each module to help you examine an array of relevant topics. The course I put together also includes a list of valuable references on the same concerns. Your own "unseen battle" need not be a lonely one! To get the online URL for my course, reach out via the contact information printed below.

Here is my contact information:

Email: annechapple0@gmail.com
Phone: 360 927-5094
FaceBook: https://www.facebook.com/anne.chapple.7/
Linked-In: https://www.linkedin.com/in/anne-s-chapple-ph-d-3812a73b/

Join me and other kindred spirits in what could be a life-changing journey of self-discovery!!
I'd love to hear from you!

xxxx words

UNBOXED GRACE COACHING COMPANY
Missy Blackmer
CEO & Coach

Melissa "Missy" Blackmer is a licensed mental health counselor & certified life coach with a passion for helping others thrive. She is the Co-Founder, CEO, & Clinical Director of Unboxed Grace Counseling Company and also leads Unboxed Grace Coaching Company, home to The Mental Health Chicks.

Missy works closely with high-achieving women, empowering them to prevent and recover from overwhelm, burnout, and anxiety. Through personalized coaching sessions, group support, and inspiring speaking engagements, she helps her clients create mindset shifts, protect their mental wellness, and develop leadership skills that spark lasting personal growth. At home in Fort Wayne, Indiana, Missy shares life's adventures with her husband of 25 years, their two teenage sons, and two dogs. She brings warmth, insight, and a bit of humor to everything she does, believing that real change happens when we approach life with grace and authenticity.

https://www.linkedin.com/in/missyblackmer/
https://www.facebook.com/MissyBlackmer/
https://www.instagram.com/thementalhealthchicks/
https://www.unboxedgracecoaching.com
https://www.unboxedgracecounseling.com/

SHE HEALS,
SHE R.O.A.R.S

By Missy Blackmer

In 2021, I hit a wall—burned out, anxious, depressed, and I had nothing left to give. My health was tanking. My fibromyalgia was flared, and my IBS was out of control. I did my best to hide it all. Like so many others, I felt buried under the pressure to keep everything together. Often to the outside, I looked strong. I was juggling my roles as a wife, mother, daughter, friend, leader, and mental health counselor. However, the world around me became a blur of expectations and obligations. There was this crushing weight that seemed to say, "I can't stop. I can't rest. So much depended on me."

Sadly, I had experienced burnout at least a couple of other times in the previous 10 years. I seemed to be very attracted to high-demand leadership roles in community mental health. When this last burnout happened, I told my own therapist that I was so tired. I could not understand why I kept taking these high-demand jobs and ultimately burning out and becoming the kind of leader I never wanted to be. One day, she said to me:

"I think you may need to consider that you are not built for bureaucratic companies. It's too much like being in your dysfunctional (childhood) family system where nothing you did was quite right or enough. So, then you are going to work in fight or flight every single day."

I was stunned, and I pushed back on this idea. But God knew that those words would end up changing my life.

Growing Up

I was conditioned from a young age to be a very high achiever. I learned that if I got good grades and became a leader in the activities I tried, I got more positive attention than negative. I grew up in three homes, really: my mom's, my grandparents' and my dad and stepmom's houses. All three homes had a different set of rules and expectations, but achievement was always welcomed.

I spent most of my time in my mother's home with my younger sister. My parents divorced when I was four, which, in and of itself, changed me. I remember the day my dad left. I can still recall it vividly and his promise to return. He didn't, though he did remain very involved in my life.

However, in his exit, my mom found the Baptist church. It was steeped in fundamentalism, and this set me on a very toxic, high-control religion trajectory. Just last year, I was watching *Shiny Happy People* on Prime. This docuseries revealed deeper truths about the Duggar family, from *19 Kids & Counting* on TLC. As I watched this, the story unfolds around the Duggar family's loyalty to the teachings of Bill Gothard. Bill Gothard is the founder of the Institute of Basic Life Principles (IBLP). As it turns out, this religious organization, which on its face appears to be Christian in nature, is more like a cult. I started to feel very uneasy about it as I watched people who had left the IBLP tell their stories. I texted my mom as I was watching and asked, "Did you raise me using principles from Bill Gothard?" Her response was, "Oh yes! We used to even take buses to his events." I was horrified. It also explained her proclivity to spank me and punish me for every little thing I did. It was laced with toxic shame. Truly though, she was just doing what was being taught to her.

I tell this foundational story because it shines a small light on some of my adverse childhood experiences. While I am happy to say that I have healed my relationship with my mom and dad, the impact of childhood experiences remains.

There is research on something called Adverse Childhood Experiences, or ACEs. It is a 10-question inventory about your childhood. The higher the score, the higher the correlation is to adult health problems, such as addiction, obesity, heart disease, autoimmune disease, asthma, and even fibromyalgia. My body very much reflects this.

I Tried to Hide It

My story is really not that unique. I was a woman, on a mission, battling exhaustion and both physical and mental fatigue while trying to balance the many hats I wear. In public, I was masking my physical and mental health issues, in favor of leading others, despite knowing deep down that I had reached my limit. In reality, I was unraveling.

My boss at the time tried to get me to tell her what I needed, but I was in a fierce fight mode. I panicked behind closed doors. Friendships were crashing. My husband was supportive, but he could not fix this for me. I wasn't even sure where my relationship with God was during this time. However, the words of my therapist kept ringing in my ears. Eventually, I was moved into a different role at my company because I was just not cutting it. I had worked beyond my capacity, and I was a mess.

I thought I had been hiding in plain sight, but the façade was brought down in one of the most humbling seasons of my life.

Shame Dies in the Light

I wanted to curl up in a hole and not come out. I was embarrassed, depressed, anxious, and physically not well. I felt so much shame. I was supposed to be the leader, on top of it all. My fall was anything but graceful.

Brené Brown, a renowned shame researcher, says this about shame:

"I define shame as the intensely painful feeling or experience of believing that we are flawed and therefore unworthy of love and belonging—something we've experienced, done, or failed to do makes us unworthy of connection."[1]

Growing up, I felt a great deal of toxic shame anytime I did anything that wasn't what was expected of me. I perceived that perfection was expected. I clearly remember my grandfather asking when he got my report card of all A's, "Where is the plus on these?" I do not believe he meant to crush my spirit with that question, but it is the clearest memory I have of thinking, "I have to do better." I was often given money for my grades and gifts of all kinds from the adults in my life when I was doing well. Therefore, in my childish brain, I equated achievement with love and connection, and anything less was shameful and a failure.

Brené Brown also teaches about shame resilience. She says that shame is fed by silence, judgment, and secrecy, and it melts away in the face of community, empathy, and vulnerability. To be resilient is to be able to bounce back from hard things. Resilience also means you cannot hide away because hiding away feeds shame, depression, and anxiety.

Healing in the Light

The spotlight was on me. It was uncomfortable, and it wasn't the type of light I liked. While it can be fun to receive an accolade publicly, it is absolutely horrifying for the light to reveal my failures and flaws. At least it was for me.

For almost two years after my burnout, I worked in a job that had nothing to do with being a mental health counselor. It allowed me to heal, to seek counseling, to renew my capacity. It renewed my ability to dream, create, and relate. I found new friends and refreshed my relationship with God. As I got honest with peers and family, that shame started to shrink. Instead, it became a springboard to tell others that they must invest in self-compassion and their mental and physical well-being.

Vulnerability is the cornerstone of courage, resilience, and problem-solving.

Investing in Mental Wellness

One night last summer, I stood in front of a group of women, talking about how we can heal from hard things. As a mental health counselor and life coach, I often walk with others on their healing journey. So, with a bit of tongue-in-cheek humor, I said to this lovely group of women, that women are often "**Warriors On a Mission while Exhausted & Neurotic.**" This elicited some giggles and a couple of "Amens!"

Can you relate?

I suggested it would be so much better if we became women who are **Warriors On a Mission** while **Empowered & Nourished.**

How do we make this shift? *We invest in our mental wellness.* There are three ways that I have found to be the most helpful in making this investment:

1. Cultivating habits and practices that promote emotional resilience and self-awareness so you can bounce back from adversity and adapt to change.

2. Developing skills and strategies to manage and reduce stress effectively, including exercise, sleep, nutrition, and engaging in supportive relationships.
3. Having goals, passions, and a sense of life direction that is driven by values and life purpose.

Let's explore the ways to bring these three ways to life by looking at the lioness.

The Lioness & Her Roar

I love lions! They are so majestic, beautiful, and powerful. The lioness is stunning. She is a powerful balance of ferocity and compassion.

She roars to communicate. Her roar may communicate her location, invite the community, or warn others in the pride of impending danger. She communicates with her facial expressions and postures as well. If she bares her teeth, her ears are pinned back, or she is in a crouch, she is preparing for an impending attack. On the other hand, a relaxed, open-mouthed expression with forward-facing ears shows she is content.

She uses her voice to claim her territory, which is similar to communicating boundaries. What a powerful skill that plays out in nature that we humans find so very difficult at times. She can communicate with other members of the pride, and they communicate back so they can locate each other.

She also coordinates strategy, which she must do in order to make sure that she provides and protects her pride. This also provides protection for her and her pride against attacks. This way of communicating is essential to survival.

She also roars to create opportunities for social bonding. She invites others into her space. She trusts those who are in her pride because they are loyal.

We can learn so much from her. Let us take a look at how you, as a strong woman, can learn to roar in ways that protect you and invite support.

She R.O.A.R.S

Here is what it looks like to roar as an ambitious woman:

- → **R**adical Self-Compassion
- → **O**wning Your Story
- → **A**ligning with Your Values
- → **R**esilient Mindset
- → **S**eeking Support

Radical Self-Compassion

One of the most powerful tools in my unseen battle against chronic pain, anxiety, and depression has been self-compassion. Often misunderstood as merely self-care, self-compassion goes deeper. It's the practice of treating yourself with the same kindness, understanding, and grace you would offer a close friend. In moments of failure, difficulty, or suffering, it means acknowledging your imperfections without judgment and extending forgiveness to yourself.

Radical self-compassion is a critical weapon in your arsenal. You must learn to extend grace to yourself, to stop the narrative of "I am not enough. I am not worthy." Kristen Neff, a self-compassion researcher, says that compassion really equates to a loving and warm presence. In her book *Fierce Self-Compassion*, Neff points out that "kindness is the emotional attitude that allows us to comfort and soothe ourselves."[2]

To heal, you need to embrace kindness towards yourself in how you think, believe, and behave.

Owning Your Story

Each woman carries a story—a history marked by experiences that shape who she is today. But too often, we bury those stories, hiding our pain, shame, and failures. The unseen battle is not just against anxiety, depression, or trauma; it's also against the weight of the unspoken. I knew that to own my story, I had to start to acknowledge my past, no matter how messy or painful it was, so I could change my future.

I struggled to own my story in what felt like a very public way. I was so angry with myself, my boss, the world, even God. Of course, most did not really know all I was going through physically, mentally, emotionally, and spiritually. In my mind's eye, though, everyone was judging me.

My whole story, which cannot even fit in a chapter, is not something to be ashamed of—and friend, neither is yours. It's not a burden but a source of strength. By talking about it, by owning it, you break the cycle of emotional repression, not just for yourself but for future generations. Your children and grandchildren will inherit a legacy of emotional transparency, rather than one of silence and repression.

Brené Brown says, "When we deny our stories, they define us. When we own our stories, we get to write a brave new ending."[3] So, how do you actually own your story? Keep reading, my friend. That answer lies in values alignment, mindset, and support.

Aligning With Your Values

As a therapist and life coach, I often do an exercise around values clarification with my clients. For most, choosing their values is a quick assignment. They know what they stand for, or maybe more accurately, they know what they *want* to stand for. Then I challenge those values by asking, "How do you live those out in your daily life? Can you give me examples?" This often renders them silent and then sad.

In my own story, I can see seasons where work and ambition overshadowed the most important things to me, like relationships with family and friends. To be totally authentic and transparent, I still struggle to lay down the ideology of busyness.

However, on my healing journey, I learned that my behaviors needed to be better aligned with my beliefs. My inner conflict and cognitive dissonance were not going to get quiet if I kept worshiping the idol of achievement.

I was listening to a short video recently where the narrator talked about cognitive dissonance. Cognitive dissonance is a state of anxiety that occurs when a person holds two incompatible thoughts at the same time. The narrator compared cognitive dissonance to listening to a junior high band when you hear the notes clashing against each other as the student tries to find the right note. It's enough to make you want to get up and run out of the room! It hurts your ears.

In the same way, living in a way that does not honor what you value will create a great clash inside your thoughts. You will be at war with yourself and those around you. In contrast, when you align with your values, becoming authentic will promote your self-acceptance, reduce your stress, and strengthen your mental health. By defining what truly matters to you, and living according to those principles, you create a sense of purpose that fuels resilience.

Building a Resilient Mindset

Your mindset is a set of beliefs that shape how you make sense of yourself and the world around you. It shapes how you think, feel, and behave in any given situation. Resilience is the ability to adapt and recover from difficult experiences and situations. Resilience is more than just bouncing back, though. It's *thriving* in the face of adversity.

A *resilient mindset* is rooted in growth. It is the belief that we can learn and grow from every challenge. It's about seeing failure not as a final destination, but as information that can put you on the path to growth. A resilience mindset allows you to take on positive perceptions and focus on what you can control. Many people get stuck on the things they can't control, which often leads to anxiety and depression. This can also be called a fixed mindset. The antidote to this is learning to lean into the belief that life is constantly changing and that you will be ok so that your capacity to adjust to new or changing circumstances will skyrocket.

A resilient mindset often leads to a growth mindset. Adopting a growth mindset means embracing challenges, learning from setbacks, and recognizing that you haven't mastered something "yet." Carol Dweck, the leading researcher on mindset, states, "The passion for stretching yourself and sticking to it, even (or especially) when it's not going well, is the hallmark of the growth mindset."[4] This idea tells me that I can go through hard things and still keep thriving and so can you!

Seek Support: You Are Not Alone

When you are going through a battle, it often feels isolating. It can also feel intimidating to reach out. But, friend, it doesn't have to be fought alone. Seeking support is not a sign of weakness—it's a strength. Whether it's therapy, coaching, spiritual guidance, or a support group, having people in your corner makes all the difference. Shame and stigma are barriers that keep us from reaching out, but they only serve to deepen loneliness and anxiety.

Healing begins when you share your pain. When we seek support, we allow ourselves to be vulnerable and, in turn, stronger. As Brené

Brown reminds us, shame thrives in secrecy, but once we shine a light on it, it loses its power.

Conclusion: The Journey to Healing

My journey to healing involved counseling, changing jobs, and restoring relationships. I had to get honest with myself, my loved ones, my friends, and with God. I had to put in the work for mental wellness, self-compassion, authenticity, and resilience. I had to get aligned with my values. Friends, the journey was long, but it was so worth it!

You can have the same victory. Every step you take towards healing is a step towards living fully, embracing who you are, and walking in your purpose. You are a warrior on a mission—exhausted, yes, but empowered and nourished as you continue to rise.

If any part of this chapter resonated with you, know that you are not alone in your unseen battle. Healing and hope are possible, and it begins with taking the next step.

I'd love to walk alongside you on this journey. **Reach out to me today**—whether it's to share your story, ask a question, or explore what supportive coaching might look like. You don't have to navigate this path alone. Let's connect, and together, we'll move toward the peace and strength you deserve.

Go to www.unboxedgracecoaching.com to get my free e-book *The Anti-Burnout Toolkit* and request a discovery call for more information.

(1) https://brenebrown.com/articles/2013/01/15/shame-v-guilt/
(2) Neff, K. (2021). Fierce Self-Compassion: How Women Can Harness Kindness to Speak Up, Claim Their Power, and Thrive.

(3) https://brenebrown.com/articles/2015/06/18/own-our-history-change-the-story/

(4) Dweck, C. S. (2007). *Mindset: The New Psychology of Success.* Random House.

SHE BOSSIN' UP | P31X
Dr. Breanna James
Life Strategist & Business Coach

Dr. Breanna "BOSS" James is a sought-after expert on women's empowerment, business coaching, and life solutions, who's been featured in multiple magazines and platforms. She started her career over 14 years ago, bringing a wealth of experience in HR, coaching, and training.

After overcoming personal struggles like fear, low self-esteem, procrastination, poor credit, and debt, she discovered the path to freedom and transformation, using her journey to inspire and guide others.

When she's not helping women redefine themselves and build businesses based on biblical principles through She BOSSIN' Up, or providing life and health insurance and homeownership solutions through P31X, you'll find her studying the Bible, decorating cakes, reading, target shooting, or nurturing her plants.

To learn more about Dr. James and how she can help you achieve your goals, visit https://linktr.ee/drboss.

Boldly Overcome Struggles and Setbacks as you positively transform yourself Body, Occupation, Soul, and Spirit..

https://www.linkedin.com/in/breannajames/
https://www.facebook.com/msjames637
https://www.instagram.com/bossupmylife
https://linktr.ee/drboss
https://www.unleashthebosswithin.com/

THE POWER OF PERSEVERANCE

Battling Through the Desire to Give Up

By Dr. Breanna James

Envision a dark winter night. It was cold outside, and the inside of the house was even colder. As I shook and shivered, I kept wondering to myself, "Will this pain ever end? I can't keep living like this."

Wait, no. It wasn't a cold, dark winter night. I've just always wanted to start a story like that, the drama of it all (smiles).

No, it was actually a beautiful Spring day in 2009. The sun was shining, and the morning started wonderfully. Off to work, I went, even though Lord knows I didn't want to go. That's another story altogether.

I said my round of hellos downstairs, and then made my way up to the top floor, successfully dodging all the people I didn't feel like talking to at the top of my shift. Working in Human Resources, some mornings, with some people, you just need a highly classified, you didn't see me, I'm really not here yet, covert start to the work day.

I entered my penthouse cubicle in the hallway, turned on my computer, quietly put my things down, and went across the hall to grab hot water for my morning tea.

Everything was just fabulous. I cued up the morning praise music mix and with my headphones on, I got the day going per usual. A couple of hours later, my head began to hurt. I've had medical issues here and there throughout most of my life, and I was used to getting headaches, so I was prepared with Excedrine in my bag. I popped a couple of pills in my mouth, drank a cup of water, stretched a bit, and got back to work.

Come lunchtime, my head didn't feel better at all, the pain was worse. This was highly unusual, as I could normally take Excedrine and within an hour, I would be better. I took another round of pills, ate my lunch, put my head down, and closed my eyes to rest a bit. After a few minutes, it felt like someone took an ice pick and started stabbing me all over my head. The pain was so intense I squealed in pain. I could barely open my eyes. It seemed like someone put all the lights in the building in my cubicle.

I was dizzy and nauseous, and my head was pounding with extra sharp pains all over. My coworkers rushed out to see what was happening. I could barely lift my head off the desk. As I described what was happening, one of the ladies said she thought I was having a migraine, handed me her sunglasses, and told me to just lie there for a bit.

The pills continued not working, and the pain continued to increase. I didn't want to go to the emergency room, I just wanted to go home, so the ladies grabbed the cars and drove me home. I lay down in pain and woke up in pain. That next morning, the stabbing sensation was gone, but I still had a painful headache that seemed to be bouncing around my head. The top right would hurt, then the left back, then the middle and back right, next my whole head. It was the craziest thing I'd ever experienced. I called the advice line and was told to make an appointment to see my primary doctor. I got an appointment for the next day. This would now be the third day in a row that I had a continuous headache with zero relief.

My doctor didn't have a clue what was going on with me. Test after test after test and they couldn't figure out what was going on. Of course, their best option was to run more tests and put me on several medications to help with the pain and try to fight what they hypothesized were the problems.

A couple of weeks went by, and no positive changes. I was in pain every single day with no relief. The only change was there were moments when the pain would get worse for longer periods, and I'd be completely debilitated. I spent most of the day crying and praying. After another doctor's visit, I was now diagnosed with chronic headaches, compound headaches, cluster headaches, headaches of the neck, and severe migraines all at the same time. They didn't know what to do, and I seriously thought I was dying. It felt like my head was going to explode. I was in pain 24 hours a day, every day, with no relief for almost seven months. Insane.

Life Moves Even When You Need It to Stand Still

This little patch of life was extremely rough. I still needed to figure out how to live and work in the middle of all of this. I was able to take some time off work, but that couldn't last forever. PTO and sick time were gone. FMLA and state disability ran out after 12 weeks. Yet, a very unfortunate part of life is that your bills and the companies that own them don't care that you're sick. They keep processing and expect to be paid, with very little to no compassion or empathy.

It's in the depths of this perplexing situation that I have to figure out how to return to work and function while being in pain all day. The crazy part is that it also wasn't that easy to be at home and in partially debilitating pain all night. I lived alone, and I was in school working on getting my doctorate degree. I had to care for myself. Cooking, cleaning, and everything in between was all on me. For school, I had to request course extensions, so I wouldn't be released from the program. Each extension was an additional 15 weeks and had an additional multi-thousand dollar price tag attached to them. Life was anything but good.

After a long conversation with my boss, we worked out a phased return to work schedule and there I was back in the office suffering. I tried to work but all I could really do was just lay my head on my desk for over half the time and continue to hope for some relief. I began having multiple migraines a day on top of the constant headaches. Yet, I discovered an interesting thing about the human body and willpower. If you truly think a thing and press on long enough, your body will help you out.

I had no choice but to work and kept telling myself, "You have to work, and since no one is going to pay your bills, you're going to show up and do something. It won't be much, but if you get one impactful thing done, you are there, you're doing your best, and that's all you can do." As time progressed, even though the pain didn't decrease, I was able to start working through the lower-level, non-migraine pain. To this day, I can have headaches or migraine with pain up to level seven and continue to work. I work much slower, but I can get things done. Now, once the pain hits an eight, I'm debilitated, and all I can do is lie down and shake, praying to the Lord for relief.

Things Couldn't Get Any Worse, Right?

Toward the middle of whatever this consistent head pain thing was, before it got better, it got way worse. One of the prescriptions they put me on messed up some of my cognitive functions. I would wake up at two o'clock in the morning bright-eyed and bushy-tailed, ready to start the day, yet still in pain and now unable to recall what I was actually doing in the moment. The side effects of this particular medication would cause me to wake up early and suffer tremendous amounts of brain fog and memory loss.

I would lose focus easily and couldn't remember half of anything. I would wake up and go to work early, work through the pain, but I kept forgetting what I was working on in the middle of the task. I was a hot mess. People would stop by to say hello and after about 30 seconds of interaction, I'd turn back to my desk to continue working and couldn't recall what I was doing. The task was right in my face, and I couldn't put it together. Each time it happened, I had to start working on anything I could think of so I'd get something done.

I traced these issues back to the medication, so I stopped taking them. A few days after I stopped taking them, my sleep schedule regulated, and I was able to focus more. Now, I never suggest cutting prescriptions cold, yet I didn't like what was happening to me. I should have consulted my doctor about stopping the pills first. My life was a gigantic ball of pain mixed with despair, depression, and agony. Yet even in the middle of all of this I couldn't help but believe that this is only a season, and it will go away. My only problem was that each day I'd wake up, the season was still present, and I wasn't doing any better, yet I also wasn't doing worse. The pain was neutral and finally manageable.

Yet, just when I didn't think things could get any worse, they did, and it was really bad. At this point, it had been over five months of consistent all-day, everyday pain flexing between levels five to seven, with occasional eight-plus pain moments. I was beyond miserable, but as I trained myself that life keeps moving, I needed to continue to figure out how to navigate things and find some kind of enjoyment in life, so I don't go mad.

One Saturday, I went to my brother's house for UFC fight night. I love UFC, so I wanted to enjoy some great matches. The fights were over, and everyone was gone. My head was on fire, so I lay back and was about to close my eyes for a little bit before driving home, and that's when it happened. The most horrible pain I'd ever experienced in my life to that point.

Commercials were playing, and the screen went from being pitch black to stark white on a Comcast commercial. With the bright white flash on the screen, something in the back right side of my head popped hard, and that was it. I was in so much pain I couldn't even make a sound. Tears poured from my eyes as I fell over on the couch, rocking. I could barely see, and I felt like I was going to throw up. The TV was now so loud that my ears hurt. I felt around for the remote and turned off the TV. My head and ears hurt so bad the subtle, ambient noises in the room were too loud.

It was at this moment, that I stopped praying to get better, and began begging The Lord to die. As I cried, I repeatedly asked to just go to sleep and wake up in glory. "I don't want to do this anymore. I can't take any more of this. This is too much. Just let me die already. Just kill me. Please! I don't care, you need to do something, and death works just fine." I was not in a good place at all.

I finally fell asleep, and seeing that you're reading this here tale, the Lord didn't answer my plea for death. He woke me up with the "normal" pain that I was now used to. The horrible pain from the night before was gone, but the headache was still there. All I could do was look up to heaven and roll my eyes, as I put my shoes on, angry about being alive, but I didn't say anything. I stopped by the house to get ready for church, and my body started feeling off. I was a bit nauseous, my eyes and ears started hurting, and any part of my body I touched was painful. It was weird.

I got to church, sat in the pew, removed my sunglasses, and was ready for praise and worship. Or so I thought. My eyes started to hurt so badly from all the lights I had to put my sunglasses back on. The music was painfully loud, and putting my earbuds in my ears didn't help much. This was the first time in my life I prayed for the music to end as quickly as possible. It was ridiculously bright and loud. I could literally smell everything in the building, down to the different types of cleaners used in the restrooms, and I was sitting on the side of the church opposite the restrooms.

I was completely miserable and just wanted to go home. Everyone I talked to after service asked about the glasses, and I told them that the headache got worse when I tried to take them off, so my sunglasses are staying on. Life went from a consistent super bad to next-level worse. On top of the headaches, I was experiencing full-blown migraine symptoms even while not having a migraine. Crazy right? I know.

Though It's Better, It's Not Over

The doctors never could explain any of it, and since that day, I have been dealing with an acute sensory sensitivity condition, where all of my senses are hyper. When this started, the problems I was having with hyper-sensitive senses, the migraine symptoms, were consistent, just like the headaches. Bless the Lord, over time, the constant sensitivity went away, and I only now have issues from time to time. Unfortunately, I still have to wear sunglasses often because most lights are too bright. If I get too much bright light into my eyes, I'll experience a debilitating migraine.

I am most thankful, that randomly after about seven months of consistent all-day everyday headaches, they just stopped. As I stated, I now still suffer from chronic migraines and hyper-sensitive senses. Also, due to the side effects of that medication, I have residual brain fog with focus and memory issues.

At the time, I wasn't quite sure how I made it through all of that. I do know that tests and trials are purposeful. "Consider it pure joy, my brothers and sisters, whenever you face trials of many kinds, because you know that the testing of your faith produces perseverance. Let perseverance finish its work so that you may be mature and complete, not lacking anything" (James 1:2-4, NIV). I knew I was gaining strength from praying and being determined to make the best of a horrible situation, even though it didn't feel that way all the time.

The depth of my pain and loneliness was profound. No one really understood what I was going through. I also had to deal with months of people looking at me, like a poor little helpless thing, and saying stupid things like, "Aw, you still don't feel better?" "No, I don't feel better," and in my head, "And I don't need your stupid looks and comments, thank you very much." This was truly a challenging pocket of life where I had to learn how to navigate through the pain and life as a whole. I had to learn to separate the emotions from the situation and intentionally seek purpose in it. There is always purpose in our pain, we just have to be open to discover it.

Looking back, I understand the power of this battle and the strength it took to go through the hardest parts of it, overcome some of it, and continue navigating the rest of it. I will never know why it happened, but I do know that I've been able to grow through it. Even when I started to give up on myself, God didn't, and that encouraged me to continue to live and thrive in the middle of my painful situation.

Continuing to Explore This Navigation Thing

Life is an absolute mess sometimes. We can't always do anything about the things that come at us, but we can choose how we respond to them. While figuring out everything and trying to keep a positive mindset, which was not easy, I looked back and identified five principles that were instrumental in helping me move my life forward.

I'm highly organized and very structured, and each principle gave me the structure I needed to navigate the challenges. These elements collectively formed a strong foundation that, to date, has enabled me to face uncertainties with steadfastness, resilience, and confidence. The principles are to ground yourself in faith, practice gratitude, set boundaries to practice self-care and soul-care, embrace all challenges, and trust in God's plan.

Grounding oneself in faith and practicing gratitude are essential steps to navigating life's struggles with resilience and confidence. For me, beginning each day with prayer and reading the Word provided a strong foundation and helped me see my worth as a beloved child of God, fortifying my self-esteem. Constantly thinking about things I'm grateful for helped shift my focus from problems to blessings while experiencing pain and challenges.

Setting boundaries for self-care and soul-care helped me get more rest while embracing life's challenges, and trusting in God's plan helped me realize that everything is under control even when it feels like it's out of control. Difficulties are opportunities for growth and resilience, showing you how to give God everything. By integrating these principles, you, too, can navigate the pain and struggles life throws you with steadfastness and courage.

You may be dealing with a consistent and seemingly unending challenging life situation but don't give up on yourself. You may want to, yet there is rest that comes even in the greatest of storms.

Need someone to chat with? Let's talk!

Visit https://linktr.ee/drboss to schedule your FREE *Ignite the BOSS Within Discovery Session* and learn how to navigate obstacles.

Boldly Overcome Struggles and Setbacks as you positively transform yourself Body, Occupation, Soul, and Spirit! Let's BOSS Up!

References

1. *Holy Bible, New International Version. (1984). James 1:2-4. Grand Rapids, MI: Zondervan.*

SWELL RETREAT
Lacy J. Hardman
Founder

I'm Lacy! I can't wait to get to know you! A bit about me: I jumped out of airplanes for 12 years while serving in the Army; I grew up in a very tumultuous home with a bi-polar mom; In the pursuit of happiness, I dedicated years to uncovering its root and can't wait to share my tools with you.

My mission in life is to help others know they aren't alone on their journey, provide healing through the wisdom of horses, and overcome limiting behaviors. When a person decides to heal they prevent future generations of suffering.

As part of my work, I lead retreats, mentor emerging entrepreneurs and coaches, and hosts a webinar in this link: https://www.swellretreat.com/liveswell, which offers courses on healing and connects people to horse retreats worldwide. Additionally, at Swell Retreat, I host family reunions, youth groups, and corporate groups. Speaker. Change Advocate. God-Loving.

https://www.linkedin.com/in/hardmanrealtors/
https://www.facebook.com/SwellRetreatUtah/
https://www.instagram.com/swellretreat/
https://www.swellretreat.com/

A HORSE LED ME TO FREEDOM

By Lacy J. Hardman

"My emotional wounds will proceed his development. I cannot help him become something I am not…" Hugh's words struck a chord as I watched him work with a wild horse. In that raw moment, I felt the weight of my limitations gripping my heart. I realized I needed to break free from my chains—not just for myself but also for my children and future grandchildren. This revelation settled heavily in my gut like an undeniable truth I could no longer ignore.

The blinders fell from my eyes; my past struggles shouldn't shadow my children's future. They deserve to grow unburdened by my invisible scars from my unseen battles, and so do I. I resolved then to stop letting instinctive responses of fight, flight, freeze, and please dictate my life. It was time for a profound shift. I had to heal, dismantle the walls built by past traumas, and forge a new path of freedom—for my sake and those I love.

We had just spent three hours in a world where wild meets tamed. On one side, a fearful horse, embodying raw power; on the other, a trained horse, moving with grace, trust, and partnership.

Halfway through, I leaned close to my husband, Ben, excitement in my eyes, and whispered, "I want everyone to see this!" We had been invited to an emotional resilience retreat, only to discover it was a multi-level marketing event. Instead of feeling betrayed, we chose to embrace the lessons this unique situation offered—every moment is an opportunity to learn. I am deeply thankful to my friend Crystal for that life-changing weekend. The wisdom from those horses became a pivotal moment, redefining my life's path and revealing how to fulfill my purpose on earth.

"Our light is what reveals us, and our shadow is what heals us. We think we have to deny, ignore, be better than our shadow, or shame it. Your shadow is your secondary story, and as you face and embrace it, you can heal. You are already feeling the effects of your shadow … you need to face and embrace it," taught Hugh, as the wild horse finally surrendered and lay on the ground.

I wondered to myself, "What was my shadow? What was holding me hostage? What was keeping me stuck in patterns where people who came into my life hurt me rather than loved me?" Hugh had said he was the co-creator of his pain. How am I co-creating my pain?

"In every story, there is a hero and villain. In your story, you are both. All the bright aspects and all the dark aspects of yourself orchestrate the melody of your song. A song that you need to hear … but in order to hear it, you have to learn to listen. To listen to not only what you want, but also what you are afraid of, your fears and your darkness; they aren't detached from you—face them, analyze them, internalize them, your shadow is always there…" Adrian Iliopoulos (goodreads.com).

My psychology degree has been a guiding light. I vividly recall my college years when I learned of Carl Jung's theories. Jung was an explorer of the human soul, intertwining psychology and spirituality to transcend the human experience. He noted, "The shadow is a moral problem that challenges the whole ego-personality," urging us to confront the darker corners of our being.

After an emotionally charged retreat weekend, I returned home. I helped my kids through their bedtime routine, read scriptures together, and listened to Zane's voice carry our family prayer into the night. Once the house was quiet, I felt compelled to explore deeper questions. I typed, "Why do I attract unaccountable people?" and embarked on a profound journey.

I discovered a mosaic of patterns—over responsibility and a chronic need to please. Each memory was like a flash of lightning, illuminating the landscape of my childhood. Scenes of my past played out like a vivid film reel, weaving together the intricate tapestry of who I had become. This was more than research; it was a deep expedition into my mind, body, and spirit—a quest for healing and understanding.

My Shadow Creation

While my mom was pregnant with my older brother, her doctor advised her to terminate the pregnancy, doubting her ability to be a mother. Yet she defied his warning, thankfully. I love my mom deeply.

She was a whirlwind of contrasts: a great provider who taught me the value of owning a home while borrowing against most of the equity; my biggest cheerleader battling her own self-doubt. A shopaholic, she worked hard to fund her habit. She connected with everyone, though her vast social circle often made it hard for her to remember names. Many adored her, and her child-like wonder charmed countless hearts while aggravating others. Beneath her lively exterior, she battled bipolar disorder, with severe highs and crushing lows, creating a turbulent home life. Navigating our relationship felt like tiptoeing through landmines, uncertain of what might trigger an emotional explosion. My childhood was riddled with emotional, physical, and sexual abuse, leaving lasting scars that still grip me.

My mother's past was tainted with the echoes of her father's harsh words, whispered like venomous serpents in her ear. The stories she told revealed a childhood marred by verbal abuse, each tale a haunting specter that chipped away at her self-esteem and self-worth. Trapped in a web of these memories, she inadvertently pushed away the good men who entered her life. My father, a kind soul, became collateral damage, their marriage dissolving when I was four years old. If she had healed her pain, would our lives have been different?

My mother found herself entangled with men who preyed on her vulnerability. They exploited her kindness, leaving scars both visible and hidden. One of these men extended his cruelty to my sister and me for years. He masked his dark intentions with lavish gifts, taking me on shopping sprees to buy clothes designed for easy access to my most sacred places and others to conceal the bruises that marred our young skin.

I remember one unsettling afternoon on the back deck of our home. I was perched on his lap, a puppet in his twisted game, as he leaned in close and hissed, "If you ever tell anyone, I will kill you." The terror of that moment is seared into my memory. I didn't know my body was my own; I hadn't been taught how to defend it or protect it. Oftentimes, I was in my mother's bedroom, playing a sickening game of hide and seek, giggling nervously as I tried to escape his grasp while she was away at work.

One day, my sister wore a short-sleeved shirt to school, revealing the bruises that painted her arms. Her concerned teacher asked questions. My sister saved us by telling the teacher about the horrors that had plagued us for years. That teacher saved us by notifying the proper authority.

When the authorities informed my mother, she couldn't bring herself to believe us. Her denial cut deep into the wounds he had inflicted, and both continued to haunt me. The examiner told my mom he didn't think I would be able to bear children.

Before dawn painted the sky, I would hear my mom's footsteps upstairs. Her light frame paradoxically sounded like a herd of elephants tromping around. Then, silence would blanket the house around 4 am, as she hurriedly left to work. I was left to get myself and my little sister ready for and off to school. The weight of this duty rested heavily on my young shoulders, yet allowed me to learn responsibility.

Shopping with my mom was a whimsical adventure. The store buzzed with conversation, rustling hangers, and the thrill of finding hidden treasures.

"Mom, I really like this one, can I get it?" I asked, my eyes sparkling as I clutched the colorful fabric.

"Is it on sale?" she replied, scanning the crowded aisles of Mervyn's like a hawk.

"Yes," I answered, excitement racing through me. "Okay," she said— that was all she needed to hear.

But the magic faded as soon as we returned home. Tension filled the air as her demeanor shifted. Her voice, once joyful, turned venomous as she accused us of being ungrateful: "The only thing you care about is me buying you things, you think I'm just made of money," she would scream. She'd dramatically wish for death, claiming we'd be better off without her. Sometimes, her anger turned physical—a sharp tug at my hair or a swift kick. The warmth of our shopping trips evaporated into a harsh reality.

I began working when I was 14 and resolved never to ask her for anything again. I bought my own clothes and school supplies. Despite the turmoil, I learned valuable lessons about gratitude and financial prudence.

When I was 12 years old, I became the girlfriend of a 16-year-old. This experience opened my eyes to entrepreneurship while robbing me further of my innocence. We dated all through high school until he got heavily into drugs, and after a little experimentation, I decided that wasn't the path for me. Why was this relationship allowed?

I was doing homework with my friend Brittany when my mom came downstairs. Her face was a mask of frustration, and she was hitting me. "Why didn't you do the dishes?" she demanded, her voice sharp like shattered glass. There were only a couple of dishes in the sink, but to her, an insurmountable mess.

I didn't understand then, but I now know her nervous system was always on edge. She often lashed out, both physically and verbally, and when I tried to share my struggles, she would break down, burdened by her own emotions. I began retreating into myself, learning to face life's challenges alone. This left an invisible scar, a psychological armor I wore to protect my fragile heart. I developed fierce independence and a stubborn refusal to ask for help, earning me the nickname "The North Face," likening me to the rugged, weather-beaten side of a mountain that endures the harshest elements without flinching.

Growing up, I often stood up to my mom's abusive boyfriends. One, whom she married, was a drunk and drug addict with a prison history. I came home from school to find my mom gone. Days passed without news of her, and I did my best to carry on alone. My sister couldn't handle my mom and moved out a few years earlier. I was called to the school office, and they asked if I knew where she was. I didn't have a clue. A few days later, my mom came home with a broken arm and bruises. He had broken her arm with a curling iron. She escaped, and a stranger bought her an airplane ticket. I was 16 and used a map to drive to Anaheim, California, searching for where he stayed. My mom had no sense of direction, and the city felt like a maze. After hours of looking, I finally spotted her white Ford. Fear and urgency surged as I approached; the doors were locked, but I couldn't give up yet. I couldn't stand the thought of him abusing her and then stealing her truck, too. I fumbled with the spare key to unlock the truck and quickly started the truck to allow the engine to roar. My mom followed me as we drove away, leaving behind a nightmare and hoping to find solace in the miles ahead. This didn't stop him, he eventually found his way back to our home, continued phone calls were made to the police, and my mom refused to press charges.

My mom attempted suicide multiple times throughout her life, the last failed attempt was during COVID. This generational predisposition began showing up in my son at age four. We must heal generational trauma.

Ultimately, focusing on the positives shaped who I am today. Through the whirlwind of emotions, I emerged with a deep appreciation for the lessons learned and the strength to find light even in the darkest times. However, I was still laden with an undercurrent that held me back from being my best self.

In September 2022, my mom was walking across the road when a speeding car shattered our world, leaving her lifeless on the asphalt. This news sent shockwaves through my soul and didn't feel real. The days after her burial were steeped in sorrow, her absence a gaping wound that bled.

Grief morphed into a storm, with my sister's pain that twisted into rage directed at me, her words cutting to my core. Meanwhile, my husband grappled with ghosts from his past—a previous wife who left him—a wound that silently festered into a chasm between us. His emotional distance felt like an icy wall, leaving me cold and isolated. The weight of these pains bore down on me like an oppressive sky, making me feel paralyzed in a life where time moved forward, but I remained frozen. Depression wrapped around me like a suffocating shroud, each day a battle to breathe, each moment a struggle. Navigating this labyrinth of anguish seemed impossible, the path obscured by relentless heartache.

Following my mom's tragic death, I felt lost, alone, and frozen. The transformative experience with the horses emerged, prompting me to confront the buried pain of my past.

I had tried counseling before, but talk therapy was a dead-end road. The horses encouraged me to seek the root causes of my hurt, revealing the emotional wounds that had become silent shadows, interfering with my actions and reactions. They helped me pursue a path of healing. This journey became about not just recognizing the pain, but transforming it, allowing the shadows to dissolve in the light of newfound awareness and healing.

I took the ACE test, designed to reveal childhood trauma. When my results flashed a 10/10, a chill ran down my spine. I called my husband to share my score. He congratulated me, unaware of the test's meaning. "No, Ben," I said. "A perfect score is far from good."

Concerned, Ben took the test and scored a 0/10. The contrast between us was striking. Research shows those exposed to toxic childhood environments face grim outcomes: homelessness, incarceration, addiction, or worse. I am among the fortunate .002% who escaped those fates. My sister, however, struggled with addiction and prison.

I served in the Army for 14 years and one leadership principle stood out: to know thyself. Imagine looking in a mirror, not just at your reflection but deep into your soul. To lead effectively—in life, family, work, and community—you must confront both your brilliance and your shadows. My journey of self-discovery began at ten, sitting on the steps of my split-entry home, questioning my purpose and place in the universe. This memory gave me hope.

Through this journey, I've committed to change—like tending a garden, pulling out old habits, and planting seeds for growth. This commitment is to authenticity, becoming the best version of myself for my family, community, business, and, ultimately, myself.

Veteran's Affairs offered equine therapy and, simultaneously, I eagerly signed up for certification as a Horse Guided Empowerment coach. These experiences cleared the cobwebs of my soul and brought a refreshing sense of liberation and opportunity to help others.

We've had about 900 guests participate in our signature Hearts & Horses program at Swell Retreat. Picture being in a field with a wild horse, a semi-trained horse, and a well-trained horse, each reflecting different aspects of our nature. Their movements teach us to harness strength and grace, guiding us to become more like them—authentic, free, powerful, and serene.

One tool we share during our experience—Trigger Identification Tool: SOFT-BEEB

1. **S**top.
2. **O**pt out of the environment.
3. **F**ocus on my breath…it takes 90 seconds for me to let the emotion pass.
4. What did the person/situation do that caused the **T**rigger?
5. What **B**ehavior did I exhibit when I was triggered?
6. What **E**motion was sending me a message?
7. What emotional wound in my past was **E**xposed?
8. Emotions are messengers: How can I navigate this emotion, person, and experience and create a **B**oundary for myself?

Every book and research study I have read over the past decade opened doors within me, dissolving the chains that bound my spirit and allowing me to soar into new realms of self-awareness and emotional, physical, and mental freedom.

Understanding triggers isn't a one-time revelation; they appear as shadowy figures at the edge of your consciousness. Initially, they seem indistinct and menacing, but with awareness, they become clearer, like bringing a blurry photograph into focus. You learn to recognize them, as understanding dawns like the morning sun breaking through the fog. You set boundaries gently yet firmly, like a tree rooting deeper into the earth.

At first, these boundaries may be breached, causing emotional turmoil. But in a moment of clarity, you find the strength to enforce them kindly. It's a powerful shift—discovering an uncharted island within yourself, a place of strength and peace.

Not everyone will respect your new boundaries. Some may react negatively, drifting away like autumn leaves, while others may bring more pain than joy, prompting you to distance yourself. This discernment becomes a beacon of liberty, guiding you toward a life free from toxicity.

With each step, you learn to navigate triggers, tracing them back and gently untangling their hold on you. You shed the weight of toxic people, situations, and addictions, like a snake casting off its skin. Each layer you peel away brings you closer to unbounded freedom and joy, where your spirit can dance free from the past. Then, you break the cycle of pain in your future posterity, a true win.

Our app, Live Swell, will be your best friend through your own journey of freeing yourself from past trauma, generational trauma, and faulty programming from society to be your best self and fulfill your purpose. It provides courses, community, and holistic approaches to healing.

LOVING LIFE'S JOURNEY
Linda Wilson
Emotional Support Expert

Linda Wilson, is a coach, mentor, and expert in emotional intelligence, emotional support, and ethical influence. She has triumphed over three open-heart surgeries, career sacrifices, losing five loved ones in four years, and depression. Her remarkable journey of resilience has redefined her life, turning adversity into a source of strength and inspiration. Today, she uses her story to guide others in their own process of self-discovery, helping them to uncover their purpose, passion, and personal path.

As a speaker and mentor, Linda focuses on affirming each individual's inherent worth, emphasizing that everyone is loved, valued, and appreciated. She believes in the power of healing, growth, and transformation, teaching people to build a life that aligns with their deepest dreams and desires.

Through her personal experiences and professional expertise, Linda empowers others to confront challenges, discover their strengths, and create a meaningful lifestyle that reflects their true potential and unique aspirations.

https://www.linkedin.com/in/lindamariewilson/
https://www.facebook.com/lovinglifesjourney
https://www.instagram.com/loving.lifesjourney/
https://lindamariewilson.com/

MY CLOAK OF INVISIBILITY

By Linda Wilson

After open-heart surgery, I lost my voice when my vocal cord got paralyzed. Talking was a very physical effort. To be heard in a whisper, I was screaming. It was physically and emotionally exhausting.

I…could…not…be…heard.

It was so frustrating! If we needed a repair person to come out, or we had to talk to the bank or any phone calls, it was IMPOSSIBLE.

This was 2013, and the voice-activated phone menu was the big thing. I would call the cable company about our service, and the recording would say, "What can we help you with today?"

I would try to talk to say what I was calling about. The recording would keep saying,

"Please repeat that."

"I didn't get that. Can you try again?"

Or just act like I didn't say anything at all. Over and over and over again.

I would be in tears of anger, frustration, and exhaustion because I could never get through to a person. I would text my husband at work, so he could get on the phone with me. I'd make the call, and he would talk. It was like I wasn't there. It was demoralizing, and my whole body ached from the mental and physical effort of trying to be heard.

And when you don't feel heard, you don't feel SEEN.

I kept networking (I had to keep my business going), but no one could hear or understand me. I started to withdraw and would just sit by myself. I couldn't place my order at a restaurant. The drive-through was an absolute nightmare.

I withdrew more and more. And became more and more depressed. I stopped visiting friends and started communicating only by text or Facebook. I still called my parents every night, but my dad couldn't hear me.

And I continued to shrink. To hide. To be invisible.

Before my first surgery, I was outgoing and physically fit. I was VISIBLE; I didn't mind being seen. I was a photographer, a public speaker, and an author. I was the president of the largest chapter of Colorado Business Women. I loved being around people, connecting people, and meeting new people. I was truly a people person.

My husband made sure I felt heard and seen. When I talked, he would lean in close so I wouldn't have to scream. He talked to me like a normal person and remembered that I couldn't be heard. He made sure others treated me normally and would step in to help when I couldn't be understood.

I was in network marketing at the time, and my upline leaders were phenomenal. When we did phone blitzes, one of them would sit next to me and help with the calls when my voice failed.

When the strain of talking got too much, I would start choking, and I would almost get sick. It was disgusting. One or both of my leaders would accompany me to my appointments. When I had a choking fit, I would leave the meeting, and they would take over until I got myself pulled together and rejoined the meeting.

During those times, I was seen. And I was heard. But not in a way I WANTED to be seen and heard. I was embarrassed by what I THOUGHT people were seeing and hearing. And I just wanted to hide and to be invisible again.

Then I had the surgery, and I thought that would fix everything. And it eventually did. I have a normal voice. I can carry on a normal conversation. It's still hard to be heard in a noisy bar or restaurant, but I get by.

Maxwell Maltz, in his ground-breaking work *Psycho-Cybernetics*, showed us we can never outperform our own self-image. And my self-image at that time was not good. I felt unworthy. I was disgusted with my circumstances. I was embarrassed to be in public, afraid I would have another gross choking fit. I thought people only saw my deficiencies and felt sorry for me. I didn't want their pity. I had more than enough of that without any help.

Boy, did I live into THAT! I only felt normal around a few people: my husband, a few close friends, and my family.

After 18 months of frustration, I decided to get a vocal implant so I could talk again. It's a simple day surgery—usually. After the surgery I aspirated, got pneumonia, and almost died. I was put on a ventilator and was unable to speak even when awake. I had a notepad to write on, and the staff would check the notepad when they came in. And I had my call button, but I couldn't reply when the operator answered. If they didn't read their notes, they wouldn't realize I couldn't answer, and they would think I was messing around, or hit it by mistake.

Then I got a superbug, CRE, that systematically went through my body, trying to kill everything inside of me. I was in ICU isolation on a ventilator for five months.

When I was awake, I couldn't talk because I was on the ventilator. Because of the CRE, I was in isolation so that I wouldn't make anyone else sick. I felt like a pariah. Many of my family and friends were immuno-compromised, so they couldn't visit me because I might make THEM sick.

This was pre-COVID. I wasn't used to the idea of the patient being the one putting others at risk. People had to be gowned, gloved, and masked to enter my room. I had a couple of the nursing staff who saw the lack of human contact starting to affect me, so they would only wear gloves, so I could see their full faces. My husband would come in to touch my hands, my face, and kiss my forehead, before gowning up.

And I shrank some more. And hid further.

My physician at the rehabilitation center was horrible. He would purposely wait for my husband to leave the room before he came in to talk to me. He would rush through his visit, never giving me time to write out questions. If I had the questions ready, he would vaguely answer them. And he NEVER looked at me. He never tried to connect with me or my husband in any way. I was a bothersome patient to him and to the facility. They weren't set up to prepare a patient to go home. I was a distraction to their 'mission' of long-term acute care, and so the doctors didn't want to deal with me. I'm not sure why they agreed to take me as a patient, but they regretted that decision, and they let me know it.

And I shrank and hid some more.

Once I returned home, it was difficult to be around people in crowds. Although it was wonderful being welcomed back by family and friends, I shrank down even more inside myself. I had gotten COMFORTABLE being invisible.

Then, my brother died, and then my husband, and over a four-year period I lost five family members. And I continued to shrink and to hide, my cloak of invisibility wrapped tightly around me.

I spent 18 months curled up in a ball on my couch, hiding, keeping myself invisible. COVID didn't change my life ONE BIT. But then my heart sister filed for divorce, and she moved to my house. She owns a gift basket company and creates the most beautiful gifts for people. Everything about what she does is so festive. It's like a party with confetti everywhere!

I began to come alive again. There was someone there who talked to me, who saw me, and who included me in all her shenanigans. Now, all of my friends and family were very loving and supportive. But once COVID hit, we couldn't get together. She allowed me my space while I slowly pulled myself together. And all my family and my friends continued to reach out to me. They SAW me, they HEARD me, ACKNOWLEDGED me. I was no longer invisible. And I no longer wanted to be.

But it didn't happen overnight. That cloak of invisibility that I purposefully wrapped myself in was now a part of my skin, my whole being. I had to relearn how to be seen, to be heard. I had to shed that invisibility cloak.
I started slowly. During the pandemic, my friend and I bought inflatable unicorn costumes, and we did roadside supply drives for the Navajo reservation in New Mexico. We were also a drop -off station

for the drives, and we filled our garage several times with donations.

We did outdoor birthday and graduation celebrations. We would show up in costume and dance for the drive-by celebrations. We bought bunny costumes and put Easter eggs in peoples' yards for their kids. People didn't see my face, but I was getting out in public again.

My heart sister's basket business exploded during COVID, and I did a lot of deliveries with and for her. We started documenting our shenanigans on Facebook. We created a page and posted videos of all our activities.

And slowly, the invisibility cloak started to loosen, to give way.

I started using my voice, reaching out to my family, friends, and connections to advocate for others. I organized and participated in a protest against the predatory tactics of our neighborhood homeowners' association. I was interviewed by several TV stations and newspapers. My face, my voice, and my name were on the news several times. I was uncomfortable, as I didn't want to be the focus. It was about my neighbors, THEIR story. It wasn't about me. But I could do it because I was helping others.

Baby steps. But each step brought me more out into the open, into the light. And I was remembering how to interact with others and allow them to interact with me.

And more and more of the invisibility cloak disappeared.

I realized that being visible is an internal journey. I had to be willing to see myself in my current state and acknowledge the feelings that came with that process.

If I wanted to be visible, I had to be willing to ALLOW myself to be visible, and to be vulnerable. There's a reason a person feels invisible or makes themselves invisible. I had to have a lot of hard conversations with myself.

Why did I feel as I did? Not just on the surface. I had to dig deep and speak honestly with myself. I had to be willing to do some serious work on myself. I had to be honest with what I was feeling and allow the feelings to flow.

I did all this by myself. I didn't share my thoughts or feelings with anyone, because, at first, I didn't even know what they were. I did see a therapist, and she was very helpful. Her work was very scientific and even though I'm a more feely kind of person, I loved the process. I didn't lie on a couch and pour out my woe-is-me story. We worked with bio-rhythms and other physical processes that helped me understand what I was feeling, and to process those feelings in a healthy way.

I learned to find different outlets to allow my feelings to flow and to release them. I love dogs, so I got a job working at a doggy daycare. They understood my physical limitations, and I got paid to play with dogs. We were currently dogless, so I got paid to get my furbaby fix.

I also became a Read Aloud volunteer, and once a week, I would go to the elementary school and read books to the early childhood education class. It was so much fun! The children were so sweet, and it was a joy to be in the classroom.

During COVID, we watched a lot of home improvement TV. And we decided to do a few projects. I white-washed the fireplace brick (it really brightened the room!). My house was built in 1984, and the decor was still in the style of the 80s. The kitchen cabinets were all oak. We decided to paint them a light blue and a cream. We put up a light wallpaper in the kitchen, and we painted the china cabinet and buffet. There was a dark wine rack and cupboard that we replaced with a pantry with white barn doors. The kitchen was MUCH brighter and more inviting.

We redid the whole backyard. We bought new cushions for the patio chairs, outdoor pillows, two red metal rocking chairs, two big swing chairs, and two huge patio umbrellas. We planted lilies and other plants, put in a fountain, hung outdoor string lights, and transformed the backyard into an oasis paradise. We kept Amazon in business!

When we were working on all the changes, I would get so tired and out of breath so quickly. All that sitting on the couch feeling sorry for myself had done my body no good.

I visited my brother in Spokane, and the same thing happened. We did a lot of walking around town, but I would have to stop and rest a lot. I started beating myself up for letting myself go.

When I found out I needed another open-heart surgery, I was thrilled! "What?!?!" you say. That's right! I was THRILLED! I thought that I was lazy, feeling sorry for myself, and had let myself get completely out of shape. When he told me my aortic valve was operating at only 40%, I was so happy!

Why? Because it meant I hadn't done this to myself. There was a valid medical reason for me being worn out at the least little bit of effort. I'm the only person I know who felt better after open-heart surgery than before it. After so many years of feeling tired, depressed, worthless, and invisible, I was suddenly alive and feeling the best I had in 12 years.

After I found out I needed another surgery, I was scheduled to go on a ladies' trip to Mexico that had gotten postponed due to COVID. I confirmed with my surgeon I could go. I had a blast! I had a new lease on life, and I went and enjoyed Every. Single. Moment.

I went zip lining, atv-ing, horseback riding, and swam in the ocean. I did things I had either never done before or hadn't done in YEARS. If you've never zip-lined in Mexico, they have these wooden steps you hike up to get to the platform. The platforms are three stories high and there were 11 platforms. I would start up first. I was sooooooo slow. Everyone kept passing me by, offering to help me. And I wasn't bothered by the attention. I was grateful people were concerned about me and looking after me. But I was comfortable being ATTENDED to, SEEN, VISIBLE. It was FABULOUS!

At this time, I only weighed 109 pounds. I kept getting stuck partway on the zip line. And a beautiful young man would have to come out and rescue me. (nudge, nudge, wink, wink…) They glide down the zip line, lock legs with you, and pull you up to the next platform.

What would have made me cringe in embarrassment a month before had me laughing in joy. Just to be able to participate, to be social, to have fun, was such a blessing!

That week in Mexico I really began to come ALIVE. You could see it in the photos. I was smiling, laughing. I was SHINING.

I was ME again. And I felt AMAZING!

The Miracles

We are ALL miracles. I am a product of at least SIX, not counting my birth.

1. Aortic dissection in May 2011.
2. Revived from cardiac arrest three times in the fall of 2015.
3. False dissection.
4. Necrotic (dead) tissue that repaired itself overnight.
5. Machines telling me I wasn't breathing and getting oxygen, when I was awake, talking, and doing fine, and that disappeared overnight (all of these in May 2021).
6. Extreme blood loss in September 2021.

I don't say this to impress you. But to impress upon you that you are here for a purpose. I found my purpose after the six miracles. I don't know if I'm just slow, or if I needed something from each one of those experiences before I could find mine. But I've FINALLY figured out why I'm here on this earth. Once where I would have hemmed and hawed, not sure what to say, I can now say my purpose with conviction.

I use my experience, knowledge, skills, and abilities to help others find their purpose, passion, and path.
I do that by shining brightly so others can see that you CAN, BE, DO, or HAVE whatever it is you desire. You need to BELIEVE that. You need to FEEL that. I am an example of that. And if I can do it, so can you.

Everything is energy, including your thoughts (your beliefs). And the Law of Vibration states that energy vibrates.

- All energy has a vibration.
- Different kinds of energy vibrate at different frequencies.
- And like energy attracts like energy.

Think of a magnet and steel. Or your dog and a potato chip bag. (If you know, you know!) Or when you think of a person, the phone rings, and it's them. Or you see them someplace unexpected.

Truly believe in your heart of hearts, feel it in every breath, that your purpose, your dream, is yours to obtain. Get into the FEELING tone of your purpose. And ACT accordingly. Like you BELIEVE and FEEL you living your purpose, every day. Like energy attracts like energy.

I'm human, just like you. I have fears. I make mistakes. I'm not perfect. And I don't want to be. We're ALL human. We share the human condition, which means we're all similar, but we're all unique. I can tell you that my aortic dissection experience is different from anyone else's. I survived it, just as tens of thousands of people have. But all our experiences in that realm are unique because each of US is unique.

If you're hiding, keeping invisible, step out into the daylight. If you feel ignored and invisible, step out into the daylight.

Rise above your challenges and circumstances, and be a beacon of hope and inspiration—not only for yourself but also for others. You never know who is watching or listening because your circumstances are similar to their own.

They're looking for guidance, inspiration on how to do, be, have better. And YOU may be that light for that person.

While you're lighting YOUR way, being VISIBLE, you're also shining brightly for others to follow, to see THEIR way.
Stop hiding in the dark. You have a purpose, and that purpose gives you life. It lights your way, so you can SEE and BE SEEN.

Love your uniqueness! Step out of the dark, out of hiding, and shine a light on your gifts. Let the world SEE you in your true glory!

EARTHSIDE ACRES
Mélyssa Léveillé
Founder

When I lost the one person you're suppose to have by your side throughout your life 10 years ago, I felt, afraid and frustrated. I had completely lost trust in life. Having had no support through this challenging time in my life and later becoming a new mother struggling with post-partum anxiety and depression. In a dark and terrifying place, I had hit my rock bottom. I was full of shame and mother's guilt. I knew I had to start helping myself because my child deserved a better ME.

Today, I have set boundaries in my relationships which makes spending time with family and friends a positive, fun time. I have built awareness of my thoughts and body, plus have taken onto physical activity such as weight lifting. Therefore, I have a healthy balance in my life. With this balance, I can be the mom I've always dreamed to be!

https://www.linkedin.com/in/m%C3%A9lyssa-l%C3%A9veill%C3%A9-052257213/
https://www.facebook.com/Earthsideacres
https://www.instagram.com/earthsideacres/
https://www.earthsideacres.com/

BECOMING A MOTHER, AN ENTREPRENEUR, AND MY BEST SELF THROUGH POST-PARTUM DEPRESSION AND ANXIETY

By Mélyssa Léveillé

The Breaking Point

On a warm, plus 30-degree mid-May summer day, I sit on the porch swing, feeling the sun touch my skin, hearing the wind pass through the leaves, and seeing two birds fly, chasing each other across the farmyard. Some may say, I was living the dream life: on the family dairy farm, in the country, on a calm road. "What a great place and way of raising a family." I had heard that one too many times. The sound of my baby crying brings me back to reality. The emotions building up, as the crying escalated, was one of my new normal now. All the feelings rush back, heart pounding, tightness in my chest, and trouble breathing. I had been asking myself, "Is this what being a mother is supposed to be like?" The loneliness, the shame, and guilt playing over and over in my head. The replay of not being enough and doing enough had created a downward spiral of emotions daily. Living on the family farm for over 10 years, I had created a belief of worthiness but only when it is related to the farm, money, or helping others. As a farmer's wife, I was doing it all, no questions asked: property maintenance, house cleaning, dishes, meals, laundry, and now, I was raising a baby. I rarely asked for help and pleased everyone as much as I could. I was worried about what others thought of me, my confidence was non-existent. As the baby cried out for me, feeling my palms become sweaty and tears filling up my eyes, I fell into complete exhaustion and hopelessness. Being over a year post-partum, I couldn't understand why these feelings were still part of me. I felt alone, misunderstood, unappreciated, and like a complete failure, as a mother, a wife, and even as a human being. Why was I stuck in this cycle of self-sabotage? This hatefulness towards myself? Family, friends, and even medical professionals would tell me: "This is all normal, Mélyssa, it will be okay!" but are these feelings really normal?

Deep down, I knew, I was not okay. The nightmares, the panic attacks, the crying, the nausea, the loss of weight, the loss of purpose, the loss of self. My whole life, from a very young age, I was so excited to have children and become a mother. This was truly a dream for me! So, why wasn't I feeling like this was a dream come true? Becoming a mother was a life goal for me. I pictured the beautiful family, having fun adventures together, and life would just be amazing! When in reality, I was struggling. My baby was sick, going on day three of a high fever, he was crying most of the day, only sleeping on me, not eating well, and having sleepless nights. I had nothing left, I felt unworthy of being his mother, I couldn't do it anymore. I had completely lost trust in life and especially in myself. As I grab my son, I sit on the sofa and cry. I talk to my husband and share that I can no longer do this. In this life, being a mother, I have no love to give to our son, and I hated myself so much.

When I returned to work, as my maternity leave was complete in January, I knew I wasn't ready. I didn't know how to juggle all the daily tasks, being a mom, and now trusting someone to watch my baby while I go to work. I worked in a heavy and, at times, toxic environment. This brought intense pressure on me. At work, I had a minimum of three panic attacks daily. Running to the washroom, to gather myself up again and compose myself to face coworkers and clients. I did not enjoy work; I did not enjoy being a mom. I did not enjoy being me and my life. In March, this is when the lockdowns came into play. The lack of connection with family and friends, the fear-based abuse, and the OCD added even more to my plate. I could no longer do my groceries without having a panic attack.

One night in February, I woke up, and as I got up, my head spiraled, my heart was beating out of my chest, and my whole body went numb. I had never felt this way before. I ran to my husband in full panic, thinking I was having a heart attack. Who will take care of my baby if I die? No one knows how to take care of him. How will my husband run the farm with a baby? Questions were rolling over and over in my head as I panicked. My husband supported me and talked to me slowly. Feeling his heartbeat on my hand was the only thing that helped me calm down. After this episode, I was extremely anxious to fall asleep, as I didn't want this to happen again. This is when my sleep began to become depleted. The next week, my husband was leaving for one week for a farmers' event. Still in a state of panic, I couldn't let him leave. I was scared this was going to happen again, and then what would happen to me or the baby? I am living in complete fear. This is when the deep fears started. Fear of others, fear of getting my son taken from me, fear of my husband leaving me, and even fear of myself. I reached out to my medical team, and they suggested to try a medication. As I started them, things got worse. I started getting nightmares and dark thoughts. I was crying all the time, lying on the floor in my kitchen, and overall not functioning. Through this challenge, I lacked support from the medical team, I felt I was going through this alone, and no one cared. I felt unseen. I decided to stop the medication.

From February to May, I lost 25 lbs, I was at my lowest weight since my high school years. I slept three to four hours a night, and I was obsessing over what was happening to me. I was continuously doing research, reaching out to healers, and trying to figure out what was going on and why. What can I do to help myself through this? This was my unseen battle.

This all led up to this one day in May. I woke up startled from a nightmare, lying in my bed, this was the last call for help. I had dreamed that I pulled a gun on myself. In a panic, I called a family member to share this nightmare. My son was sick, so I reached out to my in-laws to come help me with him. I then decided to make a call to the medical team and explain my nightmare, crying, I shared that I could not do this anymore. I needed to sleep; I needed help, and this was no longer normal. This was enough. Either she was to help me, or I was going to drive myself to the hospital. She asked me if I was safe and if I wanted to physically hurt myself or others. I expressed that I was scared to die. This was why I was calling. I needed them to stop telling me these feelings were normal and to help me. I agreed to try multiple medications and counselling.

Healing Journey

It took me two years to completely heal and finally see the light. This took huge courage, patience, and time. I realized that I was co-dependent on others around me. Co-dependency for me was that my emotions, may it be happiness or frustrations, were based on others around me. I was a people pleaser, always looking to make others happy and self-sabotaging myself daily. I rarely said no to others, which made me run on low energy and exhaustion. I would let others, even people I love, treat me poorly with disrespect and take advantage of my kindness. I lived anxiously, thinking of what others were thinking of me. Anxiety had played a big role in my overall health practically my whole life. I experience a lack of sleep from overthinking, stress, digestion problems, panic attacks, migraines, mood, and hormonal imbalances, to name a few. During this healing period, I noticed that I had been living with these traits from a very young age but simply had never noticed the effects it had on my happiness and my life. Today, I have set boundaries in my relationships which makes spending time with family and friends a positive, fun time. I have built awareness of my thoughts and body, plus have taken on physical activity such as weight lifting. Therefore, I have created a healthy balance in my life of my time and being a working mom. With this balance, I can be the mom I've always dreamed of being! Patient, Present, and Positive!

Lessons

Here is what I learned throughout the darkness.

1. **Speaking up for myself** and being firm and confident with others wasn't my norm, but during this storm, I realized, I needed it, I needed ME. No one could help me or support me if I didn't speak up and ask. I realized the medical system DOES NOT know more about me and my body than ME! I had completely lost trust in myself because I had been pushed away multiple times and had to understand that "This was all normal feelings." I realized I must do the work, the healing, the talking, the sharing, the growth, and the grief. By learning to speak up and set boundaries not only for myself but for my children, some of the relationships I had taken a turn. I learned that when you start speaking up, which sets new boundaries, this may unbalance others around you because they are not used to this new skill of self-respect. Unfortunately, I had to grieve some close relationships, let go of my expectations, and accept that our relationship had changed. I had to choose happiness, love, and peace for my life. I had to learn to choose what event or person was helping me through my healing and growth.

2. **Grief** is always present until you heal . The grief I felt started

10 years ago when I lost my mother at the age of 18 years old. Having lost someone so close, I felt abandoned, hurt, and alone. When I lost the one person you're supposed to have by my side throughout my life, I felt confused, afraid, and frustrated. At this point, I got confused about how life works. How could someone so important to me, leave this earth so early in my life? I still needed her for all my big life events, her advice, help, and unconditional love. Having had no support through this challenging time in my life and later becoming a new mother struggling with post-partum anxiety and depression. In a dark and terrifying place, I had hit rock bottom. I was full of shame and mother's guilt. I knew I had to start helping myself because my child deserved a better ME. He deserved a healthy mom!

3. **Horses** have been always a huge part of my life. All the time, when they have been absent in my life, I struggled. In 2019, during the darkness, my father moved into my area, and he brought my horse back. I started working with her again as well as other horses. The horses were a big aspect of my healing. They listened to my hurt and grief. They reminded me of my strength, my patience, and my confidence. They showed me trust, leadership, and emotional regulation. Horses do not judge; they listen and observe. As a prayer animal, they reminded me to live in the present moment. They have honest feedback, therefore, they always kept me on my toes and kept me on the right path.

4. **Find support** around you. I had to find someone, a group, and a therapist that I felt could support me through this storm. I found support in family members and found an amazing therapist. I am beyond thankful for my family, who supported me throughout the healing. My mother-in-law helped me by listening to my concerns, my sister did the check-ins, and my husband encouraged me. Secondly, I found a woman's anxiety support group that greatly helped me on my healing journey. Why? Because they were also mothers, who knew the struggles and challenges. They shared advice and held space for my

healing. Thirdly, I found a great therapist, who not only offered psychotherapy, but she also understood empaths and sensitive people. I learned to not settle for any counsellor or therapist. I met a couple before really finding the one who I am still seeing regularly today.

5. **Exercise** or a physical activity. I fell in love with weightlifting. Thanks to my sister-in-law, I was initiated into the gym environment. I developed a routine and a non-negotiable ME time. This took my husband some time to understand, but he knows now how it's important to me. He's seen the benefits; the happier, energetic, stronger version of me. The gym time is not only for the physical part but is much more a way to give my mind a break. I focus on the movements and the music, and all tasks and to-do lists disappear. Setting goals and seeing progress in the gym helps my confidence and strength.

The Reward

As I visited Ava, my horse, daily throughout my healing journey, I felt so much relief and strength. I often felt like she was showing me who the person I needed to be. She held massive space for me and took great care of me. I remember saying to my father: "Not everyone has horses to experience this with. I need to offer this to my community." This was the seed that created my dream. As I started to feel better, I researched what was out there to help people through horses. I made a great deal of phone calls, speaking to at least 20 testimonials on various certifications offered in Ontario, Canada. Finally, I decided to take an Equine Assisted Learning Certification at Dreamwinds EAL centre in Bradford. With this certification, I would start helping my community.

As I brainstormed for my new business, I finally decided on the name Earthside Acres. Earthside Acres because everyone living on earth is technically on earthside, and it can be so challenging here. It took me some time to find a logo that spoke to my heart. Finally, I fell in love with a drawing from a great artist of a horse coming out of the branches in a tree. It represented the horse so well: the grounding, the support, and the love.

As I have a background in Education Assistant, I started working with kids on the spectrum. I then shifted to helping women and mothers. I ran some private and women's programs for one summer. I am now running kids' groups, 1-on-1 private sessions, and school workshops. I wasn't sure why, but I still felt as though I was missing something in my clientèle. One summer, I met a woman who ran a respite service at her farm. As I sat in her office and we chatted for over an hour about her story and her farm, she said to me: "To help the mothers, you must take care of the children." This was my "Aha" moment, that moment when something just clicks, and you understand. I knew in this moment that my focus had to pivot back to children. May these children be in foster care, have anxiety, or have a learning disability, this is who I am here to serve and support. By creating a safe space for children, I can relieve the mother from the worry, the responsibilities, and the exhaustion they feel 24/7 for their child. The respite I can offer her to simply do her groceries without rushing for her child, take some time to meal prep for the week or even sleep. Although at the beginning, I was so focused on doing things for the moms, while really what they needed was time alone, to recharge, get organized, and composed so SHE can now tackle her mother duties and support her children and family.

Society has created this picture-perfect mom label "Supermom" while leaving mothers feeling overwhelmed, alone, and at times, hopeless. Unfortunately, this "Supermom" era is all a lie and unrealistic. From cleaning, cooking, taking care of the kids, raising resilient kids while working full-time and running around to the kids' activities, plus making sure they have healthy meals, enough sleep and learn how to regulate their emotions is not meant to be done alone. Feeling drained, never asking for help, and crying all the time is NO sign of "Supermom". Woman-mothers don't need to feel SUPER at being a mom, they need support, understanding, and community. They need to be SUPER at asking for help, holding healthy boundaries (with the kids and others), and taking care of themselves. They need "ME" time and guidance without judgment. Life is hard. Being a mother is hard. I learned the hard way that everyone deserves to live a happy life. A life you will be proud of sharing with your kids and grandkids someday. As a mother who found the flicker of light in the darkest tunnel, you matter, you are enough, and you are always worthy of a happy life. You are an amazing mother, and life does become beautiful again. You must not give up; your strength is right there in your heart. Find joy in the simplest things at first, then you will start to heal and find yourself again. Your life will be even more amazing; trust, let go, and go with the flow.

RAY OF SUNSHINE INDIVIDUAL SUPPORT SERVICES, LLC AND SELECT LATOSHA HOMES

Latosha Bobo

Realtor, CEO & Owner

With an MBA and a BS in Business Administration, I am currently a Corporate Data Analyst with a strong focus on strategic insights and data-driven decision-making. My professional journey includes expanding my own ventures, such as a home health agency and real estate business, through effective marketing and leadership. I am dedicated to helping others, whether it's by ensuring quality care for clients in need or by guiding families toward building legacies through real estate.

I value continuous learning and professional growth, which is reflected in both my educational background and my diverse skill set in data analysis, business strategy, and leadership. Integrity and excellence guide everything I do, and I take pride in fostering meaningful relationships with clients, colleagues, and communities. My passion lies in making an impact, not just through business success, but by creating positive, lasting change for the people I serve.

https://www.linkedin.com/in/latosha-b-13963778/
https://www.facebook.com/LatoshaBRealtor/
https://www.instagram.com/latosha_b_sellshomes/profilecard/

THE FOUND WOMAN

Embracing Strength, Freedom, And Success

By Latosha Bobo

As the middle daughter in a family of three girls, I grew up knowing how to work hard and strive for success, but I wasn't taught how to navigate the complexities of love and relationships. My parents, who married young, instilled in me the importance of education and independence, but life's twists and turns would soon show me that resilience requires more than just hard work. Growing up, I watched my parents work tirelessly, instilling in us the value of hard work. I saw my mother endure heartache, and my father wrestle with an unfulfilled need he couldn't quite understand, yet they stayed together as long as they could. But when I began facing struggles in my own relationships, I realized I had never truly learned what a healthy partnership looked like. These early lessons shaped me in ways I would only come to understand much later. At 15, I faced a life-changing decision when I became pregnant and had an abortion, a choice I made based on others' opinions and one I never fully healed from. That decision was only the beginning of a journey that included marrying young, enduring a difficult marriage, and eventually, rediscovering my strength through separation and self-forgiveness. This is my story of vulnerability, growth, and realization that we are defined not by our struggles, but by how we rise from them.

At 15, I became pregnant and found myself feeling lost and uncertain.

Deep down, I wanted to keep the baby, but I let the opinions and judgments of others guide my decision to have an abortion. Looking back, I realize that I never truly healed from that choice. I didn't fully grasp the depth of what I was doing at the time, and for years, I quietly carried the weight of that experience. At that point in my life, I had been with a few partners, not realizing that my actions were a reflection of something deeper—a search for validation. Looking back, I sometimes wish I had listened to my own instincts rather than letting others' opinions guide my decisions. But I've learned that every choice—right or wrong—has shaped me into the person I am today, and for that, I have no regrets.

Despite being a straight-A student, I struggled with insecurities I couldn't yet name. I didn't understand that the lack of confidence I felt might stem from unresolved issues with my parents, or that I was craving something I couldn't define. I didn't feel beautiful. As a dark-skinned girl with breasts but no shape, I struggled to see my own worth. In hindsight, I realized that the decisions I made at that time were influenced by external pressures, and I was doing the best I could with what I knew. I've since learned that it's important to show compassion to my younger self, and one way I've done that is by writing a letter to her, acknowledging her struggles and offering forgiveness. I encourage you to do the same—write a letter to your younger self. Express the understanding and love you would have needed back then. It's a powerful step in releasing guilt and embracing healing.

When I met him, he felt different. He was older and lived a lifestyle I wasn't familiar with—drinking, smoking—and I was drawn to the feeling of being "seen." I lied about my age and secretly spent weekends with him. Eventually, I moved in with him, which led to my mom threatening not to attend my high school graduation. Feeling torn, I packed my things and planned to move back home, but on my way to work that day, I was in a car accident that totaled my car. At 18, I found myself pregnant again, but this time it was planned. I remember telling him I wanted to get pregnant, though I wasn't sure if it was a response to my first abortion or a deeper longing for something missing. After my son was born, I moved in with him again and took on the roles of wife, mother, college student, and full-time employee—despite not being officially married. For three years, I played the role of a wife, and eventually, I accepted his ring—not because I was certain, but because it seemed like the right thing to do at the time. Looking back, I was ignoring so many signs. Before we even married, I had already endured his infidelities and tried to end things several times. But I believed marriage would make things better because I held marriage in such high regard. For him, though, I think it simply meant I was never going to leave.

During my marriage, I remember being called hurtful names related to my size and appearance. Those words cut me to my core, stripping me of my self-worth. I didn't just hear those words—I felt them and wore them like a cloak of shame. They became my identity, shaping how I saw myself. There were times when my belongings would be destroyed, and I would have to come up with excuses to explain why I couldn't see family or friends. I lied for him, covering up the reality of my life behind closed doors. The curfews, the cheating, the destruction of my clothes if I came home late—it all chipped away at me piece by piece. On the hardest days, when I felt like I was sinking, my son was my lifeline, keeping me afloat.

I desperately wanted more children, but after my ectopic pregnancy, I couldn't conceive, and he blamed me for it. I spent years trying to prove that I wasn't the problem, seeing doctor after doctor, taking hormones, anything to make it right. But the marriage only spiraled further, especially as his drinking worsened. I even tried to organize an intervention, but not everyone was willing to participate, turning a blind eye to the damage.

No one truly knew what my life was like—the insults, the physical altercations, the constant infidelities. The more he cheated, the more controlling he became. I lost myself entirely. I didn't know what I wanted anymore, or who I was beyond being his wife and the mother of our son. I wasn't allowed to talk to other men—not even family members. I couldn't make eye contact with men, even in business settings, and I wasn't allowed to be on my phone past a certain time. I was trapped in a cycle of control and abuse, feeling invisible and powerless, desperately trying to hold on to the pieces of myself that were slowly slipping away.

One day, while venting to my best friend, he said to me, "Everything you dislike about yourself, you can change. You're beautiful. You're smart." I held onto those words because I had never heard them before. That moment marked the beginning of reclaiming my life and redefining who I was.

I began to realize that the controlling behaviors, the curfews, and the destruction of my belongings were not normal or acceptable. I knew I had to establish boundaries if I was ever going to reclaim my self-worth. If you find yourself in similar situations, take a moment to identify the red flags in your relationship. Make a list of behaviors that don't feel right and recognize the importance of setting clear boundaries for yourself. Boundaries are not just a defense; they're an expression of self-respect.

One night, while seeking comfort, I made a decision that I would later carry immense guilt for—I stepped outside of my marriage and became pregnant. I knew I was leaving my marriage, but I had no idea how to tell people—especially my teenage son—that while I was still married and living with my husband, the baby I was carrying belonged to another man. The weight of that truth felt impossible to share. So once again, I chose to have an abortion. This decision weighed heavily on me because, after my first abortion, I swore I would never go through that again. The guilt from that first experience never left me—

I often wondered what that baby would have been like. And now, here I was again, in the same position.

As the arguments with my husband worsened, I began planning my escape. I convinced myself that this pregnancy was God's way of reassuring me that I wasn't the problem. I had to wait a few weeks before the procedure, and during that time, my husband was so consumed with his own needs that he never noticed any changes in my body or mind.

When the day came, I cried throughout the procedure. The nurse held my hand, likely thinking I was in physical pain, but I wasn't. It was the deepest emotional pain I had ever felt. At 15, I hadn't fully understood what I was losing. This time, I did, and it shattered me.

To make it even harder, I couldn't grieve openly. I had to keep up appearances and continue planning my escape as if nothing had happened. The few people who knew about it thought I was fine— because that's what I told them. But inside, I was anything but.

Leaving wasn't easy, but my therapist and close friends constantly reminded me of my strength—that I could survive and even thrive. I managed to pass my real estate exam on the first try, all while working two jobs and raising my son. I bought my own home, making real progress, but deep down, I couldn't shake the feeling of failure. I had a good job, two degrees, and yet, the emotional weight of my situation lingered. As I balanced work, motherhood, and personal struggles, my career became both a refuge and a challenge. Dedicating myself to work felt empowering, but it also served as an escape from the parts of my life that seemed beyond my control. Failing was no longer an option; especially in these areas, and with each step, I was reclaiming the parts of myself I had almost forgotten.

During my toughest times, a few close friends stood by me, reminding me that I wasn't alone. Their words became my lifeline, and I realized that true friendship can be just as healing as romantic love. My best friend consistently reassured me of my inner strength and wisdom, even when I couldn't see it myself.

I tried to make the marriage work so many times after leaving, but before officially divorcing. Each time, I realized we simply didn't fit. I was embarrassed, feeling like I had failed because I never imagined myself as a divorcee. No one really knew the reality of my life behind closed doors.

The day of my divorce hearing felt surreal. Even though we had been separated for some time, the finality of it was hard to grasp. A close friend called afterward and suggested we get a drink, asking me how I felt. Honestly, I didn't know. I struggled with the fact that, in all my successes, I had imagined my husband and son standing beside me. Instead, I felt like a failure. Divorce wasn't part of the plan, and it took me years to understand that it didn't define who I was.

After my divorce, I entered into somewhat of a poly relationship where I finally experienced what real love and leadership looked like. He led by example, not through control. He guided and encouraged me, supporting my endeavors simply because he knew they were important to me, not because he was getting anything in return. Despite the freedom and love in this relationship, I brought toxic traits from my past. I found myself displaying the very behaviors I had resented in my ex-husband, but now from my own side. Even with all the openness in this relationship, I struggled with trust. I wrestled with being submissive, vulnerable, and honest—traits I had once embraced, but which the pain from my past had stripped away.

It was in recognizing how deeply that pain had changed me that I realized something had to shift. That's when my real healing began. This man loved me and showed me in countless ways, yet I was fumbling with his love because of my own unresolved wounds. His love saved me. But before I could fully receive it, I had to forgive myself—for the pregnancies I lost, for my failed marriage, and for all the moments when I believed I wasn't enough. I had to forgive my ex-husband, my parents, and even my friends.

I learned that forgiveness isn't a one-time act; it's a process that starts within. As I began to forgive, I also began to redefine what success meant to me. Success wasn't reflected in a pay stub or measured by societal standards or failures. Success was whatever I decided it to be—a life filled with peace, happiness, and joy, reaching my own personal goals, and sharing those experiences with genuine people. That became my new measure of success. Today, my understanding of love looks completely different. It's not about control or meeting someone else's expectations. It's about respect, mutual support, and the freedom to be myself. I've come to realize that real love is rooted in equality and peace.

I began to prioritize taking care of myself—working out five days a week, meditating, and practicing daily gratitude, which helped shift my focus away from the pain and onto the blessings I had in my life. If you're trying to heal, start each day by identifying three things you're grateful for. It's amazing how this simple practice can transform your mindset. I finally forced myself to slow down and truly focus on myself. With that shift, I gained a new, healthier perspective on love, life, and success. I've realized I can't blame anyone for the choices I've made or the experiences I allowed into my life. My life is mine to shape. I choose who I let in, and I determine the path I take. I've decided to live fully, love deeply, and laugh often. A wise friend once told me that there aren't many truly good people in the world, so when you find one, you must hold on to them. I've found that to be true but holding on requires enough strength to allow them to hold on to you as well, and that can only happen through healing those old wounds. Healing isn't a destination; it's a journey that makes you stronger with every step and requires active participation. It wasn't enough to simply leave the situation—I had to nurture myself back to wholeness. Taking care of myself became essential to my recovery. Through it all, I've learned that my circumstances don't define me—they are simply chapters in the beautiful story of my life. If you're in a place where you need healing, start small. Build a daily self-care routine and commit to it. It's not just about physical wellness; it's about reclaiming your emotional and mental strength. Remember, every chapter, no matter how painful, is part of the beautiful story of who you're becoming. You have the strength to reclaim your own story, one small step at a time.

Becca Jamieson
Life and wellness Coach

I'm Bexs, a Life and Wellness Mentor, as well as a mother and nanny from Tauranga, New Zealand. I work as a support worker, but my true passion lies in being a life and wellness mentor. I often refer to my chronic pain as the Devil, and my illnesses as chaos. My endometriosis feels like Freddy Krueger, with hands like blades stabbing my insides and causing unexplainable pain. Creating an online space is my way of offering healing, inspiration, and support to others on their own healing journey, or those focusing on health and wellness. This platform serves as a means to educate and raise awareness about my personal battles with chronic pain, illness, domestic violence, unhealed trauma, and health and wellness. By sharing my thoughts, struggles, and personal challenges, I find healing, while also helping others become the best, happiest, and healthiest versions of themselves.

I'm a proud mother of three wonderful children as well as a lovely grandson. My experience as a support worker in the healthcare industry has allowed me to care for those with physical disabilities, mental health issues, and addictions.

My passion for becoming a life and wellness mentor developed when I faced my own struggles with chronic pain and illness. I have survied domestic violence, healing unhealed trauma. I was faced with a broken health system, having to adovcate for my own health and left navigating things on my own so I wanted to raise awareness and inspire others through education and my own personal story. I have three amazing children and a beautiful grandson. My work as a support worker in healthcare has given me the opportunity to care for individuals with physical disabilities, mental health challenges, and addiction. My own experiences with chronic pain and illness inspired me to become a life and wellness mentor. I have overcome domestic violence and unhealed trauma, and I want to use my story to raise awareness and inspire others through education.

https://www.facebook.com/share/HrpZd6rmvkjU5q3n/?
mibextid=qi2Omg
https://www.instagram.com/beautifullybroken_ajourney/
https://www.nirvanalifeandwellnesses.com/

FROM HURT TO HEALING, EMBRACING IMPERFECTION, AND FINDING

By Becca Jamieson

A Glimpse into My Personal Journey

My personal journey has brought me to a place where I aim to help others discover their path to self-discovery and manage their personal development. This remarkable, chaotic journey has led me to believe that we all need to step out of our comfort zones at some point in our lives and embark on an adventure to rediscover ourselves, not to change but to improve ourselves. I believe I've been on an ongoing journey of self-discovery. Every unkind experience has prompted me to reflect, leading to questions about the reasons behind breakups and friendships ending. Initially, I viewed these as part of life's challenges, but I've learned to pick myself up and move forward. All those things—the thoughts, the feelings, and the emotions—are ways to stop and take notice and ask yourself the hard questions, like, "Are you happy?" This is where this journey of self-discovery starts. The first time I truly engaged with life and paid attention was when I walked away from domestic violence. The moment he laid a hand on me, everything came to a halt, and that's when I realised it was time for a change. I was shattered, lacking confidence, no identity, no voice and energy to keep fighting. It was then that I understood this couldn't be my life anymore, and I had to rediscover myself. I won't sugarcoat it; the journey is tough, filled with challenges, confusion, and moments of solitude. When I acknowledged the chaos in my life, I understood the need to delve deeper and recognized that I couldn't navigate this alone. A change of environment was essential for my growth. I had to learn to let go of the old me and the old life and create a life that aligned with me moving forward. The positives outweigh the negatives in my journey, leading me to workshops and allowing me to meet amazing people. I've learned more about myself, discovered the importance of incorporating healthy habits, and made positive choices. By distancing myself from toxic people, I've become more conscious of unhealthy behaviours. My perspective on life has shifted towards being more open-minded. Embarking on a wellness journey has

opened up new business opportunities, improved my health, increased my focus, and provided clarity about my future. Self-discovery is an evolving process that changes as we grow and experience life's challenges. Remember to trust the process, enjoy the moments, and take pride in your progress.

I have always viewed myself as beautifully broken, putting the broken pieces together while confronting life's trials. Embrace the strength found in vulnerability and resilience. Each shattered fragment symbolises parts of my life: the people who have caused me pain, my addictions, the inner demons, unhealed trauma, all forms of abuse, mistakes, lessons, and grief. Amidst these hardships, there are also the happy moments, like raising three amazing children, pursuing a career as a nanny, obtaining qualifications, meeting incredible people, exploring beautiful places, establishing my dream job, and sharing my journey with those who want to join me on my journey.

My life unfolded like the changing seasons, profoundly shifting my perspective and shaping the person I am today. This period was defined by significant loss, daunting challenges, and personal growth. The suddenness of these events left me grappling with doubts about my self-worth and future. The familiar security and routine vanished, leaving behind an overwhelming void. Amidst the darkness in my heart, unexpected health issues emerged, intensifying the stress and uncertainty. Each medical appointment deepened the uncertainty, and I felt like I was losing control. The burden of my circumstances became almost too heavy to bear, and I struggled to find a way forward. In the midst of this difficult time, I was compelled to confront my vulnerabilities and limitations. Though confronting these truths was painful, it was a crucial step. The season that brought me to my knees also pushed me to look within and discover a resilience I never knew existed.

The world seemed to come back to life, reflecting the gradual healing happening within me. I started to rebuild, piece by piece, focusing on what truly mattered. I sought therapy, reconnected with loved ones, and pursued passions that had long been dormant. It was a slow process that I needed to trust. Through this journey, I discovered resilience I never knew I possessed. I learned that it's okay to ask for help and that vulnerability is not a weakness but a strength. The season that broke me also taught me the importance of self-care, mindfulness, and the power of community. I emerged from that period with a renewed sense of purpose and a deeper understanding of who I am.

In the end, the season that broke me was also the season that made me. It was a catalyst for growth and transformation, a reminder that even in our darkest moments, there is potential for light and renewal. I am forever changed, but I am also stronger, wiser, and more compassionate. And for that, I am grateful.

The Power of Vulnerability

Throughout my personal journey, I have come to understand the immense power of being vulnerable. Embracing vulnerability has been a significant turning point for me, shaping not only how I perceive myself but also how I interact with the world around me.

I have experienced a world of dissociation where I often felt misunderstood for a long time. Society sometimes perceives vulnerability as a weakness that should be concealed or hidden. For me personally, when I realised that vulnerability is a source of great strength. It allows for genuine connections, fosters empathy, and opens the door to personal growth. By allowing myself to be vulnerable, I have learned to face my fears, acknowledge my imperfections, and embrace my authenticity.

This shift in perspective has transformed and impacted my relationships and overall well-being. By openly sharing my challenges, struggles, and emotions, I have created a supportive environment for others to do the same. This fosters trust, deepens connections, and enhances my relationships, making them more meaningful and fulfilling. This new approach has empowered me to take risks and pursue my passions without being held back by the fear of failure. It has taught me that making mistakes is a natural part of growth, providing opportunities for learning and personal advancement. Embracing vulnerability has increased my resilience and self-confidence when confronting life's challenges.

Embracing vulnerability can be a powerful and transformative experience. It allows us to connect more deeply with ourselves and others, creating genuine relationships built on trust and authenticity. When we open up and share our true selves—our fears, hopes, and dreams—we create a space where empathy and compassion can flourish. This act of courage can break down barriers and dispel the isolation that often comes from hiding our true feelings. It can lead to personal growth and resilience. By confronting and embracing our weaknesses and imperfections, we learn to overcome challenges and build inner strength. It can also inspire others to do the same, creating a ripple effect that promotes a more understanding and supportive community.

I have created some steps that I have used on my own journey that could help you with allowing yourself to be more vulnerable in life.

• *Acknowledge Your Feelings*
Recognize and accept your emotions, whether they are positive or negative. Suppressing feelings can lead to stress and health problems. By acknowledging them, you start the process of understanding and addressing them.

• *Practice Self-Compassion*
Treat yourself with kindness and understanding. Remember that it's okay to make mistakes and that they are a natural part of growth. Self-compassion involves being gentle with yourself during times of failure or difficulty.

• *Open Up to Others and Share Your Story*
Share your story, thoughts, and feelings with trusted friends, family, and professionals. Opening up not only strengthens relationships and creates deeper connections, but it also allows others to support you and can make you feel less isolated.

• *Accept Imperfection*
Understand that no one is perfect. Accepting your flaws and imperfections makes it easier to be vulnerable. It can also help you to appreciate the imperfections in others, fostering empathy and compassion.

- *Take Risks*

Step out of your comfort zone and take risks, whether in your personal or professional life. Trying new things and facing challenges can lead to personal growth and resilience.

- *Be Present*

Focus on being present in the moment rather than worrying about the past or future. Mindfulness practices like meditation or deep breathing can help you stay grounded and more open to experiencing vulnerability.

- *Seek Professional Help if Needed*

If you find it particularly challenging to embrace vulnerability, consider seeking help from a therapist or counsellor. They can provide strategies and support to help you navigate your feelings.

- *Reflect on Your Experiences*

Take time to reflect on moments when you felt vulnerable. Journaling can be a helpful tool for this. Reflecting on these experiences can provide insights and help you understand how vulnerability has shaped your life.

- *Celebrate Your Courage*

Recognize and celebrate the moments when you show vulnerability. This can help build confidence and reinforce the positive impact of being open and authentic.

- *Create a Safe Environment*

Surround yourself with people who are supportive and non-judgmental. A safe environment encourages vulnerability and makes it easier to express your true self.

Just remember that embracing vulnerability is a continuous process that requires patience and practice. By taking these steps, you can foster a more authentic and fulfilling life. In essence, embracing vulnerability has been a pivotal moment in my life. It has allowed me to live more authentically, connect more deeply with others, and approach each day with a greater sense of courage and purpose. I am grateful for the lessons I have learned along the way, and I continue to embrace vulnerability as a powerful tool for personal transformation.

The Power of Your Story

Every person's journey is uniquely their own, and within that journey lies a story that holds immense power. Each of us carries a bag filled with experiences, memories, lessons, and dreams. This collection of personal stories shapes who we are, how we see the world, and how we interact with others. We find strength in sharing our stories, and we find resilience as we face life's challenges—embracing our imperfections is a testament to our inner strength. Each setback, each failure, and each moment of doubt contributes to our growth and resilience. These experiences teach us valuable lessons and help us overcome future obstacles.

Sharing my story is quite a natural thing for me as I've evolved as a person, ventured beyond my comfort zone, and embraced therapy. Delving into deeper aspects of my story, I aim not only to help in my own healing but also to support others on their journeys. By opening up about my experiences, I hope to create a space where others feel safe to share their own stories, fostering a sense of community and understanding. Each of our stories, no matter how different, can inspire, educate, and connect us in profound ways. In the process of relaying my journey, I've come to realise the power of vulnerability and the strength that emerges from it.

Through therapy, I've uncovered layers of myself that I never knew existed, each revelation bringing a mix of challenges and growth. It's a continuous process of learning to accept and love myself fully, flaws and all. This journey has taught me that it's okay to seek help, to lean on others when the weight of the world feels too heavy, and to believe in the possibility of healing.

In sharing my story, I want to convey a message of hope and resilience. Life's trials can shape us in unexpected ways, but they also offer opportunities for transformation and self-discovery. So, whether you're at the beginning of your journey or somewhere along the path, remember that you're not alone. Together, we can navigate the complexities of life, one story at a time.

Sharing your story can be a powerful and transformative experience. Here are some key benefits:

- Personal Growth and Healing: Sharing your story allows you to process your experiences and emotions. This act of reflection can lead to greater self-awareness and personal growth. For many, it can also be a therapeutic process, helping to heal past wounds and find closure.
- Inspiring and Helping Others: Your story has the potential to inspire and help others who may be going through similar experiences. Hearing about your journey can provide them with hope, encouragement, and practical advice.
- Building Connections and Community: Sharing your story gives you a sense of connection and community. When you share your story, you open the door for others to relate to you on a deeper level. This can lead to new friendships, support networks, and a feeling of belonging.
- Breaking Down Barriers: Personal stories have the power

to challenge stereotypes and break down barriers. By sharing your unique perspective, you contribute to a broader understanding and acceptance of diverse experiences and backgrounds.

- Empowerment: Sharing your story can be empowering. It allows you to reclaim your narrative and take control of how your experiences are perceived. This sense of agency can boost your confidence and self-esteem.
- Educating and Raising Awareness: Your personal experiences can shed light on important issues and raise awareness about topics that may be underrepresented or misunderstood. This can lead to greater empathy, advocacy, and social change.
- Be creative and write. Sharing your story ensures that your experiences are recorded and remembered. This can be important for posterity, providing future generations with insights into your life and the times you lived in.

In summary, sharing your story is a multifaceted act that can benefit both you and those who hear it. It fosters personal growth, builds connections, breaks down barriers, and has the potential to inspire and educate others.

In essence, our stories are a source of power. They allow us to connect with others on a deeper level, build resilience, and embrace our true selves. By sharing our journeys, we contribute to a more understanding, compassionate, and inclusive world.

Embracing Imperfection as a Path to Healing

It has been a long journey for me to embrace the woman I am today. Over a lifetime of unhealed trauma and years of self-criticism, I have gradually learned to appreciate myself. Three years ago, I began my healing journey with self-acceptance, authenticity, and embracing my imperfections with love and beauty.

The discoveries I made on my journey emphasized the importance of accepting my imperfections. Unaware of their impact, these revelations altered my perceptions and self-image, particularly as a woman. Many realizations unfolded, revealing the beauty found in vulnerability and authenticity. By acknowledging my flaws, I discovered strength in my uniqueness and learned to value the diversity each person brings to the world. It became evident that perfection is merely an illusion, and genuine growth stems from embracing our true selves, imperfections included. Engaging in conversations with other women, I shared stories of struggles and triumphs, fostering strength and empowerment. These interactions served as a reminder that I am not alone in my journey.

I'm sharing my treasure chest of discoveries with you—insights that have guided me in embracing my imperfections on my healing journey.

- I discovered self-compassion through therapy. Self-compassion involves treating yourself with the same kindness, understanding, and support that you would offer to a close friend. It allows personal growth and emotional resilience. By being kinder to yourself and recognizing that imperfection is a natural part of life, you can practise a more compassionate, balanced, and fulfilling life. Remember, it's the imperfections that often make life interesting and beautiful. So, give yourself permission to be imperfectly perfect.
- I discovered the strength in forgiveness, starting with forgiving myself for certain issues that had been burdening me in life. I let go of the weight I had been carrying for so long, releasing the pain caused by those who had hurt me. Letting go allowed me to release the heavy burdens I had

been carrying for so long. I started to surround myself with positive influences: friends who uplifted me; I started reading books that inspired me; and things that brought me happiness in my life.

- I discovered mindfulness, meditation, and yoga as key parts of my daily routine, helping me stay grounded and present. I began to listen to my inner voice and trust my intuition, guiding me to make decisions that aligned with my true self. I celebrated my small victories and learned to see setbacks as opportunities for growth rather than failures.

- I discovered that treating myself with kindness and patience allowed me to break free from the shackles of self-criticism and to move forward with a lighter heart. This shift in perspective not only improved my relationship with myself but also helped with my connections with others.

- I discovered and came to understand the essence of authenticity, realizing that embracing our imperfections leads to genuine authenticity. I no longer feel the urge to hide my true self under a facade of perfection. Authenticity has the power to enhance our relationships by fostering real connections built on our true selves.

- I have discovered and come to understand the importance of self-care. I now make time for activities that nurture my soul, whether it's a walk in nature, a warm bath, or simply a quiet moment with a cup of tea. I have learned that taking care of myself is not selfish but essential for my well-being.

In summary, embracing our imperfections is not about settling or giving up on self-improvement. It's about recognizing and understanding that our flaws are an integral part of our unique selves. This acceptance opens the door to healing, growth, and a deeper, more compassionate love for ourselves.

Today, I stand tall with a heart full of gratitude and a resilient and strong spirit. I am proud of the woman I have become and excited for the future that awaits me. With every step forward, I continue to embrace my imperfections, knowing that they are what makes me uniquely beautiful.

WHATEVER IT TAKES
Maranda Wood
Owner

Maranda grew up watching her dad build a logistics company. She later learned that entrepreneurship runs deep, tracing back to her great-grandfather, who owned businesses in the 1960s, making her a fourth-generation entrepreneur.

She strengthened her business acumen by earning an MBA and was recognized in 2021 with the "Entrepreneur of the Year" award from WCR.

Maranda makes impressive strides in business while also being a devoted wife and mother. She married her high school sweetheart, and together, they are raising three special-needs children, managing conditions such as diabetes, eosinophilic esophagitis, autism, anxiety, asthma, and more.

Maranda believes that entrepreneurship and parenthood are never easy, but they are always worth it.

Some days, you have to put your head down and just put one foot in front of the other. Before you know it, you will make it further than you ever expected. Whatever it takes!

https://www.linkedin.com/in/maranda-wood-m-b-a-2bb1aa48/
https://www.facebook.com/mecko138
https://www.instagram.com/maranda_wood/
https://callwitnow.com/home
https://callthemoldteam.com

BUT GOD

The Day I Almost Lost Everything

By Maranda Wood

When the pandemic hit, I was a Realtor, and my husband was working in his company, The Mold Man (now, The Mold Team). I was an average Realtor, closing about six deals a year, while my husband used lead generation sources to close deals in his company. As 2020 was ending, I challenged him with a question. "Why aren't you marketing to Realtors?" Looking back, he opened his company because he often found mold as a home inspector and did not know anyone helping Realtors solve that problem. So, when I asked him that question, his only response was, "I don't know, wanna do it for me?" As 2020 ended, I had a decision to make. Would I stay in real estate or move into The Mold Man company?

I spent some time reflecting on this but eventually said yes under one condition. You fire every company you pay to get leads and watch me fly. In hindsight, my husband often shares that this was one of the hardest things he has ever done, but he would make a bet on his wife every day.

January 2021 came, and I started working diligently to tell the world we were open to business.

By April, we were so busy. However, while I had built up a sales funnel, I did not build in any systems, and so as we got busy, I got swamped, and things got hard. I was constantly running, putting out fires, and chasing my tail. I felt like I could not breathe. Things were so intense.

At this point in the business, it was just me, my husband, and one part-time helper in the field. Yet we had our lanes very well defined. I managed admin, marketing, HR, operations, and everything else not in the field, while my husband handled everything in the field.

Work was good, but I was drowning! Finally, one day, I was at my wit's end. I don't remember many details, only that I was crying at about 7 p.m. because I felt like there was more work to be done than I had hours in the day. In this breakdown, my husband agreed to hire an assistant.

The next day, I started searching for our new assistant. I had no idea what I was doing, what I was looking for, or how to create systems; I just knew I needed help.

The day for the interviews comes. My husband is home early, working on his truck, so I don't have to worry about the children while I run to do a few interviews one afternoon.

I scheduled to host my interviews at a local coffee shop since we did not have an office. One applicant never showed up, and the other interview went well. I packed up my items and headed back home.

As I pull up to the house, I can't get into the driveway. My husband's truck is oddly parked, blocking the entire driveway. To the left of the driveway is my mother-in-law's car, and to the right is my father-in-law's car.

I park my car, get out, and walk around the car towards my husband. As I get in front of my car, I can see my husband clearly. I see that his pants are all ripped up, and I can see his underwear. I am so confused, but I make a joke: "At least those aren't your new pants I just bought you."

My husband said, "Oh. You don't know yet."

My mind exploded with thoughts… I was thinking, "What do I not know?" Is it not cool to show your underwear? What happened?

But I can only muster, "I don't know what yet?"

He responded in the most relaxed, calm, and collected manner: "My truck ran me over. I didn't want to interrupt your interviews, so I waited for you to get home to tell you."

I thought I was going to explode!

But said, "What? You should be at the hospital, not walking around, still working on your truck!"

He arrogantly said, "Baby, where I am standing, I am batting ten for ten."

He seemed worried about the crush setting in and pushed himself to work through the pain.

I told him he needed to go to the hospital, and he declined. However, I convinced him to go to the urgent care.

Within moments I mobilized everyone.

My mother-in-law was taking my husband to urgent care.

My father-in-law was taking my youngest son back to his house.

I am taking the oldest two to their extracurricular activities.

Because my oldest son has baseball awards, I needed to support him since the rest of the family had the emergency under control. My daughter had Scouts.

While they were across the street, I called my best friend to tell her what had happened. She told me to swing by our meeting spot, and she would pick up my daughter and take her to Scouts with her.

I am making the calls as we drive across town for baseball awards.

One of the first people I called was my dad, who was unavailable, so I called other close friends and family as I drove to my son's baseball awards.

I am talking to him when I pull into the parking lot for the baseball awards, only to realize that it is empty, and I must have had the date wrong.

Since baseball wasn't happening, I felt like the right next move would be to go across the street to where my daughter was for Scouts. It was like my brain was on autopilot, just moving to the next task.

As I pulled into the parking lot, my dad asked me, "If baseball awards are canceled, where are you going?"

I said, "I guess to Scouts to be with my daughter."

His response to me was almost comical. Since I was on autopilot, it was like I needed my dad to nudge me to realize what my next move should be. My dad reminded me that my daughter was taken care of, so I didn't need to go be with her. Instead, I needed to go be with my husband.

As soon as he said it, it made perfect sense, but the fact that I didn't process that thought on my own made me see how serious the situation was at the time.

After that moment, I changed my course and went to the urgent care, where my husband was waiting to be seen. Shortly after I arrived, they called him back so I could walk to the back to see what the doctors had to say.

Very quickly, the doctor stated that they were not equipped to evaluate my husband and that he needed to go to the hospital. He could have internal bleeding or other severe complications from his accident.

I remember yelling, "They said it, not me!" as I convinced him actually to go to the hospital. You see, my husband is very stubborn and hates doctors and the hospital.

At this point, there were four of us at the urgent care—me, my husband, my son, and my mother-in-law. So, my mother-in-law took my son to her house, and I took my husband to the hospital.

We get to the hospital. The waiting room is super busy, and I think, "Oh, wow! This is going to take a while!!" We get him checked in, and we sit down in the waiting room.

As we found our seats in the crowded waiting room, I asked someone sitting near me how long they had been waiting. They said two hours. I thought, "Oh, brother, it is going to be a long night."

Moments later, they are already calling him back to see the nurse to get his vitals.

We go back out to the lobby to wait. I can't even make it across the lobby before they call my husband back to do an EKG. That was when I realized how serious this could be for him. It felt like mere moments before they had him in the back in a hospital room. So, I knew this was serious!

I remember a sense of fear rushing through my body as I realized that if they had a full waiting room and they called my husband that fast, it must be a life, limb, or eyesight-type situation.

I am fielding calls. I am praying... I am worried sick about internal bleeding and other issues that may be happening with my husband. It was one of the scariest days of my life.

After getting in the room, they came to get him for his MRI. I was left in the quiet, empty hospital room all by myself, worried about the love of my life. I met my husband during my freshman year of high school, and he is the only man I have ever loved.

To feel the void of the empty hospital room, I called one of the last people on my list: my cousin. I figured calling him while I was lost in my own thoughts, sitting in the hospital room all by myself, would be a good distraction.

We get on the phone. I tell him how my husband's F-250 ran over him in my driveway. The response I got was. "Maranda, that happened to my friend, and he never moved from the sidewalk." I get he was likely trying to tell me that I was lucky that he was okay, but the reality was that I could tell that the doctors were scared. The doctors and nurses were worried, and that we were not out of the hot water yet.

So, these words hit me to the core and proved to be the opposite of a distraction.

My husband could die!! I could be left all alone with three children to raise. I have no idea how to do his job in our company; what am I going to do? How am I going to live this life without him?

They bring my husband back in, and at this point, he has been given morphine for his pay, and he is feeling great. Once the morphine took care of his pain, he got loppy and silly, as one does on such a powerful painkiller. He decided to tell me that when the truck started to move, his head was in line with the tire.

I was so upset by this news that I was sick to my stomach. I couldn't handle this news. I am not sure if I have ever felt so scared in my entire life, and as the layers of the onion of a nightmare keep unfolding, I am not sure how I am supposed to make it to the next moment.

I am not at a place where I can cry. I can't do anything but sit beside my prince charming and be present with him as much as possible. Talk to him. Check parts of his body the doctors told me to inspect it and hold his hand. I was praying that he was okay. Praying that he gets to go home with me.

It was evident that just because he stood up off the concrete did not mean he was out of danger. He could still die in the hospital room. It was almost like I held my breath the whole time we were in the hospital.

Then the next hurdle comes. He has a job tomorrow, and he is determined to make it to work! After a mild debate on when he would be cleared to go back to work, I texted his client, letting him know what was happening and that Andrew would likely not make it to the job tomorrow. Despite my husband's confidence in working the next day, I convinced both my husband and the client that we didn't have enough information but would stay in touch once we learned more.

After being in the hospital room for some time, he started telling me more about what happened in the accident.

He had to fix the center bearing on his truck, or he would not be able to work. However, he forgot to set chocks behind his wheels. He said that he was lying on the ground under his truck. When the truck started to move, his head was in line with the tire, but somehow, by the time of impact, he was able to move his entire torso out of the line of fire. The truck ran over his hip and his ankle.

He went on to say that as he lay there, all he could think about was how his truck was headed straight for the neighbor's house. If his truck crashed into someone else's house, he would lose everything he had built.

Thankfully, it stopped short of hitting their house. Once it stopped moving, he jumped up, moved his truck out of their lawn, and kept working through the pain to prevent the crush from setting in.

Apparently, due to his military training, he saw people run over and crushed. When that happens, the medics always seem to be worried about the crush. Crush is when someone has severe damage to their muscle tissue due to their body being crushed between two objects. In this case, such as being run over by a F-250 pickup truck. Crush destroys the muscle tissue and the cells and releases toxins into the bloodstream. It is what kills most people after a serious injury, such as being run over or smashed between a building and the pavement.

I am so thankful God showed up that day and moved my husband out of the way enough to spare his life. The doctors said that he had no internal bleeding and that all of his organs were safe. We walked away with just a broken ankle and nerve damage.

Still, to this day, he has damage to his hip and leg.

Considering all factors, this was a significant blessing. However, I will never forget the day I almost lost my husband.

He was back at work less than two days after his accident. Before he saw the bone doctor to put a cast on his ankle, he was crawling under houses in just his boot. He was crawling under houses as soon as he could physically move.

Meanwhile, I had to find my script, figure out how to hold my emotions together when talking to people, and be the whole sales department for our business.

If my husband was our sole provider and he was the only person who could do jobs and he was working with a broken ankle, then I had to find the strength to emotionally handle all of the questions that were going to come our way.

I told people that some days, you have to count your blessings one by one to remember that you have a lot. Today, my blessing is that my husband is still with me and can walk and talk.

This was one of the most traumatic things that had ever happened to me. I hope those who wrapped their arms around me in the days and weeks that followed would tell you I handled it with strength and grace. It sure is a season that I hope never to relive again.

During this whole event, our preacher was praying for our family, so Sunday's sermon felt like he was talking right to me. The sermon was titled "But God." It was about everyday miracles. In the middle of the sermon, I interrupted the preacher to ask if I could share.

I stood up and shared what we had survived that week. I said, "My husband should have died this week, but God showed up, and he walked in here today on crutches."

At that moment, I had found my safe place to cry. As soon as I sat back down, I finally wept all the tears I could possibly cry and found solace in the fact that God still has His hands on us.

READY4TAKEOFF
Pat Schultz
Coach, Speaker & Author

Pat Schultz is the Founder of Ready4Takeoff.

Through her personalized coaching, Pat helps women over 40 transform their fears into actionable steps, leading to greater freedom and success in their personal and professional lives.

Pat's proprietary 4 Step Process provides her clients with the confidence to move courageously towards their goals, helping them achieve the personal transformation needed to live their dream lives.

Pat uplifts and inspires clients and audiences alike because she empowers people to embrace their dreams, remove perceived blocks to achieving them, and take transformative action to create the life they've always wanted.

Pat earned her BA and MBA from Case Western Reserve University in Cleveland, Ohio where she resides.

With Pat Schultz, you can be Ready4Takeoff.

https://www.linkedin.com/in/patschultzmba/
https://www.imready4takeoff.com/

DOES YOUR BUCKET LIST HAVE A HOLE IN IT?

By Pat Schultz

Do you have a "bucket list" kind of dream? You know, that someday, "I'm gonna do this!" kind of dream that ignites your passion and excitement.

My perspective on the power of dreams was forever changed when I discovered that my late mother harbored a secret bucket list dream. She had never confided in anyone about it, and we stumbled upon it by chance.

My mother passed away at almost 90 years old. As we sifted through her belongings, my son stumbled upon one of her old college term papers written in 1988. Out of curiosity, my son read her paper titled "A Life Worth Living," in which she described her ideal life five years into the future. One page vividly depicted her dream with remarkable detail.

Excerpt from my mother's term paper:

> *"I live there in a house very near the sea. There is a bright yellow light above the doorway. There is a fireplace, and a wonderful fire is glowing. Stairs lead to the bedroom and outside to the sea. An elderly and handsome gentleman joins me for breakfast. He takes my hand, and we walk in the sun and sand."*

I was absolutely stunned as I read those words. Not only had I been unaware of my mother's dream, but it was painfully clear that she had never lived it.

This epiphany jolted me into assessing my own dreams. My mom had written that paper in 1988 when she was 62 years old. When my mother passed away, I was 65 years old. Reading about my mom's unfulfilled dream scared me. I didn't want my own dreams to share the same fate.

The Internet is flooded with articles about bucket lists—how many people have them, how many actually complete them, and the various reasons behind unfulfilled aspirations. However, the purpose of this chapter is not to inundate you with research findings. Instead, my intention is to ignite a profound realization within you. I want you to grasp the crucial role that "choice" plays in shaping our lives. Though we may be reluctant to confront this truth, the reality is that our choices throughout life ultimately determine what we include on our bucket lists and whether we accomplish those aspirations. In fact, some individuals choose not to have a bucket list at all. The problem is that most of us don't *consciously* choose.

We proceed through life on autopilot and then wake up one day to find ourselves at the end of the road, having never done what we really wanted to do. We unwittingly fall into this pattern because our lives are controlled by what we believe to be true about ourselves, our circumstances, and what we are able to achieve in life. This belief system is so ingrained that we never think about it. We make our bucket list choices by default.

Our belief system is made up of numerous individual beliefs that we accumulate over time, starting from birth. We absorb these beliefs, regardless of their size or significance, without conscious discernment. Gradually, they become an integral part of our very being. Now, this is neither right nor wrong; it is simply the way we have been conditioned to live. However, what often occurs is that we navigate through life without ever questioning the beliefs we adopted long ago. Furthermore, many of these beliefs were never consciously chosen in the first place. Consequently, we find ourselves living our lives based on the beliefs of others, who themselves inherited those beliefs from yet others. Most of us never made a deliberate choice regarding our belief system, and yet we find ourselves bound by it, often without even realizing it.

Now, I am not saying these beliefs are inherently good or bad. It's not a question of good beliefs or bad beliefs. It's a question of awareness and choice.

When we hold onto beliefs that do not serve us and keep us stuck, we refer to them as limiting beliefs.

When I was a little kid, somewhere about five years old, I was lying on the floor with my older siblings in front of the TV. We were propped up on our elbows and totally engrossed with our favorite cartoons. All of a sudden, a cartoon scene flashed Parisian "can-can" dancers on the TV screen. At that moment, without any apparent reason or prompt, I turned to my older siblings and declared, "I am going to Paris someday." To this day, I do not know what led me to make that comment. Nevertheless, from that day forward, I nurtured an enduring dream of going to Paris. I developed a deep affinity for all things French. In seventh grade, I even managed to deceive my classmates into believing that I could speak French, exploiting their lack of knowledge about the French language. They were so excited about my language ability; they wanted to tell the teacher! I had to come clean and tell the truth.

In high school and college, I diligently studied French, joined the Alliance Francaise, and subscribed to a French magazine. Then, an incredible opportunity presented itself: the chance to study in Paris, France, during my junior year in college. I guess you could call this my first real bucket list dream. My mom supported my dream but she was worried about the financial commitment. She couldn't see how we could afford it. On the surface, we really couldn't afford it. Some of the tuition assistance I was receiving could not be applied to a year abroad. After adding up all the loans, grants, and scholarships, there was still a shortfall and only one summer to bridge the gap. This took place in the 1970s when the minimum wage stood at $1.60 in 1970. A minimum wage job appeared to be my only option. Or perhaps not.

I scoured the help-wanted ads in the newspaper and stumbled upon a job that paid more than minimum wage. It was a job to be a go-go dancer in a bar. Admittedly, I had never set foot in a bar before. Sure, I had been to restaurants with bars, but I had never entered a standalone bar. Moreover, I had no prior experience as a go-go dancer and had no idea what to expect. Nevertheless, I somehow convinced my mom to lend me her car for the audition, and I was promptly hired. Although none of the bar's patrons bought into my story about earning my way to study in Europe, that didn't matter to me. I was making my dream of studying in Paris into a reality. I set sail from the New York City harbor, and I never looked back.

What obstacles do you perceive as standing in the way of fulfilling your own dreams? For me, it was the scarcity of funds—a message I often heard growing up. What messages do you receive about your dream?

If my story concluded with the return home from France, it would have felt like a fairytale ending. However, reality had a different plan in store for me. After completing my senior year in college and graduating cum laude, I found myself facing the all too familiar struggle of countless other college students—I couldn't find a job. Eventually, after a frantic search, I was hired as an insurance claims adjuster earning a modest salary of $6,900 per year. If living in Paris was my first bucket list dream, then accepting the insurance claims adjuster job was my first sell-out. I settled for what I could get. This was the beginning of the hole in my bucket list.

Throughout the seventies, my job history was lackluster, prompting me to contemplate pursuing an MBA degree to improve my job prospects. The advent of Affirmative Action created an opportunity for me to break new ground as one of the first women hired as a foreman on the night shift at Ford Motor Company, in a role ambiguously labeled "production supervisor." Despite my lack of familiarity with the position, the enticing salary and job description convinced me that I could handle it. It was the highest-paying job I had ever encountered, accompanied by an overwhelming amount of overtime. Like the novice go-go dancer, stepping foot into a bar for the first time, I had never set foot in a manufacturing plant before this job. My stint at the Ford Motor Company lasted 14 months.

A decade after earning my undergraduate degree, I finally obtained my coveted MBA. Armed with this new qualification, I landed a job in Orlando, Florida, another place I had never set foot in before. It was the epitome of a dream job in a dream location. I spent two decades there.

Throughout this time, I viewed my jobs solely as a means to generate income. I never really pursued my passions or aspired for a career that aligned with my deepest desires. Instead, I settled for whatever jobs I could secure, knowing that some were certainly better than others. Even the so-called dream job that brought me to Florida lost its allure as the industry changed. I stayed there way too long. However, after getting married, having a child, and going through a divorce, a job simply became a source of revenue—a necessary obligation that had to be fulfilled, regardless of personal fulfillment. Until I stopped.

It was almost like Forrest Gump when he abruptly ceased running across America. Unlike Forrest Gump, though, it wasn't intentional on my part. I was let go. To be honest, I had been contemplating leaving that role, and the Universe heard my call. While I would have preferred a less dramatic exit, such is the unpredictability of life. I share this part of my employment history because it illustrates the way most of us navigate through life. We tend to accept whatever comes our way without truly seizing control of the direction our lives take. We find ourselves bound by the belief that there are no other alternatives, at least not for people like us.

Now, I invite you to ponder two questions that have the power to shape your destiny:

If you could have any job in the world, what would you choose to do?

If you had the opportunity to earn more money than you could ever spend, how would you prefer to earn it?

These are the questions that challenge us to break free from the limitations we impose on ourselves and start envisioning a life filled with purpose and fulfillment.

The good news is that if we are dissatisfied with our current situation or the beliefs that have led us here, we possess the power to change whenever we choose. Yes, change is indeed possible, despite any initial doubts or perceived lack of control over our circumstances. Often, we find ourselves listing countless reasons why we cannot make a transformation. However, it is essential to recognize that these thoughts are rooted in our old beliefs, which naturally resist change and prefer to keep us stuck.

Stepping outside our comfort zone always carries an element of risk, and our aversion to discomfort tends to hinder our progress.

Do you remember the first time you rode a roller coaster? I do. You're feeling scared because you've never done it before. You're also excited because all the other kids tell you how much fun it is. You're caught in this fear/excitement mode as you climb the first upward track. You immediately feel a rush of excitement as you speed down the track and on to the next. By the end of the ride, your fear has been totally transformed into excitement, and you want to do it again. How many of us would have turned back at the crest of the track if there was some way to do that? We would have missed out on the thrill, wouldn't we?

If you are determined to make a change and break free from limiting beliefs that keep you stuck, there are effective strategies that you can employ. In truth, there are only two ways to change these beliefs. One of the ways is exactly how they were formed in the first place: constant spaced repetition. There are countless stories we have heard over and over again. After hearing the same thing so many times, we start believing that it is true. For example, "I'm no good at Math." "I'm too fat." "Money doesn't grow on trees." "The economy is bad." "You won't find a job with that degree." "Better to be safe than sorry." You get the picture. So if you want to replace the old storyline with a new one, you have to repeat it over and over again until it overtakes the old programming. And, you need to do it with emotion. There's a lot of emotion attached to our old programming.

Follow these steps to replace old, self-limiting beliefs with empowering ones.

1.   Identify the limiting belief.
Begin by recognizing the specific belief that holds you back. For example, "I'm too fat."

_____

_____

_____

2.   Create a new empowering belief.

Formulate a belief that contradicts the old one or expresses what you genuinely desire. For instance, "I am at my ideal weight, and I enjoy my healthy body."

_____

_____

_____

3.   Infuse emotion into the new belief.

Visualize yourself embodying the desired belief and connect with the emotion it evokes. Imagine the joy and confidence of being at your ideal weight and feel it deeply.

_____

_____

_____

Now it's time for consistent practice:

1.   Write it.

Write down your empowering belief repeatedly, reinforcing it in your mind.

2.   Say it.

Speak the belief aloud with conviction and passion.

3.   Visualize it.

Regularly visualize yourself living the reality of your new belief, engaging all your senses in the process.

Remember, change requires persistence. Understand that simply repeating these steps once or twice won't bring about a significant transformation. You have likely reinforced your limiting belief for years, possibly decades. It will take time and consistent effort to rewire your mindset. The more repetition and emotion you infuse into your new belief, the quicker it will replace the old programming. As you become emotionally connected to your empowering beliefs, your actions and behaviors will align with them. This alignment will lead to positive changes in your life. Changes that will last.

I mentioned a second option for changing a limiting belief. This option isn't something we initiate. It happens to us. Life sometimes presents us with an unexpected catalyst for change. We call this an emotional impact. For instance, a health scare like a heart attack might serve as a wake-up call to prioritize your self-care. Likewise, the passing of a loved one may trigger an epiphany about the importance of living a fulfilled life. My mom's passing served as an epiphany for me. However, even in these cases, ongoing reinforcement remains essential. I constantly use repetition and visualization to create the life I want. Although impactful events can prompt immediate shifts in our beliefs, it's crucial to sustain and solidify these changes with the consistent repetition and emotional reinforcement described earlier.

If you remember my earlier story about fantasizing about going to Paris, you can see firsthand the incredible power of visualization. I vividly imagined myself strolling along the charming streets of Paris, indulging in delectable French cuisine, and conversing effortlessly in the language of love. I immersed myself in all things French, even pretending to speak the language. Visualization, a technique frequently employed by athletes, including Olympic champions, can work wonders in manifesting our desires. The Internet is brimming with stories of athletes who visualized their success before experiencing it physically. So why not give it a try? In fact, chances are you've engaged in visualization without even realizing it.

Think back to your childhood when you would pretend to be a superhero, a princess, or even a movie star. Remember running around the living room in your Superman pajamas with the cape billowing behind you? Or adorning yourself with a tiara, embracing the role of a regal princess? That's visualization! As adults, we can tap into our imagination and "pretend" to be anything we want. Consider the actors and actresses who immerse themselves in a character until they truly "become" that role. They think, speak, and act like the character they are portraying. You, too, can adopt this approach.

Just like learning how to play the piano or honing your skills in a sport, **visualization** requires practice, practice, and more practice. We have spent a lifetime ingraining old beliefs, but now it's time to reverse the process and dedicate ourselves to practicing what we genuinely want. It may take time and effort, but the rewards are immeasurable.

So, are you ready to embark on this transformative journey? Are you prepared to harness the power of visualization to shape your reality? Embrace the possibilities that lie within your mind and dare to envision the life you desire. It all begins with your willingness to believe in the power of your imagination and take deliberate steps toward manifesting your dreams. Remember, the power to shape your reality resides within you. Visualization is the key that unlocks the door to your desired future.

The first step is to figure out what you want to achieve. Whatever immediately pops into your head as a reason why you can't achieve it—that is your limiting belief. Reframe the limiting belief into an affirming belief. Every time the limiting belief pops into your head, stop and replace it with the affirming belief. You may have to check yourself dozens of times in one day. Keep doing it until the affirming belief becomes a habit.

To strengthen your emotional connection with the new belief, craft a mental story or narrative that aligns with your desires. For me, it was the story of living in Paris, sitting in a charming café, and capturing a photograph in front of the majestic Eiffel Tower. As you tell yourself your story, ask yourself, "How do I feel as I experience my heart's desire?" Up-level your vocabulary with nuances of the words, "I feel good." Or "I feel happy." Here are some to get you started. I feel...

Content	Satisfied	Carefree
Peaceful	Fulfilled	Grateful
Excited	Elated	Confident

Next, focus on how your body is expressing this emotion. Are you smiling, standing tall, walking on air, or jumping with joy? You can have a lot of fun with this exercise, and it will deepen your emotional connection.

Write out your story and read it to yourself over and over again. Consider recording your story and listening to it throughout the day. These techniques help you practice, and practice is crucial for your success.

You have the power to transform your thoughts and shape your reality. Embrace this power, challenge your limiting beliefs, cultivate positive emotions, and envision the life you desire.

Returning to my epiphany while reading about my mom's dream, I must admit that I was filled with panic. In my pursuit of self-fulfillment, I became caught up in enrolling in various personal development programs. I mistakenly believed that the more I sought, the more I could compensate for lost time. However, I gradually learned that not all activities are created equal, and the key lies in identifying the right ones. Thankfully, I managed to uncover a path that worked for me.

Determined to share my story and my mom's story, I took a courageous leap. I flew across the country to attend the Transformational Speakers Summit in sunny Palm Springs, California. The event served as a platform for me to impart the importance of pursuing our dreams without delay. I almost didn't attend the summit, though. The echoes of my old beliefs reverberated loudly in my head. Doubts crept in as I hesitated to invest in travel expenses, accommodations, and the event registration fee. In spite of my fears, I summoned the courage to proceed.

With anxiety whispering in my ear, I confronted my fear of being on stage, the fear of potential rejection, and the concern that others might perceive me as too old to inspire. Moreover, I battled a detrimental notion that I needed to achieve a specific weight loss before stepping out on stage. Recognizing that these thoughts were mere obstacles obstructing my path towards becoming a transformational speaker, I forged ahead in spite of all my fears.

To refine my speaking skills, I enlisted the guidance of a professional speaking coach, who not only helped me improve my ability to communicate effectively from the stage but also inspired me to become a certified speaking coach myself. All of these experiences led me to the very moment you find yourself in right now, reading the pages of this chapter.

Every day I remind myself that it is never too late to pursue our dreams. I firmly believe that my message carries weight and that countless individuals, much like myself, hold aspirations within their hearts, yearning for their realization before it's too late and they leave this planet for good.

Reflecting on my mom's story, I am reminded that even the simple act of purchasing a plane ticket could have brought her one step closer to making her dream come true. That's what I do. I take one courageous step every day. And you, dear reader, have the power to do the same. Let us embark on this transformative journey together.

Asmita Manji

Certified Funnel Builder

Asmita Manji has over 18 years of experience in creating systems for multi-million-dollar companies. With her certification as a Funnel Builder from Click Funnels, she combines her expertise with practical skills to help corporate professionals successfully transition into business ownership. Asmita's unique strategy empowers introverts to overcome their fears and confidently step into the spotlight during live sessions. Her mission is to guide and support others in building businesses that not only thrive but also align with their true passions and values.

https://www.linkedin.com/asmita-manji-b536a419
https://www.facebook.com/funnellaunchers
https://www.instagram.com/funnel_launchers
https://www.funnellaunchers.com/
https://www.funnellaunchers.com/555challenge

FROM SILENCE TO SPOTLIGHT

How I Fought Fear and Built My Dream

By Asmita Manji

The Origin

What if I told you that everything you desire in life and business is just one bold action away?

The most challenging step toward any goal is often the first one. My journey began much the same way. For nearly two decades, I was entrenched in the corporate world, working a 9-to-5 that I actually enjoyed. I liked my work, and I liked the people. But here's the kicker—I hadn't seen a raise in over 12 of those years.

During those years, life moved forward in full swing—I got married, welcomed a beautiful child, upgraded to a bigger home, and even traded in my sleek 2-door car for an SUV (because, let's face it, that car seat just wasn't going to squeeze into the back).

Do you see where this is going?

The expenses were piling up, but my paycheck remained stubbornly unchanged. I found myself leaning on credit cards to cover the gaps—until one day, even that safety net frayed. I was at a crossroads. I needed to boost my income, and fast. All I was asking for was an extra $1,000.

Then, one day, as I was mindlessly scrolling through Facebook, a guy popped up on my feed, talking about how I could build a business by helping small businesses create their funnels. It caught my attention immediately. I was already designing applications for a living, so this felt like the perfect side venture. I was hooked.

Without hesitation, I dove headfirst into the deep end, signing up for the highest-level program. My thinking? The faster I could learn, the quicker I'd succeed.

But here's the truth: I had no list, no experience with funnels—heck, I didn't even know what a funnel was! The jargon was completely foreign compared to what we used in the corporate world. I had zero social presence, no offer, and no clue how to start an online business. I was starting from ground zero. But none of that mattered—I was fired up.

You know that feeling, right? That spark of excitement when you stumble upon a brilliant idea, and you're convinced that if you just start, people will flock to it because you're so passionate about it? You know exactly what I'm talking about, don't you?

The Journey

Month after month, I threw myself into learning, and I genuinely enjoyed the process. But no one came. That extra $1,000 I desperately needed remained elusive. Instead, I was sinking deeper, spending money I didn't have on courses that promised success but delivered nothing. I was struggling, drowning in debt, and the frustration was turning into desperation.

Each day, the weight of it all grew heavier. I became more depressed and more isolated. I avoided answering the phone, terrified it might be a debt collector. My situation was so dire that I started withdrawing money from my retirement fund—my last safety net was slipping away.

Have you ever been there? Can you relate to that feeling of needing just an extra $1,000 a month while watching others around you effortlessly pull in $50,000–$100,000 a month? The nagging question haunted me: *Why is this not working for me?*

What was I missing? Why wasn't I making any money? Night after night, I cried myself to sleep, hiding my tears from the world. I prayed to God for a sign, for some clarity on what path to take.

I was working hard—putting in long hours at my job and then grinding away on my business every evening. I was doing the time, learning everything I could. So why wasn't I allowed to make my life better? I prayed and prayed, begging for a sign.

Decision Time: Quit or Figure It Out

I reached a critical crossroad: Should I quit or figure this out? The courses I'd signed up for had drained tens of thousands of dollars, turning my side business into an unsustainable, expensive hobby. I couldn't keep going like this.

Indecision is the inhibition of your transformation.

I had to decide whether to quit now or find a way to make it work because whatever I was doing clearly wasn't helping. Then, one day, someone asked me a simple, yet profound question: *How many offers have you made today?*

Wait, what?! What do you mean?

How many people have you approached and shared your offer with today?

Ummm...

Does that sound familiar? I was stuck in a learning rut, convincing myself that I didn't know enough to start serving people. The more I learned, the more inadequate I felt.

Have you been there? Let me tell you, it's a trap we set in our own minds.

By this point, I had been spinning in this cycle for over three years. Sure, I had a few customers, great reviews even, and I was able to serve them well. But deep down, I never felt confident. I was too focused on what I didn't know, rather than on the skills I had and how they were more than enough to help my customers—who, by the way, were just a few steps behind me on their journey.

So, it came down to this: Quit and walk away from my additional losses or figure it out. By now, I needed an extra $2,000 a month— yep, things had gotten worse.

Aaargh! My business was moving backwards financially.

But here's the thing: Quitting wasn't really an option. If I gave up, I'd still need to find another way to make that extra $2,000 a month. I had to figure it out.

So, I went back to the drawing board. I knew I had a strong work ethic and was willing to put in the time and resources. So why was I struggling?

As women, we often take on too much. We want to be superheroes, juggling everything for everyone. We struggle to say "no." But what we don't realize is that when we try to do it all, we end up doing nothing well. We become resentful of our endless, thankless to-do lists. We forget it's okay to ask for help.

And because we don't, we're stressed and overwhelmed. Add debt to the mix, and we start withdrawing from family and friends, isolating ourselves. Depression sets in.

Now, if you're reading this, I know you're nodding your head, feeling what I felt. But guess what? This isn't the end. There is a better way. I figured it out, and I'm going to share exactly what I did, so you can use this strategy to climb out of your rut and fast-track your journey by three years through my experiences.

Research

"How many people have you approached and shared your offer with today?"

That question haunted me for a long time. I had to get real with myself—I wasn't doing that, at least not daily, and certainly not consistently. So, I went back to the drawing board, diving deep into research and some serious soul-searching. I started studying the GOATs in the business and was floored by the sheer volume of marketing content they were producing to promote and launch their services and products.

Meanwhile, I was doing two or three things and feeling crushed when no one responded to my offers.

Did you know Tony Robbins creates upwards of 1,300 pieces of content to promote his offers? Yes, he has a massive team behind him, but still—how many pieces of content do you create before you tell yourself you've done enough?

Think about this: Michael Jordan once said, "*I have missed more than 9,000 shots in my career. I've lost almost 300 games. 26 times I've been trusted to take the game-winning shot and missed. I've failed over and over and over again in my life. And that is why I succeed.*"

What are your numbers?

Bill Gates shared, "*I showed my plan to 1,200 people, 900 said no, 300 showed some interest. Only 85 did anything. 35 of those were serious, and 11 made me a billionaire.*"

Wait, what?! How many of us would have kept going after 900 nos?

Once I learned this, I knew what the problem was. I was caught up in busy work, avoiding the uncomfortable task of asking for the sale.

If you knew you could make a billion dollars by approaching 1,200 people, wouldn't you do it?

Absolutely. And you'd do it quickly, getting through the nos to reach the yeses. Along the way, you'd improve your presentation and gain confidence.

That was my first *Aha!* moment: I needed to reach out to more people and do it consistently to get better and more confident.

Then, I realized I was comparing my two or three half-hearted promotions to others' 1,300 full-blown campaigns. When you see it in black and white, it seems ridiculous, right? But this is what many of us do, and then we wonder why we're frustrated.

So, what was holding me back?

I was stuck in my own head. My internal narrative kept telling me, "I'm not good enough," "I can't talk for an hour," "I'm not interesting," "I'm not good at presentations."

I had to find a solution for that too. What if I shared the information in shorter increments? That seemed doable.

Okay, what's next?

I had stage fright. As an introvert, the thought of speaking in front of 5,000 people was terrifying—NO WAY!!! This was a big hurdle for me.

I remember as a child, even during family get-togethers, the larger the gathering, the quieter I became. I grew up in a small circle of five— my parents and two siblings. That was my comfort zone. When more people were around, I'd retreat into silence.

So, how was I supposed to attract more leads and showcase my knowledge to a crowd?

There had to be a way.

Smaller gatherings, I thought.

And eventually, by breaking things down into manageable chunks, and because I made the decision to figure it out, that's exactly what I did—I figured it out!

This was another major lesson for me: When something feels overwhelming, break it down into chewable pieces and tackle one chunk at a time.

And that's when my 5-5-5 Formula strategy was born.

Now, if you're an introvert and the idea of speaking in front of a large group makes you want to run for the hills, I've got you covered with this strategy.

If you're a business owner with an incredible service to offer but aren't making enough offers, I've got you covered.

If you don't have a big list and aren't sure where to start, I've got you covered.

If you're just starting out and aren't sure what to offer, I've got you covered.

So, what is this 5-5-5 Formula, you ask? Let's dive in!

The 5-5-5 Formula

It was –43 degrees Celsius outside. I was curled up in bed, wide awake at 2am. My eyes were closed, but my mind was racing.

"What should I do?" "How do I make this work?"

Another valuable lesson I learned from my mentors was to start with service.

So, as I lay there, I mentally cataloged how I could serve others. I had knowledge, I had skills, and I received an award at one of the world's largest marketing conferences and became a *Certified Funnel Builder*.

If I was going to build funnels for people, what else would they need? What challenges was I facing myself?

And then it hit me. I felt a surge of excitement, a clarity I hadn't

experienced before. I had to jump out of bed, grab a pen and paper, and jot down my ideas while they were fresh in my mind. It was like I had tapped into a new level of consciousness—the universe was finally speaking to me in a language I could understand.

This felt different from when I first started my business out of necessity to make an extra $1,000 a month. This was it. This was the idea that could change everything.

I'm thrilled to share this strategy with you because I know it will help you get unstuck.

The 5-5-5 Formula is a method for breaking down information into bite-sized chunks, giving your audience a tangible result by the end of the challenge.

What is the 5-5-5 Formula?

The first "5" stands for 5 minutes. If you're an introvert or just starting out, all you need to do is a 5-minute presentation. We can all manage 5 minutes, right? In my 5-5-5 Formula Course, I even break down what you should say in those 5 minutes, taking away the overwhelm.

The second "5" is for 5 days. You share 5 minutes of information each day for 5 days. Why 5 days? One thing I learned is that you need to lead with service. Spreading it over 5 days allows you to truly share and give real value to your audience. Sure, you could do it all in one day with a 25-minute session, but it's not as effective as connecting with your audience over multiple days. This approach helps build a stronger relationship.

The third "5" is for 5 people. As I mentioned earlier, 5 was my comfort zone—I could talk to 5 people at a time. If 5 still feels daunting for you, start with 2 or 3. The key is to start without overwhelming yourself.

And that's how the 5-5-5 Formula got its name.

5-5-5 Formula Market Research

I was so excited about this concept that I had to share it with my audience and test it out to ensure it wasn't just another great idea that would go unused. Staying true to the principle of service first, I asked 5 friends to join me and provide real feedback. I was humbled by the results—raving reviews and people asking, "What's next?"

But here's the thing—I had no idea what was next! I was just testing out the 5-5-5 Formula. Was I falling into the busy work trap again? I didn't have an offer ready for them, so I quickly said, "5-5-5 Formula Course."

The truth is, I had no idea what would go into this course. I didn't have a course! So, I started really listening to my audience, which is the next crucial step for you, too: market research. Ensure your idea is well-received and gather more information about what your audience truly wants.

Here are some key questions to consider:

- What are they asking for?
- What are their challenges?
- What do they need help with?

I built my course around what my audience wanted and needed. But here's a word of caution: Not all feedback needs to be actioned. You'll need to filter out the valuable insights from the noise.

And here's your next lesson: Don't build your course ahead of time. Build it as you go through your 5-5-5 Formula. Your course will be so much better because it will be based on what your audience is asking for, not just what you think they want.

5-5-5 *Formula Components*

I've refined my 5-5-5 Formula multiple times, and you should expect to do the same. Your first draft is just that—a starting point. It's not set in stone. You'll refine it as you gain more experience and insights.

I still remember the first time I ran my challenge. It was just 5 minutes with 5 people, but I was so nervous. Despite the anxiety, I pushed through and did it anyway. Had I not taken that leap, I wouldn't be here today, sharing this strategy with you.

So, no matter what doubts or fears you have, I encourage you to make the decision to start today. Here's why:

You're doing this with a small, manageable group in a controlled environment. Even if you're nervous, remember—it's only a small group. This is your chance to practice, improve, and get those initial nerves out of the way.

Think about Bill Gates—he didn't just present his idea once. He did it repeatedly, facing rejection until he reached success. You want to do the same. By starting with a small group, you'll begin to build your email list, generate revenue, and, most importantly, gain confidence.

And through it all, you'll be leading with service.

Now, let's dive into the 5 Days of the 5-5-5 Formula:

DAY 1 – INTRODUCTION
Begin by introducing your signature program and clearly stating the goals of the challenge. Make sure to emphasize the benefits for your

audience. Additionally, introduce yourself, especially for those who may be new to your community.

Learning Lesson: Keep the focus on your audience and their needs, not you.

DAY 2: SIMPLIFY AND BREAKDOWN

Break down your program into simple, digestible chunks that are easy for your audience to understand and implement. This step is crucial in ensuring that your message is clear and actionable.

Learning Lesson: A confused mind is less likely to take action.

DAY 3: GRADUAL LAYERING

Once you've simplified the process, guide your audience in building upon these foundational pieces gradually. This prevents overwhelm and encourages steady progress toward their goals.

Learning Lesson: Make the process so straightforward that your audience wonders why they hadn't started sooner.

DAY 4: THE NEXT THING

A common question for my challenge was: How do I attract participants to my 5-5-5 Formula? For you: Identify the next problem your audience might face. Integrate that solution into your challenge. This approach reduces barriers to taking action.

We go into more detail on how to attract participants in the challenge and course.

Learning Lesson: Believe in yourself and take consistent action, even if it's imperfect.

DAY 5: REVENUE

Ultimately, the goal of any business is to generate revenue. After serving your audience through the 5-5-5 Formula, seamlessly transition into inviting them to join your signature program. By this point, they've seen the value you can provide and are more likely to take the next step.

Learning Lesson: When you lead with service, selling becomes a natural extension of the value you've provided.

The Invitation

You've journeyed with me through the creation and evolution of the 5-5-5 Formula. Now, I want to invite you to take the next step. I would be honored to continue this journey with you in the 5-5-5 Formula Course, where we'll dive deeper into each step, ensuring you have everything you need to succeed.

In this course, you'll not only build your own 5-5-5 Formula, but you'll also receive comprehensive support, including workbooks, templates, and funnels to simplify your process. We'll explore advanced layering techniques, multiple traffic-generating strategies, and you'll have direct access to me during Q&A sessions.

Click the link below to accept the invitation:
https://www.funnellaunchers.com/555program

Your Voice Matters

As you embark on this journey, your experiences and insights are invaluable. If you feel inspired by what you've learned and are ready to share how it has impacted you, I would love to hear your story. Your feedback can inspire others who are just beginning their journey.

Please share your story here:
https://www.funnellaunchers.com/herunseenbattle

The Final Push

"The journey of a thousand miles begins with one step." – Lao Tzu
Don't let doubt hold you back from the life and business you envision. Take action, embrace the challenge, and let's make those transformations happen together.

FRANOVATION

Angelee Brown

CEO

Angelee is a founder, CEO, public speaker, and franchise expert with over 20 years of experience in hospitality, recruitment, and franchising. With experience in leadership roles for some of Canada's top companies, she balanced motherhood and corporate life throughout her thirties' until she began her own company, FranOvation, during the COVID-19 pandemic. Notably, she has achieved two company records for highest net revenue growth and has placed over 300 franchisees annually.

As a founder, Angelee is deeply committed to helping aspiring and existing franchise owners reach their goals. Residing in Niagara-on-the-Lake, ON, she is an avid foodie and a strong advocate for healthy living, blending her passions with her professional pursuits to inspire others.

https://www.linkedin.com/in/angeleebrown/
https://www.facebook.com/angeleebrown
https://www.instagram.com/angelee_brown/
https://franovation.com/
https://angeleebrown.com/

TURNING TRIALS INTO TRIUMPHS

Strategies for Overcoming Life's Toughest Challenges

By Angelee Brown

He's going to kill me.

This horrifying thought pounded relentlessly in my mind as my partner navigated the treacherous mountain roads, the snowstorm swirling around us like a shroud of chaos. With each dangerous turn, he seemed to grow more reckless. His anger pierced through the cacophony of the storm, and I could scarcely believe that this was the man I had trusted, the man I had uprooted my life for. The year was 2019 and the world had no idea what was in store - and neither did I.

I had packed up my life and moved across the country for this man— a fresh chapter with the man I thought I knew. But now, as we sped through the snow-clad mountains, I was enveloped in a profound sense of dread and isolation. I looked down at my phone, fumbling with the buttons and trying to inconspicuously share my location with my brother. It turned out my fiance was someone he wasn't, and I was emotionally drained, isolated and lied to over and over. I built up what strength I had left and packed my things in 12 hours (all 175 boxes) and in less than 7 months found myself back in my hometown, looking for a new home at the helm of the COVID-19 pandemic.

The irony was stark. On the outside, it seemed like I had it all together. At 41, I had achieved what many would consider success: a thriving career, a supportive family, and a life that others would envy. My professional life was flourishing; I was recognized as one of the best in my industry, a title I had earned through hard work and dedication. Yet, in the span of a few weeks, my self-esteem, once solid and unwavering, had crumbled. The confidence I had built over years of professional success had been shattered.

This episode was not just a single moment of crisis; it was the beginning of a series of profound personal challenges. As the global pandemic swept across the world, it seemed as though everything I had once known was unraveling. My career, which had been my sanctuary and source of pride, was now overshadowed by personal upheavals. Just when I thought I had reached my breaking point, my daughter was involved in a life-altering car accident, which turned my world upside down yet again.

The days that followed were nothing short of a living nightmare. I could no longer simply go out and get a job. The hours I had to dedicate to caring for my daughter, who was slowly recovering from her injuries, consumed every ounce of my energy. Nights were spent in a haze of worry and exhaustion, often feeling as though I was on the brink of breaking down, crumbling into a million pieces, and disappearing altogether. But there was no room for such a luxury. Bills needed to be paid, my family needed my unwavering support, and, most importantly, I needed to rediscover who I was amidst the turmoil and heartbreak.

This period of my life was marked by profound loneliness and struggle. I found myself grappling with my sense of self-worth, questioning every decision I had made and every path I had chosen. Rebuilding my life felt like an insurmountable challenge, compounded by the global crisis that seemed to exacerbate every personal difficulty. Yet, even in the darkest moments, the necessity of perseverance and the quest to regain my identity drove me forward. My journey through these trials, though fraught with pain, became a testament to the resilience of the human spirit and the unyielding strength required to overcome the most daunting of adversities.

Through these experiences, I learned invaluable lessons about resilience, self-compassion, and the importance of embracing one's own strength in the face of overwhelming challenges. In confronting my own darkest hours, I discovered a newfound sense of determination and clarity, which ultimately empowered me to rebuild my life on a foundation of authenticity and self-empowerment.

My Personal Struggles

By the age of 27, I had three young children, a husband and was running a new business as a young franchisee. My drive to succeed was fueled by a desire to prove naysayers wrong. My then-husband wanted me to stay at home and have more babies, and I was the youngest franchisee in the chain-something they reminded me of often. This internal motivation, born from a challenging childhood and demanding family life, pushed me to excel, but it also created a sense of urgency that sometimes felt like a double-edged sword. While having passion and purpose is essential, it's crucial to have a clear direction and a value system to stay grounded. This is something I've learned through experience and reflection.

Fast forward ten years,I had transformed into a force to be reckoned with. I was no longer the quiet, passive woman of my youth. Instead, I was confidently presenting in boardrooms, negotiating with some of Canada's wealthiest families, and managing a thriving franchise while juggling a busy household of teenagers. I felt invincible and at the peak of my career. Yet, in my relentless drive for success, I lost sight of my core values and the true purpose behind my ambitions.

Then came the radical shift. The COVID-19 pandemic served as the catalyst for a profound change, forcing me to reevaluate and transform my life entirely.

Navigating Professional Hurdles as a Woman in Business

From time to time, I receive messages on LinkedIn from curious professionals asking how I reached where I am today. Even now, as I build my company FranOvation, it feels like a bit of luck has guided my journey. But let me share the real story behind that luck.

By the time I was 40, I had already led franchising efforts for two of the world's major brands and supported the recruitment of nearly 800 franchisees. For many in my field, reaching that milestone in a lifetime is rare—imagine the number of interviews that entails! Throughout this period, I was fortunate to travel extensively across the country, experiencing new places and meeting incredible people. These opportunities were largely due to my role, but they also came with their own set of challenges.

One of the most impactful encounters was with a president who took a shine to the work I did to help promote Veterans to be hired into Corporate Canada. This led me to dive deeply into creating support programs for Veterans within Canadian businesses. While these experiences were rewarding, they didn't come without their difficulties.

Balancing professional and personal life was a constant struggle. Running a household like a well-oiled machine, I often found myself overwhelmed. At one point, I was so immersed in work that I couldn't even recall the names of some of their teachers. The lines between work and home blurred, and while my career achievements were gratifying, the reminders of not being a perfect mother were hard to ignore. We often end up being our harshest critics.

Additionally, pursuing a career came with its own set of criticisms. I faced questions like, "Why couldn't I just find a nice man to support me and settle down?" In an industry where only 3% of women hold leadership positions, I carried that distinction with both pride and a sense of duty. Being a trailblazer and a role model wasn't something I had planned; it happened because of my gender and determination. Navigating this role, especially as I gained more visibility, was challenging. It often felt like I was living out America Ferrera's lament from the Barbie movie: *"It is literally impossible to be a woman. You are so beautiful and so smart, and it kills me that you don't think you're good enough. Like, we have to always be extraordinary, but somehow, we're always doing it wrong."*

Looking back, I struggled to see and appreciate what I had accomplished. This internal struggle created a void that was hard to fill. However, once I left my corporate career to focus on my soul's purpose, everything began to align in a way I had never imagined. It felt like magic—new opportunities and lessons emerged, bringing hope and allowing me to embrace my true self.

This journey of rediscovering and aligning with my purpose has been transformative, opening doors to possibilities that were once only dreams.

Conquering the Battles: Turning Adversity into Triumph

One thing I have learned in my 47 years of life on this planet is that you really need to get truthful with yourself and get right with yourself. I wrote about values alignment earlier, and this is something that fueled my personal growth in my forties. It is never too late to find yourself and your purpose. Instead of chasing the ball, I put all of the balls in the air and really assessed myself, who I was, and what I wanted. This was the most frightening exercise to do as slowing down seemed counterintuitive to my nature, and also, during the financial pressures of COVID, there were many moments I thought if I just threw in the towel and got a job, life could be easier.

And so there I was, in lockdown, with my 19-year-old daughter at home with a head injury, and the world asleep at our doorstep. I began writing out a plan, one that would fill a gap in the industry and help those in need. I decided to create a business that focussed on supporting restaurants during the pandemic, and also successfully recruited franchisees for a handful of clients. During this time, business slowly got busier, and while I had to balance work and family more effectively than ever, I knew I wasn't willing to sacrifice my daughter's health or my happiness for the sake of a dollar.

I poured myself into work once again, with a newfound sense of pride and motivation for not only myself but also my family. Little did I know this would lead me to find my true love and my husband-to-be, Jeff, but that is a story for another time.

Key Strategies and Actions

1. Learn to Say No

One of the most crucial strategies for managing personal and professional growth is mastering the art of saying no. This might seem simple, but it is often one of the hardest skills to develop, especially for those who are driven and eager to please. Learning to say no is about recognizing your limits and understanding that your time and energy are finite resources.

Why Saying No Matters:

- Prevents Overcommitment: By setting boundaries and declining additional responsibilities that do not align with your goals, you protect yourself from becoming overwhelmed and overextended.

- Preserves Quality: When you take on too many tasks or obligations, the quality of your work can suffer. Saying no helps you maintain a high standard of work by focusing on what truly matters.

- Promotes Focus: Declining non-essential requests allows you to concentrate on your primary objectives and personal priorities, leading to greater effectiveness and fulfillment.

How to Implement This Strategy:

- Assess Your Priorities: Regularly review your goals and commitments to ensure they align with your long-term objectives. Prioritize activities that advance your key goals and let go of those that do not.

- Communicate Clearly: When you need to say no, do so with clarity and respect. You can explain that your current commitments prevent you from taking on additional tasks, or express that it's not the right time for new responsibilities.

- Practice Assertiveness: Be confident in your decisions. Remember that saying no is a way of respecting your own limits and ensuring that you can perform well in areas that are truly important to you.

2. Monitor Setbacks

Monitoring setbacks is an essential strategy for personal and professional development. Setbacks are inevitable, but how you respond to them can determine your long-term success. Keeping track of these challenges helps you learn from them and refine your approach.

Why Monitoring Setbacks Matters:

- Identifies Patterns: By tracking setbacks, you can identify recurring issues or patterns that may be hindering your progress. Understanding these patterns allows you to address the root causes more effectively.

- Encourages Growth: Setbacks often provide valuable learning opportunities. Monitoring them helps you analyze what went wrong, why, and how to avoid similar issues in the future.

- Boosts Resilience: Regularly reviewing setbacks and your responses to them helps build resilience. It reinforces the idea that challenges are part of the journey and encourages a proactive mindset.

How to Implement This Strategy:

- Document Setbacks: Keep a detailed record of setbacks, including the context, your response, and the outcome. This can be done through journaling, spreadsheets, or project management tools.

- Analyze and Reflect: Periodically review your records to identify trends or common factors contributing to setbacks. Reflect on what adjustments or changes can be made to improve your approach.

- Develop Action Plans: Based on your analysis, create actionable plans to address identified issues. This might involve adjusting strategies, seeking additional resources, or changing your workflow.

By learning to say no and monitoring setbacks, you create a more manageable and focused path to achieving your goals. These strategies help maintain your well-being, enhance your productivity, and increase your resilience, ultimately leading to greater success and fulfillment.

Lessons Learned

Early on, I was falling back into my people-pleasing ways. Client calls would go on far too long, and my desire to give had me taking late-night calls from people—sometimes into 9 or 10 pm at night. This became a challenge as I slipped a little and had no one there but myself to catch those behaviors and get back on track. During that time, I would cycle into a repeated thought pattern of not being good enough that I had to pull myself out of it. Because when you are at the top of your game as a female, I personally felt like if I showed any sign of weakness or lack of attention to someone or something, it would lead to my failure.

Personal Growth Unlocked

During times of radical change, it can feel like your spirit is under siege as the pace of life accelerates beyond your wildest expectations. The whirlwind of new developments and rapid shifts can overwhelm your sense of stability, making it hard to catch your breath. If you haven't planned for this level of upheaval, it's easy to feel blindsided and out of control. Reflecting on my own journey, I remember how, in the early days of my career, I was often taken aback by the success that followed my efforts. Each new client or award seemed to surprise me, despite having meticulously planned every step. This reaction, I later learned, was a classic case of imposter syndrome—a disconnect between the hard work invested and the recognition received. How could I genuinely be shocked by the fruits of my labor if I had strategically mapped out the path to success? The disparity between my efforts and my astonished reaction to the results was a clear sign that I was sabotaging my own achievements by retreating into my comfort zone instead of embracing my success.

Identifying and confronting these sabotaging behaviors became a crucial part of my personal growth. Journaling emerged as a vital tool in this process. It allowed me to reflect deeply on my daily choices and behaviors, helping me to answer critical questions: Was I effectively utilizing my time and resources? Was I being authentic in my actions and decisions? How was my approach to the market evolving, and was it improving? Was I holding myself and my team accountable for our shared goals? These reflections were instrumental in redefining my understanding of success and self-worth. The real challenge lay in recognizing that success wasn't just about external validation but also about aligning with my core values and being true to myself. By confronting these internal conflicts and addressing the underlying insecurities that fueled my self-sabotage, I began to appreciate my achievements more fully. The process of self-discovery and accountability not only empowered me to embrace my successes but also to sustain them, ultimately transforming my approach to both personal and professional growth.

Empowering Affirmations for Overcoming Challenges

Having a few (or many) affirmations to guide your confidence and boost self-esteem can help you get to where you want to go. When I first began affirmations, they were daunting as I giggled at the use of "I AM" statements stated to no one but me. But soon, they became a habit in my daily routine, in my head, as I was brushing my teeth. Positive self-talk and also laughing at my mistakes lightened my approach to life and helped me overcome my emotions at the moment.

Sample Affirmations:

Affirmation 1: *"I am strong, capable, and resilient in the face of adversity."*

Affirmation 2: *"Every challenge I overcome makes me more powerful and focused."*

Affirmation 3: *"I have the power to shape my destiny and achieve my dreams."*

Actionable Steps to Implement in Daily Life

Having a plan is key. You need to sit down, really imagine what you want, write out exactly what you need to do to the letter, and also define your purpose and your why before you set out to accomplish this.

Also, if you need to, don't be afraid to get professional help. With support from a close friend, I took the widely popular course Positive Intelligence, which taught me to reflect and label my emotions and navigate myself better. I also received amazing support from a meditation and mindfulness coach. With patience and guidance, I learned how to literally breathe again and also focus on my mental health better. I also always ate healthy, but as I had gained weight over COVID due to being isolated and depressed, I ensured I ate healthier and really ramped up eating clean. This helped alter my mood incredibly.

Looking back, the road from adversity to success is neither straightforward nor simple. The challenges I've faced—whether personal or professional—have been both harsh teachers and powerful motivators. They've sculpted a more resilient and self-aware version of myself. Confronting vulnerability, facing my fears head-on, and aligning with my deepest values have guided me through the storm, leading me to a place of clarity and renewed purpose. This chapter's contribution underscores an important truth:

Triumph is not about sidestepping difficulties but about tackling them with determination and grace. Remember that every setback holds the potential for growth, and every challenge can be a stepping stone toward future success. Your own journey can transform today's struggles into tomorrow's victories, provided you stay true to yourself and embrace your own strength and resilience.

CRUSE'S CAREER COUNSELING

Lora Cruse

Coach

My name is Lora Cruse and I am momma to 3 beautiful children and 6 precious grandbabies. I have been through a lot but have persevered past my issues to successfully run a career development coaching business. I have been through college, earned a prestigious degree in business, and managed to raise a beautiful family all in all. My demons have been substantially shut down and my choices are no longer regrets. They are the things in life that have made me a strong woman. I have a special place in my heart for women who suffer in domestic violence situations and plan on extending my coaching out to that genre as well as romantic relationship coaching. I am very happy in my skin.

https://www.linkedin.com/in/loracrusereachbeyond/
https://www.facebook.com/cruseoninn

FROM CHAINS TO CHANGE

A Journey of Survival, Strength, and Empowerment

By Lora Cruse

Pulling away was like pulling teeth. He would not let me go, and he would not let me be me. I was stuck, and I felt no one in the world could save me. What would I do? Would my life ever be mine again?

Let me stop you right there and explain a few things. My name is Lora Cruse, by marriage, Lora Snyder, by birth. I was the absolute smartest, brightest, most mentally stable person in my immediate family. I had a bright future ahead of me, I was going places. After being accepted into a prestigious high school in Chicago, IL, I excelled, but during my sophomore year, something happened. Life became real, and I became an adult, fast. My schizophrenic father took his own life that tragic year. He was a long-time sufferer of alcoholism and was guilt-ridden when my brother—who he had abused—became stricken with AIDS due to long-time heroin use. My mama, who was my rock during my later years, became a raging alcoholic who could not shelter me. I was only 16, and even though I looked after myself, I needed a guardian. So, it was off to Owensboro, KY, to live with my other brother. My other brother, an alcoholic himself, was awesome and kind and gentle, but I needed home. I stayed with him through his battle, and he finally got sober the year before I left. I was absolutely proud of him. He did his best to support me and do the necessary things fathers do for their teenage daughters. I definitely felt loved. I was a high school dropout—was I even going to succeed now? Well, I believe I would have earlier until I encountered one fateful blind date that occurred two weeks after I turned 18. My best friend, Susan, started dating this guy. She was head over heels for him, but all of her dates with him consisted of them and a third wheel—his brother. She begged me for months to please go out with this man, who was eleven years my senior. I always turned her down, saying, "No way! He's too old!"

Being the good friend that I am, I told her yes, finally. I also told her that I would pay my own way and that there was to be no funny business. When I met Roger, I had to laugh. Here was this good-looking guy wearing a Michigan sweater and…-fishing boots! Yep! A real redneck, country boy, plain and simple. He had my attention, though. I thought he looked young for his age and that he was cute and built great! Fair enough, yes, I had fun. Was I ready for what life had in store for me? No way!

As I go through the motions of life, depressed and unable to laugh, I continue to be a good wife and mother. Yes, I bore his three children. They were my only saviors at this moment in time, my everything, my antidepressants! Is that bad? I couldn't help it, I was miserable. Bruises kept me away from my family—he got me away from my family!

"Bruises! Where'd you get those bruises?" my cousin Brenda asked me a few months after Roger and I became involved.

"Nowhere. I fell," I'd tell her. I was keeping a dark secret to myself, knowing he was already in control, and I didn't know what to do. I was living a horrible life, trying desperately, to break free. He threatened to kill me or himself if I ever left. He was a person capable of these actions, in case you're wondering. One day, I came home from work, pregnant with our firstborn and not knowing it, and he made me undress. I thought this was ludicrous, but I was scared, so I obliged. He thoroughly investigated me for the scent of another man or any clue to me being in an affair.

Another day, dinner to make, children to bathe, and the devil to please. I cringed when he touched me, loathed his scent, and only tolerated his existence. He became violent with it, and me, as if I were his property. He just took it! Every day, I became stronger, though, it would be years before I was free from this psychotic, cult-like marriage. I grew strength from it. Is it sad to say that it made me who I am today? You know what? It is true. This is me wondering if I owe him some kind of gratitude for being a torturing, control freak who was jealous of every single move or action I made. With really no reason at all. Someday, that's what I kept in mind, I would be happy. I would break free of the chains that held me back from being a productive member of society. And so it was, day after day, the same thing. Finally, he made a mistake and allowed me to continue my education. I obtained my G.E.D. shortly before my eldest daughter was born. I was so proud, but he made me feel less than, of course. Nonetheless, I was ecstatic this could be my ticket out. I would earn a degree and pull away financially, and the rest would follow. I forgot one thing, though. He was the devil. Every time, I came close to obtaining a degree, he did something to stop it or embarrass me so much I couldn't face going back.

I lay in my 3 children's bed, as I had an unhinged feeling that something was off that night. My eldest was aged 5, and my youngest was aged 2. I held them tight and opened my eyes to their father, who I had separated from two days prior, caressing a gun. I didn't know what to do. I pleaded with Roger to please think about what he was doing. He was on a methamphetamine binge; he began doing hard drugs shortly after we wed. I was 19 and had my firstborn. I was too naïve to know what he was into and thought he was just smoking pot, which I hated, and got mad when he would do it. Anyway, my 2-year-old son jumped in my arms automatically, crying his eyes out. My 2 girls lay sleeping, unmoved by the commotion. I ran out to the living room with my son in my hands, and Roger took the gun, pointed at my son's head, and said, "We're all gonna die tonight, wh**e!" I saw the door open, but what was I to do? I could run for help, but then my girls lay in the house with him. I didn't even think, I just ran out the door, just knowing and hoping, he would follow. I got safely to my neighbor's, and she helped me get all the kids and get right to her house. At this point, Roger disappeared, but as soon as he saw all of us run into the house, he came out with the gun to my neighbor's head and forced us all into her house under hostage conditions. To my despair, she had no phone. I was at a loss and thought it was the end of my story

I thrived in school, making straight A's, keeping a 4.0 GPA, making the Dean's and President's list, and being inducted into the high honors Phi Theta Kappa society. I changed majors every time I went back, that is, every time I crawled back from the despair of being pulled away from school by abuse and control. First, it was paralegal. Then, business, and then, nursing. When I got into nursing school, I was one of 15 students, out of the 300 students that applied, to get into the nursing program. When I got into nursing school, I worked hard to get there, and Roger let it happen. As I went through it, I separated from him, got our apartment by myself for my kids and me, and had everything going smoothly. My kids were on a schedule. they were doing great. They were thriving, too.

"Mama! Mama!" I called her on the phone and told her there was something wrong with me. I let her know I could not get out of bed to get my kids ready for school. I tell her something is very wrong. Nobody would believe me, nobody would help. I was a single mom of three children, two of which were in diapers. I had a full-time waitressing job, and I was a full-time nursing student! How could anyone not see that this was new, and it was bad? I had a few seizures, headaches and migraines were daily. My eyes blurred and always tired. I had to have help and who do I call? That's right—the psychotic abuser I have come to know as the devil. Once he was there, he wasn't going anywhere. Lo and behold, as soon as he comes back, my momma sacrifices her whole life to take care of us. I love her for that. I loved her until she took her last breath in August 2022. I love her still and consider her my rock, but it was, while heroic, a little late. Roger never did anything to help anyway. He was simply a controlling, abusive man who cursed my children whenever I allowed him to watch them. My momma became the hero, and she really saved my life as the doctors found a rare birth defect, called Arnold Chiari Malformation, on my brain. It does not surface until the 3rd trimester of life and can be induced by blows, or a blow to the head, which is why my momma always blamed him. It was a herniation of the brain over the spine. I had to have emergency surgery, and that is when my mental illnesses surfaced. I am bipolar and have ADHD. I also have PTSD and major depressive disorder, all handled by medications. I am fully functional, with very few attacks, and have been for about 8 years now. I guess one can figure out it was in 2016, eight years ago, when Roger went to prison, and I became permanently free. His sentencing was my shackles coming off. I knew, once he faced prison, he'd never tried to bother me again, and I was right. Three years was in there for a crime he may or may not have committed. So be it—he deserved it for the abuse, my children and I succumbed to for nearly two decades.

Freedom suited me and suited my parenting as well. He was not there to undermine me or make me out to be the bad guy, although his brainwashing took a toll on my two daughters. They hated me and my whole existence. They cried the day he went to prison and were cold to me for a couple of years that seemed like an eternity. My son missed his father, but he never once acted as if I were the enemy until he got older. The girls became understanding and saw how life was. They saw what he had done to me, and they have nothing but respect for me at this point in time. My son, well, I made a few mistakes with and he could not understand. We've gotten past that, and he is a rock for me now.

So what does all of this have to do with the empowerment of women? You see, I prevailed and became a two-time business owner. I guess what I'm saying is, that no matter how long it takes or what may hold us back, women can overcome any obstacle if they simply never falter in their destination for their hopes and dreams. For a better future. We should not let anything stand in the way of what is out there for us. Around the corner is a new horizon—a new day, a new chapter. The past should be left there, and only the present gathered up in our arms and the future at our sides.

I told you about owning two businesses, but I am also in pursuit of another business. The two businesses I owned were both housekeeping businesses. T & L Cleaning and Sister Clean were very lucrative businesses that took off like a skyrocket. Sister Clean thrives today as I pursue a much bigger, riskier dream. I want to own a hotel chain named after us—my husband gave me hell, the most he could do is let me keep his last name so that I can build "The Cruse-On Inn". It will be an entertainment-based hotel chain.

I strive for a business, unlike others. With that in mind, I introduce the idea of a new concept, the Cruse-On Inn, a hotel/entertainment showroom. Here, we have a hotel that will include numerous entertainment factors. One of these is a live recording studio—friends and family can have fun and record their own CDs. You will have the option to buy one after you've recorded. There will also be an option to have your recording session displayed in the area of the recording station so other guests can listen.

Another entertaining factor will be a type of Glamour Shots makeover area. Choose one of our costumes or your own, get a full makeover, and have your photos professionally taken. You will get one free 5 x 7, and you can buy more shots and photos.

Fathers and sons take a pit stop while your female family members are getting dolled up. Introducing our virtual NASCAR racers. Take a ride in one of your favorite famous duplicate NASCAR racers' simulated race cars. It will be just like you're in a real race.

Did someone ask for a weekend Talent contest? Win different prizes and join tournaments to win bigger prizes. On downtime from talent shows, we will offer karaoke for some added entertainment.

Done showing off? Bring the family in for some exciting laser tag. Go-karts and indoor roller coasters will test your courage. What hotel would be without a mini water park? Water slides, zip lines, kiddie park, and more. Win prizes in obstacle courses, one for adults and one for the kiddos. Also, for the young ones, the slippery slimy Mountain. Get through this obstacle course without getting randomly slimed and win prizes. But watch out, slime bombs are ticking.

All wet and need a refresher? Step into our luxurious spa and salon. We'll have licensed cosmetologist and esthetician. Awesome massage and facial treatments, along with the refreshing Botox area. We will implement a type of Cool Sculpting as a weight-loss treatment with instant results.

Want to shop the best shops in town? Come to our attached mini-mall.

Hungry? A couple of food courts will be included.

Tai Bo, Zumba, Yoga, and more and more to be announced. Also, a personal training session.

Don't forget our indoor and outdoor heated Pools and Hot Tubs/Jacuzzis.

Select rooms will also include Jacuzzis. Bring the kids to our 3D theater. Watch a real chef prepare your meals in our restaurant. And last but certainly not least, the scary, haunted floor. All rooms and hallways promise to give you a mighty fine scare. Do you dare to sleep in a haunted room?

My business idea is still a work in progress, and it's in the idea Stage. I'm looking for investors, partners, and financial sponsors. This will be a trendsetter. I plan on making this nationwide.

With that, I will end with a quote that will forever be worthy of hopes and dreams out there… "I raise my voice—not so that I can shout, but so that those without a voice can be heard… We cannot succeed when half of us are held back."—Malala Yousafzai.

KNIGHT SCHOOL INC
Jaclyn Ziemniak
Co-Owner & Co-President

Jaclyn Ziemniak is one of the worlds' only female full-contact jousters and is co-owner of Knight School Inc.

Knight School Inc. has taken history's most exclusive sport, being a knight in shining armour, and reimagined it as an inclusive, accessible and welcoming suite of recreational programs. Partners, Jaclyn and Joshua, took very different paths on their journey to becoming international athletes in the sport of full contact jousting. Together they have collaborated to create the first community based Medieval Combat empowerment organization, focusing on opening previously locked doors in sport and connecting classically underserved demographics of the community with the ability to pursue their dreams.

Jaclyn lives in Toronto, Canada, with her husband and numerous rescue animals. She strongly believes in the importance of representation: You can't be what you can't see! Jaclyn has made it her mission to give all her students the opportunity to see themselves as knights.

https://www.linkedin.com/in/jaclyn-ziemniak/
https://www.facebook.com/knightschoolinccanada
https://instagram.com/knightschoolinc
https://www.knightschoolinc.com/

CHARGE ON

One Woman's Journey to Knighthood

Dedicated to the war horses that shaped my journey as a jouster:
Paladin, Superman & Maximus

By Jaclyn Ziemniak

"What was I thinking?"

I kept repeating this question to myself as I waited in the list, mentally preparing to charge down the track on a two-thousand-pound warhorse, carrying an eleven-foot-long stick and wearing a suit of armour that weighs more than I do. The narrow eye slits in my helm offer but small glimpses of my opponent – an armour-clad giant whose massive size promises a wicked hit. *This is going to hurt.* To him, I am nothing but a bull's-eye in target practice. Who am I kidding? This man could kill me if he wanted to. *Focus, Jaclyn. You can do this.* I take a long, slow breath and reach for my lance. The piercing clash of steel resonates with every move I make. My squire yells and waves his arms in a futile attempt to communicate. *You are a knight. You can do this.* My heart pounds as the horses charge forward. I can hear my blood pumping in my ears. The sound of my own breathing echoes in my helmet. I press my weight into my stirrups to balance my seat against the forward jolt of my mighty steed. *Steady your lance.* Cold, hard steel presses sharply into my bicep. *Count your strides.* I swallow hard and take my aim. *Prove them wrong.* Only a few moments separate us from the collision. Sweat drips down my forehead, stinging my eyes. *Why am I doing this to myself? What was I thinking?*

And then it hits me.

Whenever I tell people that I compete in full contact jousting, their reaction is usually the same – a dazed and confused expression spreads across their faces as they look me up and down. Please understand that I am not exactly your "typical" knight – if such a thing even exists in the modern world. Excluding Sir Elton John and Sir Anthony Hopkins, most of today's active knights competing in full contact Realgestech jousting are tall, broad, male, and appear to have just stepped out of a renaissance fair re-enactment. Looking at me, one would most likely assume I play the damsel in distress, not the big brave knight coming to the rescue.

Questions immediately follow, and most people are still sceptical of my skills and a little unsure of exactly what jousting entails, leading them to ask the insightful question, "You mean you hit people with a big stick?" It is a rather simplified version of the sport, but yes, I suppose I do just hit people with a big stick. While they try to hit me. The confusion usually morphs into intrigue as they ask a slew of related questions: have you ever been knocked off your horse, is the equipment heavy and, of course, does it hurt? Well, for everyone out there wondering the same things – yes, I have been knocked off; yes, the equipment is heavy; and yes, it hurts. A lot.

I am often asked how on earth I ended up in one of the most violent, vicious and unforgiving sports in the world. The process of becoming a knight in modern-day Canada is as difficult and fraught with danger as you would assume, remaining the world's most exclusive club since the Middle Ages. True "knights" are difficult to find these days as there is not exactly a surplus of people willing to let you hit them in the chest while they balance precariously atop a charging animal. The truth is, my journey to knighthood was certainly not a linear one.

In fact, I stumbled upon the doorway.

I have owned horses most of my life, and my tale as a knight begins at 13, dressing up for Halloween as a knight in shining armour with my noble steed. After this, there was not much else left in the world for a young woman with dreams of grandeur and nobility, or so I thought. I have to say, though, I still think we looked quite chivalrous and regal that Halloween, despite what my little chestnut pony Frodo might tell you to the contrary. Little did I know what the future had in store for the dreams of that little girl.

I went on to purchase my first horse Java while still in university and rescued a second horse, Target, shortly thereafter. As a result, I struggled for many years, working several part-time jobs to afford their care. Turns out, horses are expensive, and "rescue" does not mean "free." I often wondered how much easier things would be financially without the extra expenses, but all it took was a soft knicker or the faint smell of leftover sweet feed to remind me that I had something much more valuable than free time or extra money in the bank. (I had neither.)

The bond I had with my horses made everything worthwhile. So, when I moved barns and was asked to pay for liability insurance I cringed at the thought of another expense, but wrote the cheque anyway. I never could have imagined something as boring as liability insurance would lead me to this amazing experience. If I had any idea how life-changing the simple task of getting the mail would be that cool April morning, I probably would have taken more time to carefully account the sights and the smells, but to me, it was just another trip to the mailbox. As I flipped through the bills, trying not to imagine the gruesome sentence that lay within, I saw that my insurance card had come in, along with a directory of local equine businesses. Skimming the pages on the way up the driveway, I stopped dead in my tracks when I saw it: FULL CONTACT JOUSTING – CALL FOR

EDUCATION, SHOWS & TRAINING.

Am I reading this properly? My heart raced as I looked it over and over – TRAINING. There it was in simple 12-point Times New Roman font. Training.

We all have silly childhood dreams. My brother wanted to grow up to be an airplane. My best friend from kindergarten wanted to be a giraffe. It is a sombre moment of our lives when we truly realize the impossibility of those dreams, but unless the hormones of puberty somehow manage to produce wings and an engine along with pimples and chest hair, growing up to be an airplane will simply remain an unattainable goal. I realized that quite quickly in my youth and had, to be completely honest, simply forgotten about my dream of becoming a knight. A silly childhood fantasy, put to the side with teddy bears and training wheels, and yet in two small lines of text, all that had changed. I once again imagined myself as a knight floating gracefully atop an elegant noble steed as I dialed the number.

A gruff voice answered me on the other end. I excitedly explained who I was and that I saw the call for training. Silence on the other end.

"So? When can I start?"

He asked me my height and weight, then paused for a few seconds to consider everything. And then, he laughed at me.

Undeterred, I spent another 20 minutes on the phone convincing him why I was worth his effort for training; eventually, I persevered and soon after, my training began.

Knighthood is traditionally and historically an all-male, patriarchal, testosterone-fueled space. The modern sport of full-contact jousting reflects that ethos. One of my former coaches is quoted as saying,

"What makes you a good jouster? Two words, pain tolerance." That statement summarizes how I was treated in the sport and how I was trained. Along with pain tolerance, toughness and brutality were upheld as being the penultimate values in the sport. Along the way, additional barriers were erected in an attempt to force me to quit. This was never an option.

The training to become a full-contact jouster is exactly as challenging as it sounds. I would return from training camp looking as if I had been in a car accident, covered head to toe in bruises and welts from ill-fitting armour, hoisting heavy lances, and countless incidents of being knocked off a massive horse while cantering at combined speeds of up to 60km/hr. As trainees, we all wore these bruises as badges of honour. "Bruises prove you've been there," we would say, after teasing someone for adding padding underneath their breastplate.

Looking back on it now, one of the reasons I never fully realized at the time the true extent of toxicity and gatekeeping within the sport, was because, quite frankly, it was hard for all of us. Jousting is extremely hard. The claustrophobia of being locked into a stainless steel suit with no way to take off your helmet on your own. The intense mental contest of charging full force at another person, knowing that there is no defence. They will hit you, and the harder you hit them, the greater the impact upon yourself. Never mind the fortitude it took to pick yourself up off the ground after being unhorsed just to climb back atop your steed and do it all over again.

Throughout my year of training, I saw numerous other students, mostly men, come and go, never making it past the initial phase of carrying a lance and shield. It was because of this tenacity that the troupe made me feel included as "one of the boys" anytime we hung out after practice, went out for dinner, or watched movies in the loft above the barn. But when we got back to the arena, the seemingly harmless comments would pop up: you hit like a girl, you have weak little girl arms, etc. I don't believe that any of them truly or consciously didn't want me there. Rather, it was the systemic and unconscious bias that existed in any male-dominated sport that erected unseen and yet fully realized barriers for me. It was the emotional challenge of a sport that was not fully ready to accept women as legitimate competitors that became more and more clear as I got stronger and more confident in the sport.

When we put ourselves in scenarios that are known to be challenging, we often discount whether these challenges are necessary. In jousting, there are a lot of barriers for everyone. It is not an easy sport. No one explicitly came out and said, "You are a woman, you don't belong here." In fact, the group really made me feel like part of the group. However, I never forgot I was the only woman in the troupe. Microaggressions systemic to male-dominated sports began to surface. Much of this, I believe, was unconscious, as I don't think my colleagues fully understood the mindset they were perpetuating. Nevertheless, even when I was winning, the "you hit like a girl" joke came out at every single tournament. Every single time. One technique marginalized groups can use when faced with adversity is reclamation. And so, I reclaimed that term. At tournaments, I would ride over to the crowd and let them know that I was about to "show everyone what it truly means to *hit like a girl*!"

My experience is common when it comes to systemic and deeply ingrained biases and discriminations. It is not a big, obvious and tangible indiscretion that we can necessarily point to. It is rather this internalized misrepresentation of long-held prejudices that comes out through language and emotional barriers.

One defining moment for me came at a two-day tournament in Virginia. There were several men, including my coach, the head of the jousting troupe, and myself competing over the course of the weekend in a six-person tournament. Each day, all six of us would compete in a full tournament, with rankings decided during single elimination full-contact jousting matches. By the evening of the second day, I had taken the top place, with only one match left to go for the championship win. It was me versus my coach, a widely known international full-contact jousting champion. I took my horse Maximus into the tilt and waited patiently at one end for the squires to prepare the arena and hand me my lance. Maximus was strong, agile and wicked fast, which, if I kept my cool and rode him well, would allow me to harness his energy and deliver a hard-hitting match. The counter was that his speed also made it a significant challenge to remain balanced and upright after being hit myself. I gently stroked his neck and gave him soft reassurance before we began.

With my helmet locked closed, and the sun quickly setting, all I could see was vague shapes through the red clay dust of the summer dusk. The lance felt heavy in my hand, with a weekend of endless matches finally taking its toll on my aching biceps. Whenever I was in the list, I tried my best to make a conscious effort to close off the outside world and simply be present with my horse, my lance and my target. This time was no different. No matter who was inside the shiny metal suit at the other end, it was simply another target. Maximus danced underneath me as the match began. Hundreds of people cheered and waved from the audience, but I heard none of it. I simply raised my lance in salute of the match and began my run.

Four passes later, much to my surprise, we were tied. Only a single tie-breaker pass remained. The stadium lights in the arena only served to reflect glare from the clay and dust as the sun was long set, making it nearly impossible to see anything from the quarter-inch ocularium of my helm's visor. One pass left. The squires were exhausted. The horses were getting antsy. One pass, and the tournament would be complete. Then we could begin the equally exhausting task of tearing down the joust list and packing for the next adventure. I took my lance, came around the corner, saluted, and with the remainder of my strength, took aim.

"Broken lance, 5 points, and the WIN!" Someone yelled from the field. Still locked in my heavy helmet, I turned Maximus around to see two female squires shouting as they ran up to me.

"You won! You won!"

I am not sure I believed them. I never felt like I could possibly be good enough to win a tournament. And yet I had. And there were hundreds of people cheering and lining up to meet me and get my autograph. I was buzzing. It was a sensational experience. I distinctly remember a little girl in the audience, maybe 7 years old, coming up to me while I stood with my horse, sweat and dirt smeared across my forehead, and muscles trembling from exhaustion.

"You're my hero," she said.

It is moments like this that hit you hard in the chest. Who was I to be deserving of being called someone's hero? And yet, at the same time, why had I not been able to recognize all that I had achieved to get to that point? It was in those moments when I began to really appreciate the responsibility that came with my achievements. It was not just me in that armour, on that horse. It was a whole new generation of girls and women that could see themselves in me. In my professional career in athletic management, we often talked about the phrase "you can't be what you can't see." In that moment, I realized that is exactly what my presence in the sport of jousting represented – the breaking down of an unseen barrier.

The realization began to dawn on me, hundreds of girls and women could now *be* something they never saw themselves as before. Regardless of whether they would joust or not, it is the ability to change perspectives and actively pursue representation that becomes important, especially across traditionally closed demographic industries. I was fighting for more than just my own spot in the sport of full-contact jousting, I was fighting for others' access to their dreams as well.

A few days later, when I was back home nursing my well-earned war wounds, I saw a social media post from one of our squires. It had a photo of the knights from the tournament and the caption: "Congrats to all the knights – and the one badass woman who beat them all."

It was in that post that I could so clearly see the impact that my presence in the sport was having. And as the comments started to come in, that impact became even clearer.

"He let you win."

"If he was trying, there's no way you could have beaten him."

The comments kept coming. Regardless of whether people were actually present at the tournament or not, everyone seemed to have an opinion about this match, despite the fact that it seemingly had nothing to do with them. The previous microaggressions made in jokes and teasing comments now became actual aggressive indictments of my skill and performance. The previously unseen barriers were now much more clearly defined. I was allowed to participate, but in no way was I allowed to win, as that challenged the preconceived assumptions and prejudicial biases of how women and men were supposed to interact in direct competition during exhibitions of physical force.

It was at that point I realized that I wasn't really on the team. I was playing by myself. I was there as a novelty. My acceptance was conditional, conditional upon my compliance in fitting into the mold that was determined for me to exist within. I was supposed to exist as a comic foil, not as a legitimate competitor capable of besting the captain. There was an invisible line of competency that I was not supposed to cross. There was a brotherhood of arms that this sister could not join. And like countless other unseen people standing behind closed doors and under glass ceilings, I simply learned how to best exist within this mold.

A few years later, I was in Michigan for another tournament. I had taken time off work, packed up my protégé and her brother, and made the trip south to a small town for their summer fair, featuring a full-contact joust. When I arrived, I pulled the massive heavy armour trunk out of my car and set up at the encampment with the other knights, only to discover that I had been cut from the tournament and put into a judging and marshalling position instead. It was a familiar frustration for me at this point. So, I resigned myself to caring for the horses and setting up equipment instead.

While I was off setting up, Joshua, a jouster I had never met before, arrived. He commanded a certain level of attention as he wandered through the encampment, built like a 6'4'', long-haired, red-bearded Viking in a tie-dye t-shirt.

"Why does this armour crate say Jaclyn?" He inquired of my protégé. "Are you telling me there is a woman who does full-contact jousting?"

Prepared for the typical dismissive smirks and comments, my trainee nodded. She was a quietly tenacious left-handed teenage girl with big aspirations of one day doing full-contact jousting herself.

"I need to meet her!"

Speaking with Joshua was one of the first times I truly felt seen in this sport – not as the token girl, but as a legitimate competitor, as someone who's been through the same physical and emotional challenges and overcame, succeeded and flourished. It was in trading stories of our journeys in the sport of full-contact jousting that I truly realized the barriers that had been presented to me.

It was through that realization and alignment of personal values that Joshua and I found each other, both as partners in life, as well as in business. We came together and vowed to make the world and history's most exclusive sport – being a knight – as accessible and inclusive as possible. This is how Knight School Inc was born.

Knight School Inc is a sports-based empowerment organization that specializes in Medieval Arts and Safety Management. We offer first-aid and CPR certification, stage combat sword fight programs for all ages and abilities and mounted medieval games clinics for horses and riders. Within each of these areas, we strive to break down barriers and make the programs as unintimidating, open and welcoming as possible. We do this through a mindful focus on several key areas.

The first area we explored was language, both in how common terms in the industry were inadvertently creating unnecessary barriers to entry, and also in how words and phrases can be updated or added to increase the feeling of inclusivity. A simple change in phrasing from "he" to "they" allows us to speak to a wider audience without an underlying feeling of exclusion. Historically, jousters and participants in medieval sport were overwhelmingly male, so during the joust, everyone was called "he" by default. Why continue? The change was overdue, and this archaic remnant of a bygone era was easily updated to help everyone feel included.

No one should be excluded from enjoying the benefits that sport can bring. But the barriers that are erected in sport are not just physical or financial. A psychological barrier is erected every time someone uses another person's identity as the butt of a joke. A psychological barrier is strengthened when we perpetuate a thoughtless stereotype. A psychological barrier is cemented when we and others demonstrate our compliance to it, whether that be by smirking at the joke, joining the teasing, or simply staying silent.

When I first picked up the phone and asked to be trained to joust, I was laughed at. That was the first of many barriers I would face in my athletic career and one that sadly is extremely common across numerous industries. Why was it so humorous that I wanted to explore something new? Is mockery how we should greet genuine interest? This is exactly the toxic mindset that Knight School Inc seeks to dissolve. In our programs, everyone is invited, and everyone is given the tools to succeed.

Another key value for us is collaboration and partnerships. It is through open and honest communication that we all become stronger, more competent and closer to achieving our goals. We are only in competition with each other on the tournament field. When we share what we've learned with others in the industry, we can affect positive change for others. There is a certain level of responsibility that comes with breaking through a barrier. Our job is not to let the door swing closed behind us so that others must navigate the same treacherous path. Our job is instead to provide a helping hand so that the next person sees a clear path forward. We do this by sharing our successes, discussing our current struggles, and working in collaboration with others to create new ways forward. We currently partner with therapy riding schools to bring medieval mounted games to a group of children and teens who may never have otherwise had the chance to see themselves as knights. We also partner with community resource centres, focusing on women and girls empowerment programs.

Partnerships also exist between teacher and student. Rather than a traditional relationship where the teacher is put in a position of power and control, we put the teacher in a position where listening and accommodation are their main responsibilities. It is for this reason that Joshua and I often find ourselves in situations where we are inventing new teaching strategies and new curriculums. Knight training is historically brutal, even in all of its more modern forms. We do not teach people the way we were taught. We readily adjust our teaching based on the needs of the person in front of us. The easiest way to accommodate a person's needs is to simply listen to them. One of the most important questions we ask ourselves is "why." Why has something been done a certain way, and will changing this take away from the goal in any way? It is through this mode of thinking that we have been able to provide opportunities that would have never been possible before.

The word "sinister" comes from the Latin word, which meant "left", and historically, it was considered evil to be lefthanded. This is something that was then perpetuated through sport. To this day, you will not find a left-handed jousting tournament. It simply does not exist. At one of our mounted medieval games clinics recently, a woman laughed as we talked about the next game: throwing a spear from atop your horse into a hay bale.

"I'm left-handed," she laughed. "Y'all better get out of the way if I am going to try to throw a spear with my left hand!"

Joshua and I looked at each other for a second. Why? Why did this have to be done right-handed? How hard could it be to allow her the chance to use her left hand?

As it turned out, it was not difficult at all. It simply required us to turn the hay bale to face the opposite direction. It was in that moment that Joshua and I truly understood the importance of listening to our students. Most accommodations and inclusions are not difficult. They simply require us to hear people and in making these small changes, we truly allow people to feel heard and recognized and appreciated.

Through Knight School Inc we continue to see people of all ages and abilities find a new, untapped confidence in themselves as they navigate strange new activities, skills and passions. While teaching sword fighting to a group of summer campers recently, a young girl stopped, foam sword in hand, looked at me and said, "This is fun, I feel powerful!" These moments are as important to me as the little girl telling me that I am her hero. Instead, she sees herself as the hero.

My unseen battle was navigating a lonely path in a difficult sport, where my teammates and friends were also a big cause of my insecurities and wounds. But I persevered, and now I envision a different version of medieval sport where other people can come through this door, without other people trying to hold it closed. I grew up to be a knight in shining armour for my job. With kindness, creativity, respect for others, and a little tenacity, we truly can be anything we want in life. I am blessed to have found a partner who truly sees me and is impressed by my strength, not intimidated by it.

As we continue to navigate our growing and changing programs, I am reminded of the phrase I heard at a Women in Sport conference many years ago: "You can't be what you can't see." In my life I strive to give everyone the ability to see themselves in new and constantly evolving ways. Joshua and I grew up to be professional knights in shining armour. No one ever told us that was a possibility, but our existence in the athletics industry is a clear reminder that you can be or do anything. Through representation we can all help make the path a little easier for the next generation. At Knight School, we want to give everyone the ability to showcase their strengths, build their confidence, and learn new skills. We want to give everyone the ability to see themselves as knights.

Tenesa Smith

Born in September 1982, Fayetteville, NC to army parents, it was only a matter of time before I made the same decision to defend my country. I am retired Navy, currently working on my Master's Degree in Policy and Campaign. I recently started volunteering with a local organization called 904ward. My passion is to mentor young women. I began that journey while active duty and today I continue. This is important to me because I could have used a mentor in my life and things may have gone differently. I now understand this is my purpose and I had to go through that life. Outside of these things I am the mother of a 7yr old little girl. She keeps my schedule pretty full with her numerous extra circular activities. When I am not whisking her away to practice I enjoy reading, shopping and traveling..

https://www.linkedin.com/in/tenesa-smith/
https://www.facebook.com/tenesa.gibbs
https://www.instagram.com/tenesa09/

I AM THANKFUL FOR MY SCARS

By Tenesa Smith

As little girls, we are taught to be careful when we play, especially outside. Moms would say to stay off the monkey bars because you could fall, scrape your knee, and end up with scars, or don't play so rough, little girls are to be girly and not full of scars. I also remember hearing, "Sticks and stones can break my bones, but words would never hurt me." Little did I know that words cause hidden scars that stay with you for life until you are ready for true healing. I want to share with you just some of the scars I picked up along this journey called life.

I joined the Navy very young. I was 17. I had no clue about the world. I was raised in the church with only one place I could go to, school. I was very sheltered, naive, and inexperienced with life. I remember calling home and telling my mom how cruel people are and not understanding why people lie for no reason at all. I also remember my first encounter with men. I was preyed upon and had no idea how to defend myself. I was told I had nothing to offer but my looks and body. To be heard in the world, I had to give my body away. I was groomed to believe the only thing men would ever see in me was a cute face, a banging body, and their property. I was placed in positions and experienced things that shaped my life and decisions, but it made me who I am today. I am thankful for those scars.

In 2008, I married my first husband. I had heard him tell me many times I was only as good as an 8th-grade education. I shared with him that I failed the 9th grade twice and had to go through Youth Challenge to obtain my GED, and he reminded me of it every chance he got. He was very proud of the many degrees he had. I didn't even realize he just had multiple associate degrees when we were together, but the way he spoke about them made it seem as if he had his PhD. This caused me to shut down and not share things with people because they threw it back in my face. Today, I am thankful for that scar.

In 2011, I married a second time. I was lied to, manipulated, gaslighted, verbally and emotionally abused. I lived in constant fear of this man because his anger outbursts were worse than mine. I remember the arguments and fights we had where he always destroyed something that belonged to me, be it my phone, a wall in my apartment, or my perfume bottles. I was scared of this man my entire relationship, but on the outside, you wouldn't know. I had learned to adapt and hide things from people. I played my role as a wife, a nice piece of eye candy on his arm. I knew to smile in public and never tell anyone what I endured at home. I am thankful for that scar.

It was 2012 when I was diagnosed with anxiety and depression. I am known for always striving for perfection, and when I cannot achieve it, I am my biggest critic. This year, I was in school (I was trying to prove I was smarter than my 8th-grade education). I also received a promotion to E6, but my physical readiness test (PRT) was around the corner, and if I didn't pass, I would have to wait to put on my new rank. The night before my PRT, I took my history final. It was graded immediately, and I failed. Early the next morning, before the PRT, I took my math final and failed. By now, I was feeling rather anxious for my Navy PRT. I went and completed my sit-ups, and push-ups and began my run. I finished three seconds over the time I needed, therefore, I failed my PRT. That was it. I knew I wouldn't be able to put on my rank. The only thing I could think was I was a failure. I failed everything in a matter of 24 hours. I started hyperventilating, my hands and arms turned numb, and I couldn't catch my breath. I had my first panic attack. The ambulance came and rushed me to the hospital. They performed chest X-rays and CT scans and ran multiple tests. Finally, they came and told me I had a panic attack. I was then placed on medication for anxiety. Now, I have another mental scar.

The anxiety and depression I was diagnosed with just three years prior had finally taken a toll on me. I was in my second marriage, my mother was living with me and learning to live with her new diagnosis of multiple sclerosis. I was at my fifteen-year mark in the Navy, still an E6, and deployed for 6 months that year. Deployments can always be a trying time, but this year brought me to my breaking point. I had always been the type of person who, if one thing in life wasn't going my way, would put all my focus into a different area, such as if work was bothering me, I would try to make my home life very comfortable and vice versa. This year, everything went downhill.

This deployment was a significant time in my life. I did not know how to deal with my emotions. All my life, I have never shown them. I had an anger issue that almost destroyed me and my career. With my marriage failing, my mother's health deteriorating, my work environment being toxic, and having to go through a Family Advocacy Program, I thought there was only one way out, and that was to leave it all here. I had begun to feel that I would not go farther in education, I was unworthy of a healthy romantic relationship, I was unloveable, I was dumb, I was clueless, I was hard to get along with, I was angry, I was a disappointment to myself and God. Everything the devil could throw at me, he did. I live in a city with bridges, and going over one of them took over my thoughts. Another thought was taking all of my pills. I had more than enough of them to do the job. My scars were becoming too great and starting to be seen on the outside. I had reached a point in life where I felt I was going nowhere and things could not get better, so why not?

Something whispered to me and said, "You are my child, and you are not finished yet." I now realize that voice was the Holy Spirit and that I haven't lived out my destiny. Jesus and therapy are what brought me from that dark place. Jesus and therapy are still part of my life today. I have made a conscious decision to put God first every day I wake, and he orders my steps. My mental health is very important to me. I have a daughter who was born in 2017, two years after I wanted to end everything. My purpose is her, this is why I had to learn to put myself first and take care of myself so that I can take care of her. I find myself mentoring young women, especially those in the military. This is my purpose. Had I given in to the enemy that day and driven my car off the Dames Point Bridge, I would not be living in my purpose. Spreading hope, love, and joy, and sharing my experiences with women like me all over the world is my purpose.

I have learned that everything I experienced was for a reason. From the moment I was groomed to be a sex object instead of just me, God was with me. He reminded me my body is a temple. The scars that came from that were for a purpose. In the moment I was told I would not be more than an 8th-grade education, God was with me. In February 2024, I completed my Bachelor's Degree, and I'm currently pursuing my Master's Degree in Policy and Campaigns. When I was emotionally abused, verbally harassed, and physically assaulted, God was with me. He was showing me how not to treat others and what not to tolerate in the future. When those around me despised me, God was with me. He taught me to "Love my neighbor, as myself." Anxiety and depression reared their nasty head in 2012 and have been present with me ever since, but my God said, "Be anxious for nothing"; "Call upon me, I will deliver you."

My scars shaped me. Through the years, this caused me not to trust people, to stay to myself, and not voice my concerns for fear of not being heard. These scars made me angry, hypervigilant, overprotective, and hyperindependent. These were all things I had to release to God in the form of forgiveness for those situations. I have learned these scars were part of me but do not define me. I have accepted them and understand they were given to me to help others find a way to heal their scars. I am thankful for my scars.

I leave you with two encouraging songs that help me. The first one by Crystal Lewis is titled "Beauty for Ashes." I recommend whenever you are doubting yourself, your decisions, or your life, listen to this song and be reminded of what God can do even if you are in fear, mourning, and despair. The other by I Am They is titled "Scars." Remember to be thankful for them because those scars brought us here to this book, to this chapter, to deliverance, to God.

AWAKEN WELLNESS WITHIN REACH

Joyce Ayers

Heart-Centered Divorce Coach

Joyce Ayers is a passionate Heart-Centered Divorce Coach, NLP Master Practitioner, Embodiment Facilitator, and Hypnosis Transformer who spent years pouring her heart into supporting her family and her husband's business. While she gained many valuable skills and insights, she lost touch with her own identity and dreams. This realization ignited a transformative journey of self-discovery, where she reclaimed her power and began living authentically. Now, Joyce is passionate about helping other women unlock their true potential, passion, and purpose. She guides them to align with their core values, and make choices that genuinely reflect what they want. Through mindset reprogramming, soulful practices, embodiment techniques, and powerful manifestation methods, Joyce empowers women to confidently shine their light, and voice their hearts desires. Her mission is to encourage women to reclaim their lives, align with their soul's purpose, and live a life that truly fulfills their deepest desires.

https://www.linkedin.com/in/joyce-ayers-79893b85/
https://www.facebook.com/joyce.ayers.395669/
https://www.instagram.com/awakenwellnesswithinreach/
https://soul-genius.com/

FINDING YOUR VOICE

The Journey to Authentic Happiness

By Joyce Ayers

For most of my life, I lived a quiet, almost invisible existence. I preferred not to attract attention, avoid conflict at all costs, and became really good at people-pleasing. I thought if I made everyone else happy, I'd feel liked and loved in return. So, I stayed small to feel safe by not being noticed. This way, no one would question what I was doing or my choices. The truth is, I did have a strong will, and I liked doing things my own way. I believed that if I flew under the radar, I could get things done without any interference. It was my way of keeping everyone else happy while I pretended this way of living was okay.

But my voice? It was barely heard. Over time, I started to feel like I didn't matter, that my needs didn't matter. Even after I got married and had kids, my feelings and requests often went ignored. I couldn't understand why my family didn't seem to care about what I wanted and needed.

Looking back now, I realize I had unknowingly taught them that my needs weren't important. I actually taught others how to treat me! I fell into the role of the accommodating wife and ever-attentive mother, always there to meet everyone's needs but my own. It felt like I had it all together, doing the right thing, so why was I so unhappy?

Each time I ignored my own needs, each time I silenced what I truly wanted, a piece of me was slowly dying. My voice, once full of trust and optimism, slowly realized there really wasn't anyone whom I could turn to and lean on for understanding during the early child-rearing years and multiple moves. I had learned early in life to stuff my feelings and get on with it and what was needed. What I needed was to feel that I was not alone and someone had my back, like my husband.

He was a wonderful provider, strong, confident, and wonderfully masculine. We had a good life in many ways—the house, trips, social events—yet his work took a lot of his time and energy, and he didn't have much capacity left at the end of the day to support me in my challenges with the kids and ALL the other family needs.

I had the mindset that I needed to be strong for everyone else. I thought that being strong meant dealing with my own feelings, my own needs, and the loneliness that had been creeping into my life—even within my marriage. I told myself I just had to get through this next hurdle, then things would eventually calm down again. But the more I pushed down my needs, the emptier I became. I had this armor of "strength" around me, but underneath, I was disconnected from my feelings, who I truly was, and from enjoying the life I was blessed with.

I didn't realize how much this was affecting me until one day, standing in my bedroom, looking out the window, knowing the girls started going off to college, and there were no more community roles to occupy my time, I thought to myself, "I am so unhappy!" I believed that by placing my dreams last, I could ensure my girls had all the opportunities possible; supporting my husband's business with my hands-on help was part of the deal—part of being a supportive wife and mother. All those years of waiting for my turn, not acknowledging to myself what I wanted, being accommodating, and living where the job took us were giving up pieces of myself—pieces I didn't know how to reclaim. I had no boundaries hoping the family would know I needed their cooperation and appreciation. The old belief that my needs didn't matter left me feeling resentful and powerless. I thought that if my family understood how much time and effort it took to take care of everyone and everything, they would gladly be helpful and appreciate all I did for them. I was so focused on making sure everyone else was taken care of, even the dog, that I didn't stop to make my needs a priority, even if I knew what they were.

When I finally could slow down enough to pause and notice what I was feeling, I realized how much my husband and I had grown apart and how deeply unhappy I was, yet unable to express my heartache to him. I was noticing how unsupported I felt, how out of alignment we were and the lack of capacity he had to validate my feelings. The relationship I'd given so much to wasn't there for me in the ways I needed. Instead of feeling seen and heard, I felt ignored. I'd been holding everything together—managing the house, the kids, the emotional weight of the marriage—and I hadn't asked for help because I didn't think I could. I thought I had to be strong and handle it all.

Being very independent early on was not in my best interest long term. Keeping my feelings to myself made me unemotional, even in the happiest of times. I was like a robot, getting the "things" done to have a false sense of control over my life, so I could be happy.

I stayed silent, not because I didn't have things to say, but because I hadn't learned how to speak up for myself. I couldn't ask for what I needed because I didn't feel I could have it. Somewhere along the way, I believed my needs didn't matter as much as everyone else's. That my dreams could wait for someday. So, I buried my feelings, telling myself that my frustrations didn't matter and that my loneliness was temporary. I thought when the business sold and the girls started their own lives, things would get better then it would be my turn. But that never happened. The silent void just got heavier. I started to realize how lonely I felt, even surrounded by my family.

This silence, this need to be strong, was suffocating me. It locked me in a cycle where I looked outside myself for validation, where I was only as good as how well I could meet everyone else's needs. And in the process, I lost myself. I wasn't living in a way that was authentic. I was disconnected from who I really was and what I wanted.

The lifeless life I had been living got uncomfortable enough to become the catalyst for my decision to find my own happiness. It was like a fire was lit under me, and a small voice inside told me, "Go find your happiness!"

For many women in midlife, this strong urge to find happiness finally wakes you up. It's when the roles we've been playing—wife, mother, friend—start to shift. We start to ask ourselves, "Wait, who am I? What do I want? What actually makes me happy?" I was no different. It was during this time that I discovered my passions, the things that lit me up, the things that I had forgotten about while I was busy living for everyone else.

Finding my passion again reignited something inside me. It reminded me that my happiness mattered. I stopped living solely for others and began focusing on what I needed to feel alive. And the more I leaned into that, the more I began to see myself differently. I started to understand my worth, not because of what I could do for others, but because of who I was. This shift in perspective was empowering. For the first time in a long time, I felt seen and heard—by myself.

Reclaiming my voice was more than just speaking up. It was about being real and authentic in every part of my life. It was a slow process with baby steps as I learned to navigate my feelings and express them. I started acknowledging how I truly felt, what I thought, and what I wanted—and finding the courage to express those truths, even when it was most uncomfortable, even when I thought people would disagree with me. It was my life, after all.

I know how challenging this can be for heart-centered women, having experienced many challenges for many years. You've spent a long time making sure everyone else was okay, being the supportive partner, the attentive mother, the reliable friend, the good daughter, that it can feel like a huge leap to say, "What about me?" But here's the truth: We can't fully be there for others if we're not there for ourselves first. True strength comes from being vulnerable, from being willing to be honest about who we are, even if it means facing rejection or disapproval.

When you let yourself be truly seen, you start to create deeper connections with the people around you. You attract relationships where you don't have to pretend or hide parts of yourself. I would "test" people and myself, by sharing something personal, wait for their response, and if I still felt safe, they would get the okay! And in doing so, I felt empowered in ways I never had before. I felt more alive and more fulfilled because I was finally in alignment with who I really was and celebrating my feelings.

My healing was at the center of finding my voice. And it wasn't easy. This journey started with heartache—the loss of my marriage and the realization that if I had let my former husband know who I was, what I felt, and what I needed, the outcome would definitely have been different. This pain forced me to confront my deeper wounds and beliefs, the ones I had carried for so long without even realizing it. I felt at a deep level that I didn't matter, that what I wanted and needed would never happen. As hard as this growth path was for me, there was also great healing and wisdom to gain.

It took acknowledging my fears and letting go of the stories I'd told myself about who I had to be. I had to peel back layers of hurt and self-doubt, and as I did, I began to see that I was stronger than I ever gave myself credit for. I wasn't just surviving—I had the power to create a life that I actually wanted.

For me, the turning point was the end of my marriage. It shattered the life I thought I would always have and the hope things would get better. It also gave me the chance to become the person I never knew and build a new future for myself. I looked at all the ways I silenced my voice, all the ways I gave my power away, and started reclaiming it. I began to speak my truth, set boundaries, and, for the first time in a long time, put myself first.

The more I healed, the more my identity shifted. I started to see myself not just as a caretaker or supporter, but as someone with my own gifts and strengths. I realized my worth wasn't tied to how much I could do for others—it was tied to how committed I was to myself.

This shift was both exciting and terrifying. It meant letting go of the roles I'd played for so long, the ones that felt safe, and stepping into something new. It meant trusting in my own worth, even when it wasn't validated by others. But as scary as it was, it was also incredibly freeing. I began to see myself as powerful, capable, and deserving of all the good things life had to offer.

I know for many women, this shift in identity also brings a renewed sense of purpose. You start asking yourself, "What do I want to contribute to the world? What do I want to be remembered for?" And as we align with our true purpose, opportunities that match who we really are begin to show up.

One of the most powerful lessons I've learned is that vulnerability isn't weakness. It's strength! When I allowed myself to be vulnerable—when I stopped pretending everything was fine and started being honest about my fears, insecurities, and dreams—I opened the door to deeper connections, greater intimacy, and the possibility of real happiness.

I stopped hiding, I stopped pretending, and in that space of vulnerability, I found my true self again and allowed myself to share my voice.

Three Action Steps for Healing and Empowerment

If you're on a similar journey of reclaiming your voice, here are three actionable steps you can take to shift your beliefs, live authentically, and take back your power. These steps incorporate tools from hypnosis and neuro-linguistic programming (NLP), which can help shift your thoughts, creating a lasting transformation:

1. **Shift Your Beliefs with Self-Hypnosis:** Start by identifying the limiting beliefs that have been holding you back—such as "I'm not worthy" or "My needs don't matter." Using self-hypnosis, get into a relaxed comfortable position and imagine releasing these beliefs from your subconscious mind. Visualize yourself being free from these old patterns, creating space for new empowering beliefs like "I'm deserving of love and respect" or "My voice matters." As you release these beliefs, they may float away, drain away like a river flowing, or vanish like steam. Repeat these affirmations and visualizations regularly, helping your unconscious mind and soul integrate these new beliefs and step into your power.

2. **Practice Authenticity with NLP Anchoring:** Authenticity requires vulnerability, and it can be difficult to stay true to yourself in situations where you feel pressured to conform. Use an NLP technique called "anchoring" to tap into a feeling of confidence when you need it most. Think of a time when you felt completely authentic and empowered. Hear what you heard. See what you saw. Feel what you felt. While recalling the memory, press your thumb and forefinger together, creating a physical "anchor." This hand gesture for rewiring your neurology, anchors more powerfully a state of authenticity. When you're in a situation where you feel tempted to silence your voice, press your fingers together again to trigger the feeling of authenticity and courage.

3. **Reclaim Your Power through Visualization:** To take back your power, close your eyes and visualize yourself setting boundaries and confidently expressing your needs with your eyes closed. Imagine seeing yourself on a movie screen. Notice your posture, the actions you are taking, and the confidence and certainty in your voice. Bring to mind a specific situation when you've struggled to speak up. Now, observe yourself calmly and assertively stating your needs, feeling strong and empowered in the process. Step into the movie as yourself looking out through your own eyes at this moment. Feel the confidence in your body, the calm, relaxed ease of expressing yourself, and hear the clarity in your voice. When you feel complete, step out of the picture and come back to the present moment. This visualization technique helps rewire your brain and prepares you for real-life situations where you'll be able to express your truth with confidence and clarity.

By incorporating these strategies into your life, you can begin to shift your mindset, live authentically, and step into the power that has always been yours. Remember, the journey to finding your voice isn't easy, but it's one of the most rewarding journeys you will ever take. You deserve to be heard, to be seen, and to live a life that is true to who you are.

I now celebrate finding my path, living my dreams, and being true to myself after finding my voice. It is much more fun and powerful to be authentic, even if others don't get me!

It matters that I get myself, I understand who I am and what I need. This gives me comfort, confidence, and compassion as I continue to grow and evolve in many other ways on this journey. Every hurdle is an opportunity to be more flexible, adaptable, and resilient.

My mentors were the light in my darkness, the truth I needed to know as I explored this new terrain with all its obstacles. My mentors saw who I was, my potential, and my passion for living. I was able to come alive once again and welcome in this new life after divorce, knowing I was not who I pretended to be. I am myself, and I'm good with this.

Celebrate the version of yourself that is forming. Like learning to walk as a toddler, you are learning to become who you truly are. Allow others like myself into your new world to support you as you grow into your powerful adult self. You may not get it perfect AND know that you are perfectly made.

To contact me for support on your journey and share ways you are finding your voice you can email me at: joyce@soul-genius.com or visit my website: soul-genius.com

Inside my website, I will gift you my "Self Love Empowerment Guide" that will empower you to use your voice in ways that are authentic, confident, and aligned.

There is value in all things we experience. Take the gold nuggets from my chapter, let them settle, and observe what is shown so that your authentic self is express through your voice.

In celebration to the beautiful authentic women you are discovering,

Joyce Ayers

Conscious Divorce Coach
Certified Conscious Uncoupling Coach
Master NLP & Hypnosis Practitioner

VITALITY BY EVA
Eva Skarström
Owner

Eva Skarström is a passionate advocate for natural healing, driven by her belief in the body's innate ability to heal itself. She combines formal training in craniosacral osteopathy with a deep, self-acquired understanding of the body's interconnected systems. After overcoming burnout, fibromyalgia, and endometriosis, through years of personal experience and study, Eva developed a holistic approach that integrates nutrition, mindset, body cleansing, energy work, and befriending one's body. This broad expertise allows her to lovingly guide clients towards a life free of pain and full of vitality.

Originally from Sweden, Eva now resides in Gran Canaria with her family, embracing the sunny, diverse and tranquil island life.

Eva believes that everyone deserves a life full of vitality, harmony, and happiness, and she is dedicated to inspiring and empowering women to take control of their health and well-being, and embark on their own healing journeys.

https://linkedin.com/company/vitality-by-eva/
https://www.facebook.com/VitalityByEva/
https://www.instagram.com/vitality_by_eva/
https://evaskarstrom.com/

VITALITY RECLAIMED

A Journey From Chronic Illness To Liberation

By Eva Skarström

"I am sorry, Eva, there is nothing to be done. You just have to accept the fact that this is your life now. I can prescribe you these painkillers and hope they get the edge of your pain, but other than that, there is nothing I can do to help you further."

These words are forever stuck in my head, for two reasons. It was the worst feeling that I've ever had, the verdict of a life imprisoned in a body at constant war with me, but ultimately, it also came to be the moment that triggered me to take control of my own body, mind and life. And that is what I am going to share with you in this chapter.

Background

I've had issues with my body since I was a teenager, and year by year, it got a little bit worse. Subtle pain, poor sleep, restlessness and fatigue alternately. And extreme menstrual cramps. I got an endometriosis diagnosis at 23, and even if I got it treated (by being put in menopause for six months) and it got better, there were several other issues getting worse instead. And that's how my life was, one thing handled and two new rising. I tried to live healthy, exercising, thinking about my diet, etc., but no matter what I did, my body got worse.

By the time I was 36, I was diagnosed with exhaustion disorder, fibromyalgia, endometriosis, vaginismus, vestibulitis and eczema. I also had sinusitis often, upper respiratory infections and a flu-like feeling in my body, although I didn't have the flu. I was living with severe pain and fatigue 24/7, 350 days of the year. I could barely get out of bed in the morning, every movement in my body was aching, walking was a torment, my body was so sore it hurt to even have clothes on, and my hands were bleeding from the eczema. I was exhausted all the time, and no matter how much I slept, it made little difference. When I had plans to go somewhere, I got so exhausted just by getting ready, so more often than not, I ended up not leaving home after all. Just to take a shower felt like a marathon. To go grocery shopping was like climbing a mountain. And the brain fog, oh my, I have this memory of standing in the store for 15 minutes just choosing between two different brands of ketchup!

I was also a mom to a wonderful three-year-old boy, my husband was a chief officer at sea for long periods, and I was a medical secretary. Life looked good from the outside, but in reality, it was far from it.

I was a non-functional woman, supposed to be a mother, but no energy left to support my son, in fight/flight/freeze mode with high levels of stress and anxiety. Every day was a constant struggle that seemed to have no end. I was annoyed, frustrated, angry, victimised, sad, short-tempered, blaming others, and questioning myself, my body and my life. And tired. So utterly tired of living this way, yet no energy to change things either. To be living like this was a nightmare I could not wake up from. But it didn't feel like living either, I was barely surviving, and my life was slipping away from me, one day at a time. I felt robbed of everything beautiful in life because of my body and its problems. I was also ashamed of myself, for not seeing the signs, for not taking better care of myself, for not being a better mom and wife, daughter and friend, and for being a bad employee. I had more or less isolated myself for years, since it became too much to keep the facade towards friends and family. It actually took me years to get the courage to tell my friends I was ill, and I realise now that I never really told them how bad it was and how deeply affected I was by my illness. I felt terribly lonely.

And so one afternoon at the doctor's office, I got to hear these words:

"I am sorry, Eva, there is nothing to be done. You just have to accept the fact that this is your life now. I can prescribe you these painkillers and hope they get the edge of your pain, but other than that, there is nothing I can do to help you further."

My Pivotal Point

Is he being serious? Do I really need to live like this for the rest of my life? It is not fair towards my son to have a mom like this. How come they don't know the origin of my illnesses? I have so many things I haven't done yet. If they don't know what has caused my illnesses, how can they say there is nothing to do about them? My life hasn't even begun yet! On my deathbed, I don't want to look back to a life like this. There is so much more for me to experience! This can't be it, this can't be the end. Who are they (the doctors) to tell me how my life will be, what gives them the authority to predict my future?! Especially since they don't know the cause! My son is innocent in all of this, and he deserves a present mom who is there for him and wants to play and have fun! And I deserve to enjoy my life and experience all the things that I have dreamt of!

I refuse to believe the doctors and live the rest of my life like this!!
These were my thoughts the following weeks after the doctor's appointment. As you can see, I quite quickly came to the conclusion that I didn't accept my prognosis. Filled with anger towards the health care system for giving a prognosis without looking for and explaining the

cause of the illnesses, I decided that the only person possible to make that kind of statement about my life was me. I hereby took back control of my life! This was an empowering moment for me, and I felt relieved.

My Healing Journey

The realisation that I needed to make changes and new decisions, to be able to get healthier, led me to a "green rehabilitation". I hadn't really made any big efforts to improve my health up until now, other than resting and surviving. My employers hadn't been helpful either, they didn't take care of their staff, and as the years passed, they threw a wrench in the works instead. So when I now put my health as a priority and got accepted to this rehabilitation, which really felt like the right step forward, I found myself at the point where I needed to choose one or the other. I came to the conclusion that if I wanted any chance to be healthy again, I needed to quit my job. Said and done, and on my way home the same day, at the end of April 2017, an idea popped into my head. To live abroad the following winter.

After talking it through with my husband, who was on the other side of the world, we decided to give it a go. The timing was perfect in so many ways, and six months later, in October 2017, after my rehabilitation had just ended, we left for Gran Canaria in Spain. It was a lovely six months on the island: I continued with my rehab on my own, relaxed, and enjoyed the sun and the warmth. I was almost pain-free and I started to feel alive again. The quality of my life was so much better than back in the cold, raw, south-west winter in Sweden. I loved it!

When we came back to Sweden in April 2018, we thought of moving to Gran Canaria permanently. *The quality of your life is everything!* We began to make a plan of what needed to be done before a move could be possible. For me, it was important to get back to work and see what I was capable of, so that was one of the things I focused on.

The other main focus was to read about the body and what could cause the symptoms of the disease I had. I came across Candida and got a 94% accuracy on a Candida test. This made me look into diets and how to eat to eliminate Candida in my body. And I also realised how what we eat affects the body, *we can eat ourselves both sick and healthy*! From there, I got to read about how our body is connected, how our organs need to be taken care of and often cleansed to work properly, that it's very common to have inflammation, what causes inflammation, overload of toxins in our bodies, acidic bodies and the most important thing – cleansing symptoms!

Our body is working relentlessly to take care of itself and keep itself healthy. And depending on the circumstances we give it, the results vary. If our body is so overloaded with toxins, acids and/or inflammation, so that the kidneys and liver aren't capable of cleansing themselves as fast, we can get to feel cleansing symptoms. Think of a hangover, for example. We drink more than what our body can handle at the moment, and the alcohol/toxins circulate in our bodies instead, and we get intoxicated. During the cleansing period, i.e. sobering up, we can have a headache, stomach problems, pain in the body, poor sleep, etc., not comfortable at all. And it's the same thing when our body cleanses itself from the waste products, toxins, acids and inflammations that are accumulated in our bodies. This was a huge AHA moment for me!

Learning how to detect if our body is overloaded with waste and how cleansing symptoms manifest, I realised that all the symptoms I've had during the years had been just like this, cleansing symptoms. My body was heavy on toxins, acids and inflammation and was just trying to clean itself. No wonder the medications and ointments hadn't helped, they only added up the amount of waste my body needed to take care of! And when I had done something that was good, like changing my diet and exercising, my symptoms got worse – because then the embedded toxins in the tissues released, which led to even more toxins circulating the body and, therefore, the enhanced pain and dis-ease. The fact that it's important to take care of our organs as well, especially our kidneys and liver, was nothing that had crossed my mind before either. But when thinking about it, it made sense, our filters need maintenance just as they do in a car, for example. They all get clogged when enough dirt has passed through and need some service when they do.

With this new information, I felt an urge to clean my body, but my head was overloaded, and I didn't know where to start. I booked an appointment with a detox specialist who guided me in the beginning and so, in October 2019, my second big change began.

1. Stop eating food that causes inflammation in your body, such as meat, dairy, gluten, sugar and alcohol.
2. Eliminate one thing at a time, at the pace you are capable of.
3. Even small changes make a difference for the body, and if your body is very overloaded with toxins, it is usually better to take it slowly.
4. If the cleansing symptoms are too difficult to handle, take a step back and recuperate. Then start over again in a lighter way, for example, by scaling down instead of eliminating. Toxin-binding supplements like active charcoal are also helpful.
5. Make sure your kidneys filter properly. You can do the "cloud test" on your morning urine to see the amount of residue that has been filtered.
6. If the kidneys need support, you can drink parsley infusion, take herbs/tinctures, lubricate with castor oil or do a cavitation/radiofrequency treatment.
7. Keep your lymphatic system well circulated.
8. Cleanse your intestines from old residue and plaques, a salt water flush is favourable since it cleanses all the way.

9. When you have cleansed your body a bit, a detox is a good suggestion. You can choose from different types of detox, let your body guide the way.
10. During a cleansing and detox, you can get different kinds of cravings, these are often just our body and parasites complaining about the change that's happening. Do not relapse because of them!

The most important thing, though, is to listen to your body!
You need to make this change with love towards yourself and your body. Because change cannot happen at war, you can't poop and outrun a lion at the same time, you need to do it together with your body. In peaceful understanding and collaboration. So, if you truly want a change in your body and life, you need to regulate your nervous system as well.

When I started my path of cleansing, I had already gone to medi-yoga with meditation – for stress reduction and balancing of the hormones, for a year. Through the help of that calm, empathetic kind of yoga, I got in contact with my body again. I went from having my body as an enemy, to being curious about what it needed and what the signals it showed me meant. "We" became friends, and this made me and my body ready for the maximum effect of whatever we did, in this case, cleansing the body itself.

The results were quite instant. Within 6 months, the pain I'd had for years was almost completely gone, and I had lost 20 kg in weight. I could move much more easily and had a different energy. I started to enjoy life for the first time ever, and I also deepened my journey inward, to get to know the true me, shadows and all.

So, how did I manage to get this huge change in only a few months?
In October 2019, I started to change my diet. My first step was to stop eating meat, then dairy, and after that, gluten. At New Year the same

year, I had come to the point where I ate vegan and gluten-free food. I tried to stop eating sugar, but that became too much so I ate less of it instead, and whenever I could, I switched to healthier kinds of sweeteners. I mostly used honey, agave or coconut sugar.

In February, I went for two cavitation/radiofrequency treatments. The week before I started to support my kidneys, and during the days around the treatments, I also fasted on smoothies. The treatment was so painful! I had so much inflammation in my body, and lumps and knots in my connective tissue. Completely exhausted, I went home and went to lie under three blankets shivering and with an aching body. It was not a pleasant feeling, but I knew things were moving in my body now and it made me happy. I also had to pee, like, all the time. And when I went, it was *gushing*!

Going back for another treatment two days later, I was to put the same clothes on since I still had a sore body from the previous one, and they were loose. I couldn't believe my eyes. I had peed out 4 kg of weight after the first treatment, in two days! The second treatment started even worse than the first, since I was already bruised both here and there, but we could get even more of the bumps released. Already at this point, it was noticeable that the inflammation in my back and shoulders had reduced. Another day of shivering and with an aching body awaited, and even more peeing, but after a few days, I started to feel a lot better. I had an easier feeling in my body, less pain, and felt energised in a way I hadn't been for years. And I had lost 10 kg and 10 cm around my belly! It was crazy! But the thing that made me the happiest was that I could see a small cloud in my urine, yay!! I now knew my body had started to filter and that it was functioning.

Empowered with this experience I decided to do a two-week detox in April. The detox made us gradually phase out all foods to have three days of juicing, before introducing fruit and vegetables again. We were also to take a number of different herbs and remedies to clean and support our organs and intestines. I remember so vividly on day four, I started to feel like the rabbit in the old Duracell advertisement. I had so much energy that I didn't know what to do with it all, and this was a real surprise for me. I also peed and pooped a lot, and after these two weeks, I had lost another 10 kg and 10 cm around my belly. The pain was almost completely gone, with no stiffness, my thoughts were clearer, I could function in a way that I hadn't for many years, and my body was at ease. I could hardly believe it myself, what a huge difference this had all made!

My Victory

In the summer of 2020, after years of battling chronic illness, I was finally pain-free, moving with ease, filled with hope, gratitude, excitement for life, and a deep sense of liberation. I was no longer bound to survival, but living and creating my own life, and our move to Gran Canaria in August was no longer a necessity, but a choice to fully embrace life. I was a new me, an empowered, healthier woman, and I had reclaimed both my vitality and my life.

Thank you for taking the time to read my story.

If you have any similar issues with your body that I had, whether you're feeling overwhelmed by illness and fatigue, or you're ready to take action but just haven't found the right way yet, I want you to know—you are not alone, there is hope, and I wish you all the best along your path forward.

If my journey has inspired you and you want to know more, I've crafted a free guide filled with the same tools that empowered and supported me in the beginning, together with what I've learnt along the way and wished I would have known sooner. You can find the guide on www.evaskarstrom.com or my social media, Vitality by Eva, where I will be sharing more about my healing journey and our miraculous healing body.

With love and vitality,
Eva

JOIN THE MOVEMENT!
#BAUW
Becoming An Unstoppable Woman
With She Rises Studios

She Rises Studios was founded by Hanna Olivas and Adriana Luna Carlos, the mother-daughter duo, in mid-2020 as they saw a need to help empower women worldwide. They are the podcast hosts of the *She Rises Studios Podcast* and Amazon best-selling authors and motivational speakers who travel the world. Hanna and Adriana are the movement creators of #BAUW - Becoming An Unstoppable Woman: The movement has been created to universally impact women of all ages, at whatever stage of life, to overcome insecurities, adversities, and develop an unstoppable mindset. She Rises Studios educates, celebrates, and empowers women globally.

Looking to Join Us in our Next Anthology or Publish YOUR Own?
She Rises Studios Publishing offers full-service publishing, marketing, book tour, and campaign services. For more information, contact info@sherisesstudios.com

We are always looking for women who want to share their stories and expertise and feature their businesses on our podcasts, in our books, and in our magazines.

SEE WHAT WE DO

OUR PODCAST   **OUR BOOKS**   **OUR SERVICES**

Be featured in the Becoming An Unstoppable Woman magazine, published in 13 countries and sold in all major retailers. Get the visibility you need to LEVEL UP in your business!

FENIX TV
EMPOWER THROUGH ENTERTAINMENT
BE THE NEXT FENIX TV HOST AND INSPIRE A WORLD OF POSSIBILITIES!
Visit our website for more details:
FENIXTV.APP

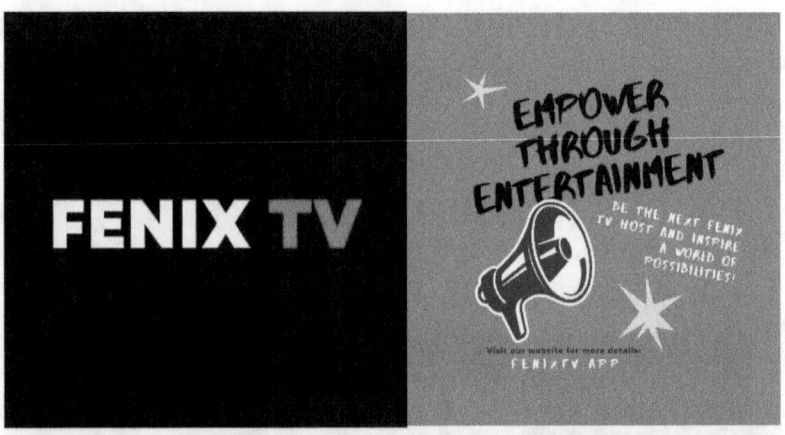

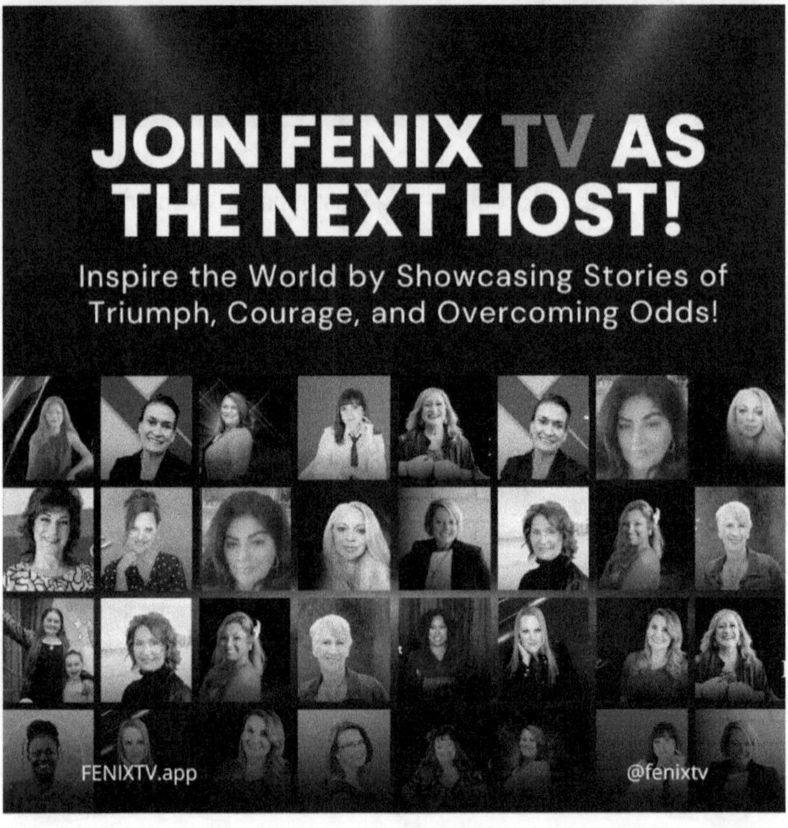
JOIN FENIX TV AS THE NEXT HOST!
Inspire the World by Showcasing Stories of Triumph, Courage, and Overcoming Odds!
FENIXTV.app
@fenixtv

Have your own TV show streamed across major platforms like Roku TV, Amazon Fire Stick,

Apple TV and more!

Learn to leverage your expertise. Build your online presence and grow your audience with FENIX TV.
https://fenixtv.sherisesstudios.com/

Visit www.SheRisesStudios.com to see how YOU can join the #BAUW movement and help your community to achieve the UNSTOPPABLE mindset.

Have you checked out the *She Rises Studios Podcast?*

Find us on all MAJOR platforms: Spotify, IHeartRadio, Apple Podcasts, Google Podcasts, etc.

Looking to become a sponsor or build a partnership?
Email us at info@sherisesstudios.com